International Perspectives on Psychology in the Schools

SCHOOL PSYCHOLOGY

A series of volumes edited by
Thomas R. Kratochwill and James E. Ysseldyke

Stark, McGee, and Menolascino • International Handbook of Community Services for the Mentally Retarded

Horne • Attitudes Toward Handicapped Students: Professional, Peer and Parent Reactions

Thaw and Cuvo • Developing Responsive Human Services: New Perspectives About Residential Treatment Organizations

Elliott and Witt • The Delivery of Psychological Services in Schools: Concepts, Processes and Issues

Maher/Forman • A Behavioral Approach to Education of Children and Youth

Rosenfield • Instructional Consultation

Sandoval • Crisis Counseling, Intervention, and Prevention in the Schools

D'Amato/Dean • The School Psychologist in Nontraditional Settings: Integrating Clients, Services, and Settings

Saigh/Oakland • International Perspectives on Psychology in the Schools

International Perspectives on Psychology in the Schools

Edited by
Philip A. Saigh
Graduate Center
City University of New York
Thomas Oakland
The University of Texas at Austin

Routledge
Taylor & Francis Group
NEW YORK AND LONDON

First Published 1989 by
Lawrence Erlbaum Associates, Inc., Publishers
365 Broadway
Hillsdale, New Jersey 07642

This edition published 2013 by Routledge
711 Third Avenue, New York, NY 10017
2 Park Square, Milton Park, Abingdon, Oxfordshire OX14 4RN

First issued in paperback 2016

Routledge is an imprint of the Taylor & Francis Group, an informa business

Production, interior, and cover
design: Robin Marks Weisberg

Library of Congress Cataloging-in-Publication Data
International perspectives on psychology in the schools/edited by Philip A. Saigh, Thomas Oakland.
p. cm.
Includes index.
ISBN 0-8058-0110-3
1. School psychology—Cross-cultural studies. I. Saigh, Philip A. II. Oakland, Thomas.
LB1027.55.I57 1988
370.15—dc19 88-3041
CIP

ISBN 13: 978-1-138-97307-7 (pbk)
ISBN 13: 978-0-8058-0110-1 (hbk)

Publisher's Note
The publisher has gone to great lengths to ensure the quality of this reprint but points out that some imperfections in the original may be apparent.

This book is dedicated to those committed
to enhancing the lives of all children
in the world and to our own children:

Mark
Laura, Chuck, David, Scott, Chris,
and *Allyson*

Contents

Foreword

School psychology throughout the world has probably developed more quickly during the past 10 years than during the prior 50 years. Catterall's three volume set, *Psychology in the Schools in International Perspective* (1976, 1977, 1979) gave[1] us the first opportunity to compare and contrast the development of school psychology services worldwide. Since then, through improvements in international communication, school psychology has undergone dramatic changes. No longer limited to the affluent, resource rich, and politically powerful nations, psychology is making its rightful contributions that address the psychological and educational problems of the world's schools. This book provides us with an update of the status of psychology in educational systems worldwide and serves as another source of communication that allows us to benefit from the experiences and knowledge of our colleagues from around the world.

The impact of international communication on the practice of psychology in the schools becomes more visible every day. At a recent conference on Attention Deficit–Hyperactivity Disorder (AD–HD) the audience was informed that documentation of significant differences in the prevalency rate of AD–HD was leading researchers to speculate that aspects of this disorder may be based on cultural factors. As a result, they reported that their research would be altered accordingly in order to focus on the environmental factors affecting this psychiatric "disorder" which is so prevalent in the United States. Another example of the relevance

[1]See Catterall, C. D. (1976, 1977, 1979). *School psychology in international perspective* (Vols. 1-3). Columbus, OH: International School Psychology Steering Committee.

of international perspectives comes from my work counseling families and providing consultation to teachers. In my community, many families are adopting youngsters from Korea, Vietnam, South America, and India. A fifth-grade teacher recently asked for information on the Indian school system to help her understand the behavioral adjustment problems of one of her students. This particular student had lived on the streets of Calcutta since age 6 and his prior schooling included some unique circumstances. Once these had been identified, his fifth-grade teacher and the school psychologist were able to develop more culturally sensitive (and more effective) interventions. Being familiar with the child's school of origin provided a context for better understanding of his current behaviors.

The understanding of any country's educational system is only the beginning in a process that brings us closer to one another in the world community. As one of the key players within the educational system, the school psychologist is in an excellent position to facilitate this communication process. And, approximately 15 years ago, a group of school psychologists did just that, when they initiated and formalized international communication within our profession.

Around 1972, in response to the need to establish global awareness, an international committee of school psychologists was formed. This group provided a forum for the exchange of information, identified promising practices and practitioners, and encouraged more frequent travel abroad. The exchange of information was accomplished primarily by the publication of a small quarterly newsletter, *World-Go-Round*. The Committee's interest in mutual understanding culminated in an organized effort to understand the role of "school psychology in changing societies," which was the theme in 1975 of the first international colloquium in school psychology held in Munich, Germany. Approximately 250 school psychologists from 17 countries and six continents were represented. During the next few years an informal liaison network was built representing a large number of countries throughout the world.

With the help of contributions from individuals and a sizable allocation of funds from the National Association of School Psychologists (USA), colloquia became regular events. Throughout the past 12 years, interest in these meetings and attendance has increased steadily. Meetings were initially hosted with the assistance of national associations but have recently found greater independence. Meeting sites have included the Federal Republic of Germany (1975), Denmark (1977, 1986), England (1979, 1985), Israel (1980), Sweden (1982), United States (1983), France (1984), Switzerland (1987) and, again, Germany in 1988. Meetings have been concentrated in Europe because they appear to draw more participants; however, regional meetings and travel seminars have served to bring attention to school psychology services in other geographical areas.

After many informal meetings, travel seminars, and professional activities, interest in international school psychology grew rapidly. The work became overwhelming for the few volunteers, and the International School Psychology Committee felt it was time to establish a formal organization. Consequently, in 1982 during the fifth Colloquium in Stockholm, the International School Psychology Association (ISPA) was chartered. In support of the goals expressed by its membership, the Constitution set forth the following purposes for this organization:

1. To promote the use of sound psychological principles within the context of education all over the world.
2. To promote communication among professionals who are committed to the improvement of the mental health of children in the world's schools.
3. To encourage the use of school psychologists in countries where they are not currently being used.
4. To promote the psychological rights of all children throughout the world.
5. To initiate and promote cooperation with other organizations working for purposes similar to those of ISPA in order to help children.

The implementation of these goals is being accomplished through the efforts of many individuals and the work of several committees. The organizational structure of ISPA includes an executive director working out of the central office located in Copenhagen, Denmark. ISPA's executive committee is made up of officers elected by the membership. These include the president, president-elect, past president, treasurer, and secretary. Affiliate organizations form a second stratum of leadership. National and international organizations vote in the affairs of ISPA. Votes on important issues are taken at each colloquium during a meeting of the General Assembly, which is responsible for setting the policies of ISPA and approving its budget. The General Assembly consists of the executive committee, individual members, and representatives from affiliate organizations.

The work of ISPA is conducted by a variety of committees. In addition to the usual standing committees (i.e., membership, constitution and bylaws, and nomination and elections), work is underway in areas such as child development, professional standards, peace education, research, and international exchange. ISPA is also a charter member of Project SHARE, a hospitality network of psychologists throughout the world.

ISPA was instrumental in the publication of Catterall's three volume set of *Psychology in the Schools in International Perspective*, and Burzynski's (1979) *To Be a Child*, a photographic essay published in connection with the 1979 United Nations International Year of the Child.[2] That year, 10 "Psychological Rights for

[2]See Burzynski, P. (1979). *To be a child.* Columbus, OH: International School Psychology Steering Committee.

the Child'' were drafted and adopted by the General Assembly. This declaration was distributed throughout the world and continues to serve as a document guiding school and social programs to deliver services in the best interests of the child. The Danish Association of School Psychologists published an illustrated booklet elaborating these psychological rights. More than 20,000 were distributed in Denmark. Further printings followed in Sweden and the Federal Republic of Germany. In 1980, ISPA also initiated the publication of *School Psychology International*, now published by Holt, Reinhart and Winston. The journal is gaining international respect as an outlet for information on research and practices in school psychology.

National affiliate organizations continue to join in ISPA efforts. Formal affiliation has been accepted from organizations representing school psychologists in Colombia, Federal Republic of Germany, France, Iceland, Israel, Norway, and the United States. Applications from at least seven other national organizations are being processed. Of the estimated 40,000 school psychologists throughout the world, the majority are now connected with the international efforts of ISPA. We know that 60 or so countries now utilize school psychology services with varying degrees of sophistication.

Currently, ISPA is seeking admission to UNESCO. This affiliation is seen as necessary to securing international recognition and support to accomplish ISPA's goals. UNESCO has long been an advocate of improved educational services. In 1956, UNESCO recommended that school psychologists serve school children at a ratio of 1:6,000. This favorable ratio has been exceeded in some of the developed countries while others lag behind. Current figures are not readily available for many countries. For example, in Great Britain the reported ratio in 1968 was at 1:10,000. This volume provides this needed update of information.

Recent inquiries to the ISPA have been received from many individual practitioners as well as government leaders. Interest ranges from questions of practical application to broader concerns of professional standards and matters of national policy. Questions have included the following: How can preschool education be promoted (especially in a society where religious forces encourage women to remain home to care for their children)? How can educators keep children in school while economic pressures dictate the need for them to work in support of the family? Should school psychologists be under the authority of a local building administrator, regional office, and/or nationally legislated board of standards, and in what combination? Are training standards best set by local needs, private institutions, university-level trainers, or national governmental bodies? These are not isolated requests but rather reflect a growing awareness of how important an international perspective is in practicing psychology in the schools. Despite differences in geography, resources, and political ideology, information concerning best practices in being sought throughout the world.

Since Catterall's publications, interest in school psychology services has grown year by year. During the past 15 years, information in his volumes has quickly become outdated as school psychology services broadened their scope. It has also been difficult to find a perspective from which to judge the effectiveness of school psychology services. Although describing services is a necessary first step, describing their effectiveness within each country is more difficult. The degree of effectiveness usually comes from the identification of standards that a country (usually through its professional organization) tends to strive toward. If it were possible, the establishment of internationally agreed to standards would allow comparisons among school psychology programs worldwide. Such an effort can be threatened by the promotion of one system as being "better" than another. It is important to guard against indiscriminate comparisons because of the danger in perpetuating national chauvinism and the arrogant political views of some groups. There are, however, some promising areas of agreement. For example, at a recent ISPA colloquium, the theme of identifying the roles and function of the school psychologist was debated in a harmonious atmosphere. By describing the scope of school psychological services, the process of understanding the nature of effective and professional practices is furthered. This book goes further in this effort toward international understanding by including descriptions of services from various countries, by addressing new issues, and expanding our frame of reference.

Information generated by books such as this has usually been treated with little more than a degree of curiosity. As Catterall (1976) pointed out, it is important to those of us who are interested in the international aspects of our profession, to continually attempt to sort out those ideas that are "nice to know" from those that can be effectively transferred to another setting. Although few practices once found their way across international boundaries, that has now changed. Thinking in school psychology has taken on a broader, more ecological perspective and has become more holistic. Many good ideas are quickly being transferred from one setting to another. In the process, we are developing a more unified, professional, and international network capable of applying increasingly more powerful technologies in psychology to the solution of school-related problems. For example, efforts are currently underway to utilize existing international computer–telephone networks to link school psychologists who have access to a computer modem. Availability of sophisticated behavioral technology, increased use of computers, and improved communication allow quicker access to more information and appear to be pulling nations together to form a "professional mainstream."

Although not in the mainstream, other ideas and projects are gaining international momentum. For example, interest in understanding the learning processes of infants and preschoolers is gaining worldwide attention. Concepts such as categorical diagnosis of exceptional developmental attributes are quickly losing favor. Also on the decline are notions of *school readiness*, which is a term that implies certain skills or conditions need to be met before a child is ready to learn, particularly in a school setting. Rather, learning is being more frequently viewed as a lifelong process that crosses all settings—not just the school setting. As the average life span increases, new roles for the school psychologist are emerging that have never before been emphasized. The school psychologist's role in identifying exceptional school-age children is being expanded to facilitate the transitional process from public school to postsecondary settings and from school to the work place. As job markets change and leisure time increases, school psychologists are increasingly involved in lifelong learning activities within the schools, work place, and community. These activities are not yet part of the work shared by school psychologists around the world.

Although the role of the school psychologist appears to be moving toward a mainstream, individual differences remind us of what is unique about school psychology. Attending to individual differences in a teaching environment is important to the work of the school psychologist. The school psychologist must be able to draw from a wide variety of possible interventions. There is great diversity in the activities of the school psychologist. Paradoxically, this diversity also binds together the work of school psychology: The work of applying the principles of psychology for effective educational practice and having the ability to draw from a rich variety of strategies to meet individual needs. School psychology is a dynamic field that crosses many disciplines, can synthesize a wide range of information, and is flexible enough to meet individual needs within a sometimes rigid educational system. With educational systems in place throughout the world, this characterization of school psychology may make it the most "international" of the applied sciences.

School systems throughout the world, however, are not equal. Consequently, the stage of development attained by school psychology programs varies greatly. This variety is closely tied to political ideology, religious dogma, natural resources, and economic development. Usually, as a nation evolves, the development of its educational system reflects the development of its economy. As a basic educational system evolves, special services for exceptional children emerge as part of the programming. With the identification of exceptional children, school psychologists are employed to help meet their assessment, placement, and programming needs. Later, the school psychologist's role expands within the school system, then diversifies to other settings. This overall developmental process varies from country to country with emphasis placed on different aspects as needs dictate.

Among some developing countries, school psychologists have been more assertive in determining the future of school-based programs. This proactive role has placed demands on the international community to be more responsive to individual needs. Individual school psychologists and trainers in school psychology are beginning to take advantage of the great pool of resources available within our profession. The effects of this inquiry process and subsequent responses are changing the future of school psychology. No longer isolated, school psychologists and administrators are quick to compare the similarities and differences of their respective schooling practices with foreign systems.

Global resources are now more frequently utilized in response to the need for more effective programs. We are collaborating on research efforts, some of which are cross-cultural, some of which are not. We are collaborating on developing theoretical constructs and testing each other's ideas. No longer are international boundaries barriers to effective communication among school psychologists. Although there are differences, we are feeling more secure in our roles and finding it safe to expose our vulnerabilities. We are shaping a common identity, giving international involvement personal meaning. The efforts of the editors and authors represented in this text have acknowledged the value of an international perspective capable of recognizing personal needs and maintaining national autonomy while developing international unity. This book is a significant contribution reflecting the work of educators from around the world. The book's content also can serve to shape the direction of our children's future through their experiences in our schools.

Herbert Bischoff

Preface

The origins of this book are difficult to trace. In fact, they differ for each of the two editors.

The origins of the book for Philip Saigh are associated with his tenure (1977–1986) at the American University of Beirut. Despite the war in Lebanon, Beirut's cosmopolitan climate coupled with the University's emphasis on research served to prompt his interest in matters relating to international school psychology.

The origins for Tom Oakland are likely to lie in the thoughts and dreams elicited by postcards and letters he received as a child from his Aunt Olga as she traveled all parts of the globe in search of adventure and knowledge. His appetite for travel whetted, he and his children later embarked on their personal international travels to meet other peoples, to learn more about different cultures, and to work professionally.

Our international experiences clearly indicate the quality and level of psychological services available to children and youth—both within and outside of schools—differed markedly between countries. Moreover, most professional services for children and youth within all countries are provided by schools rather than through other public or private sectors. Thus, an understanding of psychological services for children and youth in most countries requires an understanding of the quality and nature of such services provided through schools. School psychological services typically encompass all professional psychological services available to most children and youth in the world.

Most primary sources of international literature on school psychological services were dated and limited in scope (e.g., Catteral, 1976, 1977, 1979).[1] Efforts by *School Psychology International* and later the international series in the *Journal of School Psychology* have been effective in adding to our knowledge of school psychological services. We believe this book, by bringing together literature on 25 countries, serves the following goals: (a) to promote an understanding of school psychological services from international perspectives; (b) to recognize the various ways psychological services can be offered so as to enhance both individual growth and national interests; (c) to identify problems impeding the growth and development of school psychological services; and (d) to suggest future trends of school psychological services.

The issues effecting the growth and development of children and youth are not confined within arbitrary geographic boundaries. Many major issues and problems effecting school psychological services are best studied and resovled from international perspectives. We hope this book compels others to become involved in the promotion of quality school psychological services.

It is also hoped that this volume whets your appetite for more information on an involvement in international school psychology. Although you are encouraged to acquire additional information on these topics through reading, enjoyment and understanding are enhanced when you change from a role as an observer to one as a participant. The script discussing the futures of school psychology remains to be written. We encourage you to join the international community of psychologists who work in schools and help form the future by contributing directly to the advancement of school psychological services and promoting the development of psychology in the schools internationally.

We also want to acknowledge the invaluable support and dedication of many persons associated with the production of this book. We are grateful to our chapter authors who willingly shared knowledge of psychological services in their respective countries. We appreciate the willingness of the *Journal of School Psychology* through its editor, Raymond Dean, to grant us permission to reprint (some in revised form) eight articles that previously appeared in that journal. The encouragement and support of Caven McLoughlin, Herb Bischoff, and others associated with the International School Psychology Association mean much to our efforts. The book could not have been published without the assistance and support by Thomas Kratochwill, James Ysseldyke, and others affiliated with Lawrence Erlbaum Associates.

The excellent typing skills and forbearance displayed by Jo Ann Smith, Mary

[1]See Catterall, C. D. (1976, 1977, 1979). *School psychology in international perspective* (Vols. 1–3). Columbus, OH: International School Psychology Steering Committee.

Ann Gustafson, and Mickie Sheppard at the University of Texas Learning Abilities Center overcame many of the foibles displayed by one of the co-editors. A grateful note and thanks is also extended to Rachel Diamond and Emily Filardo at the Graduate Center of the City University of New York for their assistance with the pageproofs and indices. To all of them we give a special thanks.

Philip A. Saigh
Thomas Oakland

Published with the endorsement of the Professional Standards and Practices
Committee of the International School Psychology Association

Chapter One
Psychology in the Schools: An Introduction to International Perspectives

Thomas Oakland
The University of Texas

Philip A. Saigh
Graduate Center
City University of New York

A BRIEF GLANCE AT INTERNATIONAL PSYCHOLOGY AND EDUCATION

When persons initially acquire an international perspective on school psychology they discover a world of differences—differences that exist in what school psychologists are called, how they are educated and prepared, the services they perform, where they work, and their legal responsibilities and protections. The magnitude of the differences seemingly overshadows the similarities.

However, psychologists who provide services in schools also share a number of similarities. They tend to be respected and established professional educators who acquire advanced preparation in academic psychology and who hold a strong commitment to applying psychological theories, principles, and technology so as to promote the growth and development of children, youth, and others. Although their major concern lies in facilitating academic development, they realize that academic development is closely intertwined with a host of related variables. School-based psychologists also generally recognize the need to provide direct and indirect services to pupils in regular and special education settings. They also recognize the value in providing psychological services in out-of-school settings. School psychologists recognize their effectiveness is increased by working with teachers and other educational personnel, parents, and other persons who influence the growth and development of children and youth.

Our understanding of professional psychology at an international level may be augmented by recognizing six conditions that influence variations in the practice of psychology among countries (Russell, 1984).

Regulations governing those who may claim to be psychologists vary from country to country. The use of the title *psychologist* often is determined by one's academic and professional preparation, membership in scientific and professional societies, and certification or licensing status. Important differences exist between countries in the nature and quantity of preparation, the availability of national professional organizations, and laws relating to professional service delivery. Most countries in fact lack legislation governing the use of the title *psychologist*.

Economic realities also strongly influence psychology. We see differences in the level of psychological services both among and within countries that are attributable to economic factors. Psychology is cultivated mainly in industrialized nations (Ardila, 1982b). Moreover, within countries, academic and professional psychology often are stronger in industrialized and urban (i.e., wealthier) areas.

Geographic distances between nations, the third factor, has had a considerable influence on the scope and course of psychology. Psychology most readily has reached those countries that are closely linked politically and through transportation and communication to the countries that are generally associated with the origins of modern psychology (e.g., Germany, France, Great Britain, and the United States). Countries that have close ties with nations that provide leadership in psychology are more likely to have well-developed psychology programs.

Language and semantics, the fourth set of factors, figure importantly in psychology's growth. English has become the universal language, although not the exclusive language, of psychology. Thus, the growth of psychology tends to be stronger in English-speaking than in non-English-speaking countries. Also, monolingual psychologists in English-speaking countries frequently feel little need to be fluent in another language and thus tend to be unaware of research and writing in other languages.

National interests and priorities, the fifth set of factors, have strongly influenced the initiation and growth of psychology in all countries. Both the academic and professional areas of psychology tend to be directed toward important national issues within a country. For example, the development of psychology in the U.S.S.R. is largely consistent with Marxist philosophies (Nilsson, 1984; Pambookian & Holowinsky, 1987). Developing countries in South America support psychological programs that are intended to have a desirable social impact (Oakland & Ramos-Cancel, 1985; Wechsler & Oakland, 1987). Features of U.S. psychology also are narrow and often reflect national philosophies and interests (e.g., an abiding concern for individual differences, compliances to Public Law 94-142).

Cultural factors, the sixth set, decisively influence the growth of and interest in psychology, perhaps more so than other factors. Psychology's origins and growth occurred largely in Western European and North American countries that are relatively homogeneous with respect to physical appearances, foods, dress, economic development, and values. As long as the discipline of psychology remains so strongly influenced by contributions from a few countries having common cultural characteristics, its growth will be limited in countries with different cultural orientations; moreover, the development of psychology as a strong international discipline requires us to balance our predominant Germanic and Anglo-Saxon orientation with contributions from various countries throughout the world (Ardila, 1982a).

Given prevailing Western influences on psychology, one can expect the stages through which psychology develops in Western countries to be different from those that characterize its development in non-Western countries. The greater the cultural differences, the less applicable Western psychology may be. This trend can be seen clearly in Occidental countries. Academic psychology in these countries has been characterized as passing through five stages (Azuma, 1984). More specifically, these changes involve (a) a pioneering stage in which the relevance of psychology is realized; (b) an introductory stage in which psychology is accepted as an important discipline of study; (c) a translation and modeling stage in which attempts are made to apply Western concepts and technology; (d) an indigenous stage in which new concepts and technology appropriate to the culture are developed; and (e) an integration stage in which psychology is freed from an exclusive Western influence and develops orientations consistent with their dominant domestic cultural characteristics.

As we have noted, the course and scope of psychology is influenced decisively by a country's cultural characteristics. School psychology also is influenced decisively by a country's educational institutions, through which services often are provided. The quantity and quality of school psychology services within a nation are closely associated with the general quantity and quality of its educational systems and its financial resources. Quality school psychology services always are found in countries that place a high value on education and have a well-established public school system. Knowledge of the diversity of educational systems within which school psychologists work helps to explain many of the apparent differences in school psychology that are apparent from an international perspective.

Educational Programs in Primary and Secondary Grades

Compulsory education exists in almost all reporting countries for children between the ages of 6–14 years. However, in many developing nations, significant numbers of children do not attend school. Formal enrollment estimates (World Bank, 1985) suggest about 70% of eligible students attend primary level schools and 40% attend secondary level schools. The percentage of primary school enrollment is lowest in Africa (except in the Republic of South Africa). Girls are far less likely to attend school, particularly in the higher grades: only 53% at ages 6–11 and 28% at ages 12–17 attend school (McHale, McHale, & Streatfeild, 1979a). Pupils typically enter school between age 5 or 6 to embark on a 6- to 8-year course of primary education. Secondary education (e.g., for pupils 13–15 years and older) frequently is optional. Students often choose between tracks that emphasize general, scientific, literary, or vocational education curricula.

Education in most countries is a joint enterprise between national and local governments. The national government frequently establishes broad parameters guiding regular and special education services and provides a portion of the funds. Local education agencies typically exercise responsibility for employing personnel, providing programs that go beyond basic national requirements, allocating national financial assistance, and raising and allocating additional taxes.

The school calendar typically is 9 to 10 months in length. Although most students attend school 5 days each week, students in some countries (e.g., Japan, U.S.S.R., and Israel) attend school 6 days a week. The length of the school day ranges from 3 to 7 hours. The vast majority (e.g., more than 90%) of pupils within the countries surveyed attend public schools. Notable exceptions exist in Lebanon (Saigh, 1984) and Australia (Ritchie, 1985) in which a higher percentage (> 20%) of students attend private schools.

Requirements for Teacher Preparation Vary

Requirements for the preparation of teachers vary. The requirement of a university degree, especially among primary-grade teachers, is rare. In lieu of this, most teachers are prepared in institutions that are exclusively devoted to pedagogical preparation. Some countries require secondary-level teachers to obtain a university diploma in addition to a pedagogical degree. Few, if any courses taken during the pedagogical degree count toward the completion of a university degree. In many developing countries, primary-grade teachers typically graduate from secondary schools and are not expected to obtain a tertiary education. Thus, lower academic standards often prevail for primary- than for secondary-level teachers.

The ratio between pupils and teachers varies. A report by the Population Reference Bureau (McHale, McHale, & Streatfeild, 1979a, 1979b) noted a range between 20:1 (e.g., United States, United Kingdom) and 500:1 (e.g., Chad, Burkina Faso, formerly Upper Volta). Among the countries considered in this study that report these data, the ratio typically is close to 25:1; notable exceptions are Japan and Brazil with 40:1. In addition to having a high pupil–teacher ratio, Brazilian schools often provide a morning or afternoon program for different student groups.

Preparation of Psychologists

Compared with other disciplines, the history of academic psychology is relatively short. Its beginning is frequently ascribed to the establishment of Wundt's laboratory in 1879. Its growth throughout the world has been very uneven, stronger in European and North American nations and weaker in African, South American, and Far Eastern nations. By the beginning of this century, psychology departments in Germany, England, France, and the United States offered undergraduate and graduate degrees. The establishment of separate departments of psychology occurred much later in many countries: Israel in 1957 (Raviv & Wiesner, 1985),

Ghana in 1964 (Danquah, 1987), Ireland in 1965 (Chamberlain, 1985), and the U.S.S.R. in 1968 (Holowinsky, 1986; Pambookian & Holowinsky, 1987). A number of countries (e.g., Greece; Nikolopoulou, 1986) still have neither established psychology departments nor offer psychology degrees. Psychology courses in these countries typically are offered in departments of philosophy or through pedagogical institutions.

In those countries that have psychology departments, with the exception of Ireland (Chamberlain, 1985), one or more of its institutions offer graduate degrees in psychology. The graduate diplomas typically require 1 to 3 years of study and provide for advanced generic academic preparation. Very few institutions offer a doctoral degree in academic psychology. None offer a doctoral degree in professional psychology.

Few psychology departments offer programs directed toward the professional preparation of applied psychologists at the undergraduate or graduate levels. Such programs, when offered, usually are directed at the subdoctoral graduate level. They tend to emphasize general preparation in assessment, counseling, therapy, consultation, and research areas; to be 2 to 5 years in length; and to be in departments of education or pedagogical institutions. Thus, the goal of such programs is to prepare applied psychologists to begin practice with the necessary knowledge for independent functioning. Furthermore, the programs also presume that, if specialization occurs, it will be self-initiated and self-directed and will reflect the needs of the specialist's practice.

Preparation of School Psychologists

As expected, one finds both similarities and differences regarding the quality and duration of professional preparation from country to country. An early report from the UNESCO Institute for Education (Wall, 1956) suggested three minimum requirements for the basic training and qualifications of school psychologists: They included: (a) a teaching diploma or other professional qualification as a teacher, (b) at least 5 years of teaching experience, and (c) a university qualification in psychology at a high level.

In contrast to the vast differences otherwise observed among practicing school psychologists stands one noteable commonality. In most countries school psychologists initially were prepared as teachers. Many are selected for advanced study because they are identified as superior teachers. Almost all have graduated from pedagogical institutions and taught for 2 or more years. Teaching credentials often are obtained as part of an undergraduate preparation after first having been selected for competitive places at universities in academic areas of study. Moreover, in some countries (e.g., France), teaching experience is an obligatory prerequisite for graduate preparation in the area of school psychology. In some countries (e.g., Denmark) school psychologists are required to continue teaching on a part-time basis (Poulsen, 1987).

In contrast to their uniformity of requiring teaching credentials, great diversity exists in the academic and professional preparation of school psychologists. For some (e.g., Japan), formal academic and professional preparation in psychology may end upon the receipt of a teaching certificate. The psychological services they provide largely are associated with their teaching roles, and advanced preparation in psychology is provided through in-service and short courses. School psychologists elsewhere (e.g., Brazil, West Berlin, Ireland, Israel) typically graduate from a university with a bachelor's degree in psychology after initially obtaining a teaching degree. The length of this preparation may range from 7 and 12 years.

For example, in West Berlin (Leyssner & Steinhausen, 1986), preparation as a school psychologist takes at least 12 years: a minimum of 3½ years in teacher preparation, 2 years as a probationary teacher, 5½ years in the university study program, and a 1-year probationary period as a school psychologist. School psychologists also must pass three state examinations. Specialization occurs at a later stage through on-the-job training programs.

In a third scenario (e.g., Denmark), teachers are allowed to enter a graduate-level psychology program without having obtained a BA in psychology (Poulsen, 1987). In a fourth scenario (e.g., New Zealand), school psychologists often graduate initially first from a pedagogical institution, teach, complete a 3-year undergraduate degree and a 2-year graduate degree in education or psychology, and then complete a 2-year post-MA specialty program in school psychology (Bardon, 1980; Oakland, 1981).

Thus, the previous experiences of school psychologists and the way they are selected and prepared in most of the countries considered in this review meet most of the criteria that were set forth in Wall's (1956) UNESCO recommendation. However, school psychologists in some countries (e.g., Canada, Norway, Poland, and Switzerland) are expected to have stronger academic preparation in psychology (Culbertson, 1983).

Many school psychologists in the United States may be surprised to learn that the scientist–practitioner model, which guides much of the training and practice of professional psychology in the United States, is not as popular elsewhere. The model (Cutts, 1955; Raimy, 1950) holds that applications of psychology should be supportable empirically or theoretically and should be derived from a body of literature that generally is well regarded by the profession. Although few may disagree with this feature of the model, many leaders of school psychology in other nations reject the notion that professionals also are responsible for contributing to this literature through scholarly activities. They acknowledge that the amount of academic preparation needed to conduct this level of scholarly activity presently lies beyond the scope of typical programs that are either at an undergraduate or graduate subdoctoral level.

Instead, programs in many if not most countries seemingly strive to prepare practitioners to be capable of independent practice and to be good consumers of the literature without the need to be good contributors. Consistent with this notion is the call for increasing the number of professional preparation programs at the masters rather than at the doctoral level (Ho, 1986). Lacking a commitment to conduct research as a part of practice, the doctoral degree, traditionally acquired by research-oriented scientists, cannot be maintained now as an entry standard for the professional practice of psychology.

SCHOOL PSYCHOLOGICAL SERVICES

Ratio of School Psychologists to Students

The UNESCO report also recommended no fewer than one school psychologist for every 6,000–7,500 children. The extent to which services meet this standard is difficult to estimate. Most countries do not maintain current or accurate information as to the numbers of school psychologists. An accurate count is difficult when no provision exists for certifying or licensing school psychologists. Moreover, many school psychologists are employed on a part-time basis in schools and other public agencies. In some areas (e.g., Lebanon, Denmark, and West Berlin), school psychologists are expected also to serve part time as classroom teachers. Furthermore, many governments do not maintain accurate records of the number of pupils or children enrolled in their schools; some allegedly report falsified data so as to convey a more positive picture than what actually exists.

Among many countries reviewed[1], it is not possible to determine the typical ratio of school psychologists to children due to the lack of information. Among those reporting, the range is broad, extending from about 1:1,400 in Denmark to about 1:33,300 in Ireland. England, Wales, Scotland, West Berlin, Israel, and other countries fall within the range recommended by UNESCO (i.e., 6,000–7,500).

[1]Information for this chapter was obtained from existing literature describing school psychology in more than 30 countries. North American countries are not included in this discussion. The following references were relied on most heavily:

Australia (Ritchie, 1985); Brazil (Wechsler & Gomes, 1986); China (LaVoie, this volume); Zhang Houcan (personal communication, March 1987); Denmark (Poulsen, 1987); England (Lindsay, 1985); Federal Republic of Germany (Mietzel, Russman-Stohr, & Mason, 1987); Finland (Poikonen, 1979); France (Guillemard, 1984, 1985); Ghana (Danquah, 1987); Greece (Nikolopoulou, 1986); India (Joyce & Showers, 1985; Paliwal, 1977, 1984; Raina, this volume); Ireland (Chamberlain, 1985); Israel (Raviv, 1984; Raviv & Wiesner, 1985); Italy (Meazzini, 1985; Oakland, Laurent, & Meazzini, 1987); Japan (Shinagawa, this volume); Jordan (Hamdi & Hamdi, this volume); Lebanon (Saigh, 1984); New Zealand (Bardon 1980; Oakland, 1981); Saudi Arabia (Gerner, 1985; Sendiony, Marzouky, & Ghamedy, 1987); Scotland (Conochie, 1987); Sudan (Saigh, 1984); Taiwan (Barclay, J., & Wu-Tien-Wu, 1986); Thailand (Boonruangrutana, 1987); Union of Soviet Socialist Republics (Holowinsky, 1986; Nilsson, 1984; Pambookian & Holwinsky, 1987); Wales, (Lindsay, 1985); West Berlin (Leyssner & Steinhausen, 1986; Wechsler & Oakland, 1987; Oakland & Cunningham, 1987).

Number of School Psychologists

The number of school psychologists providing services within the countries that were surveyed show considerable variability. Some countries report few school psychologists (26 in Ireland; 51 in West Berlin; 70 in Finland; 140 in New Zealand), but others have a relatively large staff (500 in Denmark; 1,200 in England and Wales). Some countries report no or few school psychologists (e.g., India, China, and the U.S.S.R.). The majority of school psychologists in all reporting countries seemingly are female; the percentage in some nations exceeds 90% (e.g., Brazil and Jordan), owing in part to the generally low status of education and psychology and restrictions on women's entering other professions and occupations in these countries. However, the overall percentage of women is estimated to be approximately 68% from the results of a recent worldwide survey (Oakland & Cunningham, 1987). In larger countries that have disparate and widely separate urban areas and large sprawling rural areas, school psychologists seem to prefer to work and live in or close to urban areas; their numbers in rural areas are few.

Types of School Psychological Services

The scope of school psychological services is quite extensive. The most frequent direct services to students involve vocational and academic guidance, personal and academic counseling, and educational curriculum-based interventions. These services are provided by school psychologists in almost all countries. Other direct services, including therapy and teaching, occur less frequently. Numerous indirect services also are offered. Consulting with teachers and parents, observing and testing, and recommending special education placements are common. Other important, although less frequent, indirect services include research, school, and community organizational development, in-service programs to staff and parents, and test development.

School psychology services in some countries (e.g., Denmark) are directed toward a broad age range (i.e., birth through 18), whereas services in most other countries focus on a more restricted age range (i.e., 6–16). All countries but one (i.e., Ireland) devote considerable attention to primary-level students. Ireland devotes more attention to post-secondary students. School psychology services in all countries are directed to some degree to both regular and special education. This commitment reflects the regular and special educator's needs for psychological services and the psychologist's desires to serve the needs of pupils in both areas. However, the proportion of services that school psychologists devote to regular and special education varies between countries. Historical patterns, legislation, advocacy groups, and the availability of other specialists strongly influence the nature and scope of services.

The nature and scope of a nation's school psychology services should be viewed in the context of the nature and scope of its total psychological and social services. Many countries have provided publicly supported psychological and social services for years (e.g., England and Wales) whereas other countries (e.g., Greece) lack the financial resources or interest to do so. The importance of a country's publicly supported services derives from the simple fact that most psychological services for children and youth are provided through the public sector. The amount of direct services provided by schools, clinics, hospitals, bureaus, courts, and other agencies that derive their funds from the public probably exceeds the amount provided by private practitioners by a ratio of 500:1.

Empirical information relative to the nature and scope of psychological and social services in most countries is quite limited. This information is needed before one can confidently generalize about international trends with respect to differentiation of services provided by school psychologists in contrast to those in other specialties. However, anecedotal accounts suggest that school psychologists who work in countries that have well-established psychological and social services for children often concentrate more of their time and resources on school-related issues. On the other hand, those working in countries with less-established networks exercise more diverse roles; for them, school-related issues constitute only a portion of the problems to which they attend. If this observation is correct, one might conclude that the nature and scope of *school* psychological services often greatly depend on the extent to which publicly and privately supported psychological and social services are well established within a nation. Quality school psychology services are likely to exist when quality psychological services for children also are provided through other sources.

Persons interested in providing psychological services through private practices may regard this discussion as somewhat constrained given the limited emphasis that has been afforded to the role of private practitioners. In effect, however, the services of private practitioners in psychology, especially for children and youth, are virtually unavailable in most countries (except perhaps in major metropolitan areas for middle- and upper class families). Although the private practice of psychology with children, including school psychology, is quite common in some countries (i.e., Canada, Lebanon, and the United States), its role in most countries is minimal.

Locations for Services

The locations and settings from which school psychology services are delivered are quite diverse. For example, school psychologists in New Zealand, Ireland, Israel, Denmark, England, and Wales have their offices in community rather than school settings, which enables them to serve both community and school needs. This is consistent with their broader mission to be of service to all children (not just students), their teachers, and families. The missions of school psychologists in West Berlin, Ghana, Australia, Federal Republic of Germany, and other nations are more restricted to education. As such, psychological services in these countries tend to be delivered in the schools.

The sources of funds used to pay school psychologists' salaries reflect similar diversity. Many countries rely on funds from both national and local governments. However, the relative proportion of their contributions frequently differ. Many are paid principally from national funds (e.g., Ireland, New Zealand), but others rely principally on local sources (e.g., Spain, England, Wales, Australia).

Administration of Services

One also is impressed with international differences with respect to the administration of psychological services. Six different styles are evident. In some countries school psychologists are likely to be assigned to a single school in which they serve as teachers, counselors, and assessment specialists. They also may have districtwide responsibilities and be assigned on a part-time basis to community settings (e.g., Japan). In other countries, school psychologists are assigned to a cluster (e.g., two to eight) of schools. The cluster may involve schools of the same grade levels (e.g., primary or secondary) or may combine those of different levels. A third type of arrangement provides for one or more school psychologists to serve at the school district level. Their responsibilities in this regard are likely to depend on the ratios of school psychologists to students. In countries with lower ratios, school psychologists are likely to devote more attention to issues involving individual students, whereas in countries with higher ratios they are more likely to devote more time to districtwide issues and to consult with educators and parents than to see individual students. A fourth organizational arrangement is found frequently in less-populated areas. Within this arrangement, services are provided by one or by a small number of school psychologists within a geographic region containing a number of small towns; their time is divided between the various towns in their district. The term *towns* is specified so as to emphasize that their services often are provided at that level and include, but are not limited to, school settings. School psychologists working within such a geographic region see children and youths in various settings (e.g., schools, families, social services agencies, courts). They also are likely to provide services through consultation, organizational development, and in-service programs. A fifth arrangement is similar to the fourth except that the services are delivered within a single town. Within this arrangement, the focus remains on children and youth, not on pupils. The sixth organizational structure is found in a few countries (e.g., India) in which school psychologists principally exercise administrative, teaching, research, and development responsibilities. These countries tend to have a limited number of school psychologists and attempt to bring their abilities to bear on the nation's efforts to improve education and social services.

Thus, considerable diversity exists among countries in the administration of school psychology services. Considerable diversity also exists in the relative emphasis placed on school-related and community-related services. The services of school psychologists in some countries are almost completely restricted to pupils and educators but in others are broadened to include infants, children, and youths and those persons, institutions, and agencies responsible for their development and care.

Other Factors Influencing Services

School psychology services within a country generally are stronger in urban than in rural areas. This pattern is not unique to the profession of school psychology. The quantity and quality of medical, dental, legal, and other professional services tend to be proportional to an area's population and environmental amenities. Higher quality services are more likely to be found in more urban areas and more desirable living environments (e.g., those having desirable climates, well-developed municipal services, economic and political stability, as well as cultural activities and other amenities).

School psychology services also tend to be stronger in countries displaying economic and political stability. Whereas most countries have had established school systems for 100 years or more, school psychology services developed recently, in most countries after World War II. Nations that began school psychology services in the late 1940s and early 1950s and whose political and economic history since then have been stable tend to have more established programs. However, countries that began their services at the same time but have witnessed political and economic turbulence (e.g., Ghana, Lebanon) tend to have weaker programs. The educated people in these countries frequently emigrate to safer and more stable countries.

One strong exception to this trend is found in Israel (Raviv, 1984; Raviv & Wiesner, 1985). The country's school system was established in 1948 and its school psychology services began in 1960. Despite the country's continued military alertness and unbridled inflation, its school psychology services have grown markedly and are well developed (e.g., Israel's ratio of school psychologists to students—1:1,556—is one of the best in the world).

ANTICIPATED GROWTH AREAS FOR SCHOOL PSYCHOLOGY

Political and economic instability, on occasion, may create conditions that facilitate the development of school psychology services. As we have indicated elsewhere, most services were initiated following World War II during periods of political and economic turmoil. Furthermore, forecasts of growth in school psychology services are relatively low in some countries that show considerably more stability (e.g., Finland, Denmark) and higher in some countries showing more instability (e.g., Brazil).

The growth of school psychology during the next 30–40 years conceivably will be proportional to a country's commitment to respond to important yet unserved psychological needs of its children. Slower growth can be expected in countries such as West Germany, Finland, and Denmark that have well-established services and relatively steady birth rates. In contrast, the potential for growth is almost beyond description in the three most heavily populated nations: China, India, and the U.S.S.R. Together they have an estimated population of 461 million among children aged 5–14. These figures constitute almost 50% of the world's population of children (United Nations, 1985). Despite their large populations, there are virtually no school psychologists in these countries. Both China (Professor Zhang Houcan, personal communication) and the U.S.S.R. (Irina Doobrovina, personal communication) are expressing signs of interests in developing their psychological resources and applying them to education. India, too, is capable of expanding the roles for psychology to go beyond the preparation of teachers and research on teacher education. Should school psychology services in these heavily populated countries develop to the point of reaching the 1:6,000 ratio suggested by UNESCO, they would have a total of 76,833 school psychologists. On an even broader note, applying the 1:6,000 ratio to an estimated worldwide population of 933 million among children aged 6 to 14 produces a goal of 155,500 school psychologists worldwide. This is in sharp contrast to the 40,000 school psychologists estimated in 1982 (Catterall, 1982).

MAJOR PROBLEMS FACE SCHOOL PSYCHOLOGY

The expanding literature describing the practices of school psychology (e.g., see Catterall's three volumes on *Psychology in the Schools in International Perspectives*, the *Journal of School Psychology*, and *School Psychology International*) enables us to begin to establish broad international trends. Although diversity exists in the preparation of and services provided by school psychologists within the various countries, they face a number of common problems. The 30 or more separate problems identified in the reviewed literature can be characterized in the context of three themes: low levels of professionalism, limited technology, and inadequate information.

Problems Related to a Lack of Professionalism

Elsewhere, six essential attributes of professionalism that relate to the practice of school psychology in the United States have been defined and examined (Oakland, 1986). These include a profession's activities and areas of responsibilities, attempts to promote self-regulation through professional standards, quality and quantity of professional preparation programs, programs that enhance professional socialization and status, systems for rewards and recognitions, and practices within organizations. Almost all of the 30 problems fall within this realm of professionalism.

Concerns are voiced by some observers about their areas of responsibilities. School psychologists are often unable to provide servives that represent state-of-the-art practice. They lack preparation in professional psychology, are unable to specialize, work within vague job specifications, devote too much time to minor issues while finding themselves unable to attend larger organizational and systems issues, feel restricted by having others define their areas of competence, and express various degrees of confidence about the services being provided.

Others expressed concerns about the lack of professional standards governing ethics, practices, and professional preparation, particularly in those countries lacking strong professional associations. Also lacking among the countries surveyed are procedures to certify or license psychologists and school psychologists. Lacking effective standards, ethical and professional standards can widely vary. Malpractice occurs but is rarely alleged or addressed. Also, conflicts arise with other professions that may be abated if strong professional codes existed and were followed.

The professional status and identity of school psychologists in a number of countries are tenuous. A number indicate that their prestige is low, that they receive little recognition for their services, and that the public and educators often place restrictions that prevent them from offering the full range of services they feel capable of providing.

Professional recognition and rewards also are problematic in some countries. Salaries are low compared to those received by professionals in private practice. Furthermore, their services are often considered expendable. Faced with economic difficulties, school systems may encourage part-time employment or may not replace school psychologists who leave while expecting the existing staff to assume mounting responsibilities. School psychologists report difficulties when working within schools and other organizations in which they hold limited authority. They report competing with other support services, seeing teachers and other educators inadequately prepared, diffusing their professional roles within the organization, and being confined to work in areas important to the organization rather than their own areas of interest and expertise.

Detriments to professionalism recently were identified through the results of a survey in which recognized school psychologists from several areas of the world identified eight significant problem areas comprising their practice (Oakland & Cunningham, 1987). These were, in increasing order of importance: a dearth of time to carry out assigned responsibilities, inadequate compensation compared to physicians and lawyers, limited opportunities for professional advancement, compromised professional standards due to organizational mandates, the lack of high self-expectations, assuming responsibilities for services that are unrelated to their training, low status among educators, and being supervised by persons who have little expertise in school psychology.

Areas less likely to be rated as problematic, in decreasing order of importance, include managing family and professional responsibilities, assuming responsibilities unrelated to psychology, having opportunities to confer with colleagues in school psychology, and receiving pay comparable to that received by educators.

Low levels of professional preparation encompasses another set of concerns. Few universities offer professional preparation programs in school psychology. Preparation consists almost exclusively of generic academic psychology, and relies too heavily on self-initiated specialization following the completion of a degree.

Professional socialization also is problematic. Attempts to promote socialization among professionals typically are directed toward establishing power and control over its members and to ward off attacks from others. Whereas strong feelings of comradery and confidence exist among school psychologists in some countries, others feel vulnerable, powerless, and unsure of their professional identity. Moreover, many feel threatened by the possibility of other professional groups usurping responsibilities normally under the control of psychologists (Wechsler & Oakland, 1987).

Problems Related to Inadequate Technology

Professionals typically rely heavily on the tools of their trade to facilitate and improve their services. Technology in psychology, often readily available in Western nations, is unavailable or in short supply in many developing nations. For example, although school psychologists in the United States can choose from a host of standardized and validated tests, those in other countries generally have few tests developed within their country and standarized on their students. Moreover, needed research activities from which technology may emerge are limited by restrictions on time, resources, abilities, and antiempirical attitudes.

Problems Related to Lack of Information

School psychologists typically face problems others have found vexing. They are expected to improve children who have not been responsive to help from others. They typically work with students exhibiting moderate to severe social and emotional problems, substance abuse, low achievement, test anxiety, and other problems. Career and vocational guidance activities often proceed despite a superficial understanding of a student's aptitudes, achievement, interests, and training opportunities. School psychologists frequently search desperately for successful alternatives to ineffective education programs, not knowing if such programs exist, are implementable, or are effective. They may be responsible for developing new programs for working with immigrants from cultures about which they know little. School psychologists frequently report feeling overwhelmed by these and other responsibilities. They readily admit that they lack vital information needed to be effective. Many countries do not have their own professional journals through which flow new academic and professional developments. The purchase of foreign books and journals may be difficult financially or even pointless given language differences.

Future Needs and Trends

School psychologists are gaining a better understanding of their history and clarifying their present roles and functions. They also are identifying future needs and trends. Most articles upon which this review is based identified needs and trends that characterize school psychology in their respective countries. These needs and trends are divisible into three major attributes of professionalism.

Expanding Professional Activities and Responsibilities. The plurality of comments concern professional activities and responsibilities. A number of authors recognize the need to increase both the breadth and depth of services. They foresee that the focus of their work will broaden so as to include a larger segment of regular education. Services involving consultation (e.g., closer work with parents and educators) as well as systems and organizational development are central to achieving this goal. They anticipate maintaining and improving diagnostic and intervention services to the handicapped while expanding their involvement with preschool, prevention (e.g., handicapping conditions, school drop-outs, test anxiety), and research. School psychologists perceive their need to provide leadership in developing programs that enhance understanding of and relationships among persons from different racial, cultural, and economic groups. These additional activities may require the employment of more school psychologists in countries with stable pupil populations. Countries with significantly increasing birth rates will need to employ more school psychologists to maintain basic services. Countries with increasing birth rates and expanded duties for school psychology will need their numbers of school psychologists to dramatically increase.

Promoting Professionalism. A second major set of future trends and needs involves professional standards and self-regulation. School psychologists in many countries are aware of the need to form an independent professional association or to strengthen existing professional associations. From these associations may emerge strong guidelines for ethics and professional practice. Moreover, those organizations may bring to bear effective lobbying and other initiatives to regulate the practice of psychology and school psychology through legislation. Professional associations also need to work toward establishing principles and practices that make possible the provision of services during periods of economic, social, and political turmoil.

School Psychology's Interface With Education. The third most frequently mentioned set of trends and needs centers on the professional practices of school psychology within systems of education. The organization of education may be analogous to a family whose members differ in knowledge, responsibilities, and authority. Its members convene at an irregularly shaped table that provides them differing degrees of visibility and power. Often lacking legal or legislative status and political power, school psychologists frequently are the distant, although somewhat accepted and perhaps even welcomed, family members. School psychologists propose to formalize their status and increase their power by becoming more visible and by influencing the omnibus system of education, not just special education, through activities such as organization development, teacher consultation, and teaching psychology in secondary schools and in pedagogical institutions. Some perceive these activities as particularly germane in underdeveloped nations that have large student populations and few school psychologists (e.g., Ghana). Employing the concept of triage, one first must work on developing viable general education programs before deploying scarce resources to special programs. However, work also must occur on a broader scale in countries with historically strong cultural traditions that are antithetical to the health, welfare, and education of the majority of its people and the practice of psychology (Danquah, 1987).

Fewer trends and needs pertaining to the remaining three professional areas were identified (i.e., quality and quantity of professional preparation programs, programs that enhance professional socialization and status, and systems for rewards and recognitions). However, some writers comment optimistically about being able to improve both the academic and professional preparation of school psychologists (as well as regular and special educators). Within many countries the academic discipline of psychology is gaining greater strongholds in universities and the number of graduate programs is increasing. International exchanges of scholars and increased availability of international literature on academic and applied issues are seen as aiding the growth and development of the profession.

Our Views as to Possible Solutions to Problems Facing School Psychology

We would like to restate some of the aforementioned problems in order to underscore the most seminal problems and to suggest additional solutions. These include promoting professional activities and responsibilities; promoting professional standards; promoting and improving academic and professional preparation; improving recognition and rewards; developing, publishing, and marketing scholarly, professional, and technical contributions; and creating and sharing knowledge.

Promote Professional Activities and Responsibilities. The activities that fall within the scope of the profession of school psychology have not been clearly specified. Statements prepared and endorsed by national and international associations are needed that clearly describe the breadth of services one can expect from the specialty of school psychology. The operational boundaries defining our specialty should be established broadly in order to avoid restricting the range of services that the profession can provide. By charting broad parameters, school psychologists will be encouraged to pursue activities and responsibilities that fall somewhat beyond their present grasp yet within their near-term reach.

Such statements might include a commitment to services directed toward individuals and groups and involve psychological and educational assessment, interventions, teaching, counseling, consultation, organizational development, administration and supervision, program development and evaluation, research, and prevention. The goal is to create a set of aspirational guidelines that specify the types of services the public can expect from the profession although not from a particular member.

Promoting Professional Standards. A number of authors raised concerns about the principles that should guide practice in their countries. The profession's acceptance of the responsibility to provide specific services should rest on the considered judgment of school psychologists at the national level as to the best ways to contribute to the theory, science, and practice of psychology. Every profession can be expected to have uniform and recognizable standards that serve the needs of the practitioners, clients, and educators, as well as legal and financial bodies. Many school psychologists are requesting a clear statement of the ethical principles to guide their practices. National and international associations should respond to this request by preparing statements that discuss issues such as responsibilities, competence, moral and legal standards, confidentiality, consumer welfare, professional relationships, assessment, and research.

Promoting and Improving Academic and Professional Preparation. A profession's status is highly influenced by the quality and quantity of academic and professional preparation expected from its members. A profession states its expectations by recommending the entry-level standards that it considers necessary and sufficient to guarantee effective practice.

The academic and professional preparation of school psychologists varies greatly between countries. The standard in some countries is an undergraduate degree (or even a few psychology courses during one's pedagogical preparation), whereas others require 3 or more years of graduate preparation. The well-being of a profession's clients and members requires the profession to work toward creating standards for professional preparation that are realistic and help to ensure the delivery of services commensurate with its resources and best efforts.

Thus, national and international associations should prepare statements that establish entry level standards for the academic and professional preparation of school psychologists. The pathfinding efforts of UNESCO (Wall, 1956) to establish standards in this area may serve as an appropriate starting point. The profession of school psychology, like others, is judged on the basis of its lowest acceptable standards. The availability of strong guidelines for preparation will improve its status and will enable its members to work to improve the preparation of school psychologists in those countries with inadequate preparation.

International societies of psychologists also are encouraged to work toward establishing one or more international schools of applied and professional psychology devoted to the preparation of psychologists, including but not limited to school psychologists. Such schools should be able to combine the best elements of scientific and applied psychology in order to enhance scholarly knowledge and the quality of services rendered. Such international schools would select from among the world's most able scholars, practitioners, and students interested in applications of psychology to important national and international issues.

Improving Recognition, Rewards, and Organizational Services by Institutionalizing Practices. School psychology in many countries is highly expendable because its services are not mandated through legislation. School psychologists frequently serve at the pleasure of national and local authorities. Moreover, when mandated through legislation, services tend to be directed toward a small portion of the student population (e.g., special education students) rather than toward the entire educational enterprise.

A possible solution is proposed for two related problems: limitations in providing services in institutions in which school psychologists often have little authority or power, and restricted recognition and rewards. The solution to these problems may lie in more astute political action by the profession, by fostering legislation mandating the provision of school psychology services throughout the entire educational enterprise. National and international associations of school psychologists should institute a study that explores the needs and desires of its members for assistance in forming professional and political alliances, in marketing school psychology services, in creating model legislation, and in timing initiatives to effect legislative changes.

Developing, Publishing, and Marketing Scholarly, Professional, and Technical Contributions. In many countries, school psychology services clearly are restricted by a modicum of technological resources. The lack of textbooks, primary references, tests and other assessment techniques, data-retrieval services, broad data banks, and other resources limits the ability of school psychologists to provide suitable and up-to-date services. This condition is similar to one encountered during the last 80 years by psychologists in other specializations who experienced numerous difficulties in publishing, marketing, and acquiring scholarly, professional, and technical contributions.

One of the important responses of psychologists in the United States to these conditions was to develop partnerships with other sectors of the U.S. society (e.g., publishers, other corporations, and research foundations). New Zealand psychologists (Bardon, 1980) accomplished similar goals through the creation of the federally funded New Zealand Council for Educational Research. International psychology needs one or more privately or publicly held corporations devoted to promoting psychology and education internationally and willing to work with psychologists, educators, and others in developing, publishing, and marketing scholarly, professional, and technical contributions in important academic and professional areas of psychology. The International School Psychology Association, the International Union of Psychological Science, the International Council of Psychologists, and other international societies of psychologists should confer in order to determine the degree of interest in working toward the creation of a corporation or to form an alliance with one or more existing corporations to develop, publish, and market technological resources in psychology, education, and related areas for worldwide consumption.

Creating and Sharing Knowledge. Many of the previous suggestions, if implemented, are likely to stimulate the creation, dissemination, and use of knowledge pertinent to the profession. However, school psychology need not wait for developments in other arenas to acquire and use the knowledge they need. School psychology can begin to address a number of problems it faces by sharing information and resources among its members and allied professions.

The practices of school psychology vary widely throughout the world because school psychology is a specialty whose members work with pupils who manifest virtually every variant in educational and psychological characteristics and who live in divergent cultural, economic, social, and geographic regions. Few other professions have a comparable breadth of experiences with children. With this in mind, existing networks of school psychologists should be expanded through bilateral exhange programs that promote joint activities that are intended to resolve important international issues. Partial financial support for this program might be provided by the United Nations, international service organizations, (e.g., Lions, Kiwanis, Rotary), philanthropic foundations, and member nations.

Many of the problems that the profession has encountered are common to a number of nations. However, psychologists in some nations have more extensive experience and greater success in resolving them. One or two school psychologists from countries encountering a particular problem could be released from their regular duties and invited to a host country for a period of 3 months or more in order to learn from the host country's experiences, to develop strategies for their own countries, to prepare a report outlining possible remedies for dissemination to colleagues and others upon their return, and to assume leadership for its implementation—at least in pilot form. A few examples are provided here.

School psychologists interested in developing and expanding their services should consider consulting their colleagues in Denmark and France who have a well-developed and highly respected program. Psychologists providing services to pupils struggling under economic, social, and political crisis should consult colleagues in Lebanon and Israel. Psychologists might find contacts with Chinese colleagues beneficial if they are interested in better understanding cultural influences on students' educational and psychological development, the family's influence on achievement, or ways to implement primary prevention programs. Those encountering problems in delivering services to rural areas may want to contact colleagues in Australia (given its extensive experience with students in the Outback) or the Alaskan and Appalachian regions of the United States (e.g., Gotts & Purnell, 1986). Those developing community-based programs involving adults and children in Third World Nations should consider consulting colleagues in South America for whom this is a frequent experience (Oakland & Ramos-Cancel, 1985)

CONCLUSIONS

Despite the differences relating to the scope and quality of services, school psychologists are providing valuable assistance to children in many countries. Services are well established in many nations. School psychology services are likely to increase significantly in the future as the discipline of psychology becomes more popular and as it matures to incorporate important features of non-Western cultures and societies. Its continued growth depends on a number of conditions external to the specialty. These include the status accorded education and the amount and stability of funds that school-based services receive, the country's political and economic stability, and certification and licensing of professional psychologists. The internal factors that will influence the growth of school psychology include its ability to increase its professionalism, to improve its technology, and to acquire a solid knowledge base from which to guide services.

The growth of school psychology services also will be enhanced by expanding a purview beyond the limits of a national focus so as to develop and to utilize resources at an international level. This expanded focus is needed to bring about a better understanding of the cultural, social, and political factors that strongly influence the delivery and acceptance of services. An international perspective also is needed in order to extend the growth of the discipline of psychology beyond its current western orientation.

ACKNOWLEDGMENT

Portions of this chapter were taken from an article that appears in the *Journal of School Psychology*, *25*, 287–308, 1987

REFERENCES

Ardila, R. (1982a). Psychology in Latin America. *Annual Review of Psychology, 33*, 103–122.

Ardila, R. (1982b). International psychology. *American Psychologist, 37*, 323–329.

Azuma, H. (1984). Psychology in a non-Western country: stages through which psychology develops: *International Journal of Psychology, 19*, 45–55.

Barclay, J. R., & Wu, W. T. (1986). The development of school psychological services in Taiwan. *Journal of School Psychology, 24*, 1–8.

Bardon, J. I. (1980). *The New Zealand educational psychologist: A comparative analysis*. Wellington, New Zealand: New Zealand Council for Educational Research.

Boonruangrutana, S. (1987). School psychology in Thailand. *Journal of School Psychology, 25*(3), 277–280.

Catterall, C. (1982). International school psychology: problems and promises. In C. R. Reynolds & T. B. Gutkin (Eds.), *The handbook of school psychology* (pp. 1103–1128). New York: Wiley.

Chamberlain, J. (1985). School psychology in the Republic of Ireland. *Journal of School Psychology, 23*, 227–224.

Conochie, D. (1987). School psychology in Scotland. *Journal of School Psychology, 25*(3), 235–246.

Culbertson, F. (1983). International school psychology: cross-cultural perspectives. In T. Kratochwill (Ed.), *Advances in school psychology* (pp. 45–82). Hillsdale, NJ: Lawrence Erlbaum Associates.

Cutts, N. (Ed.). (1955). *School psychology at mid-century*. Washington, DC: American Psychological Association.

Danquah, S. A. (1987). School psychology in Ghana. *Journal of School Psychology, 25*(3), 247–254.

Gerner, M. (1985). The school psychologist in Saudi Arabia. *School Psychology International, 6*, 88–94.

Gotts, E. E., & Purnell, R. F. (1986). Families and schools in rural Appalachia. *American Journal of Community Psychology, 14*, 499–519.

Guillemard, J. C. (1984). The future of school psychology in France: practices and perspectives. *School Psychology International, 5*, 21–26.

Guillemard, J. C. (1985). The training of school psychologists in France. *School Psychology International, 6*, 69–71.

Ho, D. Y. F. (1986). Psychology in Hong Kong. *International Journal of Psychology, 21*, 213–223.

Holowinsky, I. Z. (1986). School psychology in the USA and USSR. *School Psychology International, 7*, 35–39.

Hu, S., Oakland, T., & Salili, F. (1988). School psychology in Hong Kong. *School Psychology International, 9*, 21–28.

Joyce, B., & Showers, B. (1985). Teacher education in India: Observations on American innovations abroad. *Educational Researcher, 14*, 3–9.

Leyssner, U. K., & Steinhausen, H. C. (1986). School psychology in West Berlin. *Journal of School Psychology, 24*, 97–102.

Lindsay, G. (1985). Educational psychology in England and Wales. *Journal of School Psychology, 23*, 305–317.

McHale, M. C., McHale, J., & Streatfeild, G. F. (1979a). *Children in the world*. Washington, DC: Population Reference Bureau.

McHale, M. C., McHale, J., & Streatfeild, G. F. (1979b). *World of children*. Washington, DC: Population Reference Bureau.

Meazzini, P. (1985). The training of school psychologists in Italy. *School Psychology International, 6*, 63–68.

Mietzel, G., Russman-Stohr, C., & Mason, E. (1987). School psychology in the Federal Republic of Germany. *Journal of School Psychology, 25*, 255–266.

Nikolopoulou, A. (1986). School psychology in Greece. *Journal of School Psychology, 24*, 325–333.

Nilsson, T. M. (1984). Skolpsykologer-ocksa i Sovjetunionen? [School psychologists Even in the Soviet Union?] *Psykisk Halsa, 25*, 37–38.

Oakland, T. (1981, August). *American psychologists abroad: Perspectives on children and schooling in New Zealand.* Paper presented to the annual meeting of the American Psychological Association, Los Angeles, CA.

Oakland, T. (1986). Professionalism within school psychology. *Professional School Psychology, 1,* 9–27.

Oakland, T., & Cunningham, J. (1987, July). *Status on psychology in schools: Results of an international survey.* Paper presented to the annual meeting of the International School Psychology Association, Interlaken, Switzerland.

Oakland, T., Laurent, J., & Meazzini, P. (1987). Special education in Italy. In C. R. Reynolds & L. Mann (Eds.), *Encyclopedia of special education* (p. 866). New York: Wiley.

Oakland, T., & Ramos-Cancel, M. (1985). Educational and psychological perspectives on hispanic children from hispanic journals: A view from Latin America. *Journal of Multilingual and Multicultural Development, 6,* 67–82.

Paliwal, T. R. (1977). Psychology in the schools in India. In C.D. Catterall (Ed.), *Psychology in the schools in international perspective* (pp. 168–182). Columbus, OH: International School Psychology Association.

Paliwal, T. R. (1984). The prospects for psychology in Indian schools. *School Psychology International, 5,* 27–30.

Pambookian, H., & Holowinsky, I. (1987). School psychology in the USSR. *Journal of School Psychology, 25*(3), 209–222.

Poikonen, P. (1979). School psychology in Finland. In C. D. Catterall (Ed.), *Psychology in the schools in international perspective* (pp. 162–169). Columbus, OH: International School Psychology Association.

Poulsen, A. (1987). Schol psychology in Denmark. *Journal of School Psychology, 25*(3), 233–234.

Raimy, V. (Ed.). (1950). *Training in clinical psychology.* Engelwood Cliffs, NJ: Prentice-Hall.

Raviv, A. (1984). School psychology in Israel. *Journal of School psychology, 22,* 323–333.

Raviv, A., & Wiesner, E. (1985). School psychology in Israel—Some problems in the profession. *Journal of School Psychology, 23,* 113–119.

Ritchie, M. (1985). School psychology in Australia. *Journal of School Psychology, 23,* 13–18.

Russell, R. (1984). Psychology in its world context. *American Psychologist, 39,* 1017–1025.

Saigh, P. (1984). School psychology in Lebanon. *Journal of School Psychology, 22,* 233–238.

Sendiony, M. F., Marzouky, H., & Ghamedy, H. (1987). School psychology in Saudi Arabia. *Journal of School Psychology, 25*(3), 267–276.

United Nations. (1985). 1983 *Demographic Yearbook.* New York: Author.

Wall, W. D. (1956). *Psychological services for schools.* New York: University Press for UNESCO Institute for Education.

Wechsler, S., & Gomes, D. C. (1986). School psychology in Brazil. *Journal of School Psychology, 24,* 221–227.

Wechsler, S., & Oakland, T. (1987, August). *School psychology in South America.* Paper presented at the annual meeting of the International Council of Psychology, New York.

World Bank. (1985). *Publication summary.* Washington, DC: The International Bank for Reconstruction and Development/ The World Bank.

Chapter Two
School Psychology in Italy

Antonio Nisi
ASP Centro di Psicologia Clinica
Verona, Italy
Lega Del Filo D'Oro
Osimo, Italy

Dina Vivian
State University of New York at Stony Brook

Paolo Meazzini
University of Rome

The current approach to school psychology in Italy is largely determined by theoretical and philosophical forces unfamiliar to those outside the country. This chapter presents an historical overview of the theoretical and philosophical underpinnings of Italian psychology in an attempt to provide a context for a better understanding of the current status of psychology in the schools. The Italian educational system as well as the training and employment of school psychologists are also discussed.

THE ITALIAN EDUCATIONAL SYSTEM

Upon parental request, any 3-year-old Italian youngster can be enrolled in preschool (*Scuola Materna)*. The preschool is not mandatory. It is designed to develop basic perceptual and cognitive skills that underlie school achievement and to foster the child's socialization. This emphasis on improving the socialization process among preschool children reflects a deep-rooted Italian tradition. These schools can be administered by the state, privately by the local townships ("*Comuni*"), and/or by private organizations usually of Catholic persuasion. As shown in Table 2.1, according to the *Centro Studi Investimenti Sociali* (CENSIS, 1986), approximately half of the preschool children attend private schools that are generally administered on a secular basis. Although enrollment in public preschools is cost free, private schools have fees that are generally rather modest.

Table 2.2 presents the Ministry of Education's figures regarding the number of schools (divided by school category), teachers, and students in Italy during

TABLE 2.1
Structure of the Italian Educational System

Type of School (Italian Title)	Type of attendance (& Duration of Program)	Age of students	School Administration[a]		
			Public (% pop. served)	Private Secular (% pop. served)	Private Religious (% pop. served)
Pre-school *(Scuola materna)*	Voluntary (3 years)	3–5	49.9%	29.2%	20.9%
Primary school *(Scuola Elementare)*	Mandatory (5 years)	6–10	92.3%	1.6%	6.1%
Lower secondary *(Scuola Media Inferiore)*	Mandatory (3 years)	11–13	95.5%	0.6%	3.9%
Higher secondary *(Scuola Media Superiore:)*	Voluntary	14–on	90.1%	4.6%	5.3%
1) Classical, artistic, linguistic, & scientific *lycées (Licei)* (5 years)					
2) Technical institutes (5 years)					
3) Teaching training institutes *(Magistrali)* (4 years)					
4) Vocational institutes (2–3 years)					
University *(Universitá)*	Voluntary (4–6 years)				

[a]The percentages represent mean values obtained by combining data obtained throughout the national territory. In northwestern regions of Italy a higher number of students than in southern Italy is enrolled in private schools (secular and religious combined), as follows: pre-elementary 73.1% (nw) vs. 37.7% (s); primary & lower secondary: 8.3% (nw) vs. 1.6% (s); higher secondary: 15.9% (nw) vs. 6.1% (s) (CENSIS, 1986)

the 1982–1983 academic year (*Europa Yearbook*, 1986). As depicted in Table 2.2, the ratio of teachers to students in the preschools is approximately 1:28.

Mandatory instruction begins when children reach the age of 6 and continues for 8 years. The first 5 years constitute the primary school (*Scuola Elementare*) and the next 3 years constitute the lower secondary school (*Scuola Media Inferiore*). As indicated in Table 2.1, over 90% of primary and post-primary schools in Italy are public and are tuition free. Most of the private schools are administered by the Catholic Church and are usually supported by modest annual tuitions.

Mandatory instruction in Italy is extremely decentralized. For example, small villages frequently have their own elementary and secondary schools. As indicated in Table 2.2 the teacher to student ratio for the mandatory schools is relatively low (i.e., 1:15 in the elementary schools and 1:10 in the lower secondary schools). According to government statistics the average number of students per class during the 1986 year was 16.5 children in elementary classes and 21.3 children in lower secondary classes (CENSIS, 1986). This characteristic of the Italian school system facilitates the implementation of individualized instructional curricula and the mainstreaming of handicapped and developmentally disabled children in regular classrooms.

Several types of teachers provide services in the elementary schools. In addition to the regular teachers, classes are enriched with support teachers that assist children with special learning needs. Approximately one support teacher is provided for every four children with "special" needs in elementary schools, and approximately one support teacher is provided for every six students in the lower secondary schools (Comassi, 1979). The support teacher facilitates the implementation of individualized instructional curricula and, when appropriate, access to special educational resources (e.g., resource room) for these children. Finally, due to a recent legislative change, elementary schools and some lower secondary schools employ an additional category of teacher (known as socioeducational or personal assistants (*assistenti socio-educativi/personali*) (Comassi, 1979; *Gazzetta Ufficiale della Repubblica Italiana*, 1985). In contrast to the regular teachers and support teachers who are government employees, socioeducational assistants are employed directly by, and are responsible to, local district or town officials. This latter group of educators attempts to increase the personal autonomy of children who present with more severe learning disorders or handicaps, and who are mainstreamed into the regular classrooms. When present, the socioeducational assistant is responsible for only one child per classroom.

Mainstreaming: Italy's Unique Approach

The model of mainstreaming implemented in Italy is, in some aspects, unique

TABLE 2.2
Number of Schools, Teachers, and Students in Italy (1982–1983) by Category of School

Category	*Schools*	*Teachers*	*Students*	*Teacher/ Student Ratio*
Preschool	29,495	61,849	1,759,892	1:28
Primary	29,297	276,424	4,215,841	1:15.2
Secondary:				
Scuola Media	10,074	272,194	2,862,639	1:10.5
Superiore (overall)	7,472	209,696	2,465,903	1:12
of which:				
1. Classical, etc. *licées*	2,003	36,283	597,511	1:16.5
Art *licée*	247	9,493	60,562	1:6
2. Technical institutes	2,672	97,020	1,097,921	1:11
3. Teacher training inst.	879	14,019	237,657	1:17
4. Vocational inst.	1,671	52,881	472,252	1:9

Source: Ministry of Education (from: *The Europa Year Book*, 1986)

in comparison with that of other countries. Until the end of the 1960s, the management of both developmentally disabled and handicapped children was conducted in "traditional" ways (see: "Testo Unico #577" [Law #577], *Gazzetta Ufficiale della Repubblica Italiana*, 1928). The most severely disabled children were institutionalized and often given only custodial care; the less severely handicapped and disabled children were kept in special classes ("differential classes") within the regular schools.

At the end of the 1960s, profound cultural changes took place in Italy, as in other European countries, due to the influence of (a) the English antipsychiatric movement (e.g., Cooper, 1969; Jones, 1968; Laing, 1969); (b) Szasz's (1961) criticism of the concept of mental illness; and (c) Goffman's (1961) attack on "total" institutions. The views espoused by the proponents of the English antipsychiatric movement, emphasizing the unique role of the social environment in the etiology of psychological problems, and rejecting the notion of diagnosis because of the resulting stigmatization and labeling of the individual, were readily incorporated into the Marxist philosophies that were predominant among the Italian cultural elite (cf. Meazzini & Rovetto, 1983). The principal proponent of the antipsychiatric movement in Italy was Basaglia (1968, 1971). He was an influential psychiatrist who promoted philosophical and structural changes in the field of mental health. The culmination of these changes was the passage of Law 180 that abolished all psychiatric institutions in Italy and replaced them with a network of local centers that were based on the day hospital model (*Gazzetta Ufficiale della Repubblica Italiana*, 1976). In 1977, a second law (Law 517) came into effect. Law 517 mandated the total mainstreaming of disabled and handicapped children into the regular schools (*Gazzetta Ufficiale della Repubblica Italiana*, 1977; Meazzini & Nisi, 1985).

Law 517 regulated the presence of support teachers, both in the elementary schools (one for every four disabled children) and in the lower secondary schools (one for every six disabled children). More significantly, however, the new laws promoted a policy of total integration. To prevent the effects of social stigmatization and to enhance the socialization of the children, developmentally disabled and handicapped children were placed in regular classes and grades appropriate for their chronological age regardless of their level of impairment (Meazzini & Nisi, 1985). The social integration of disabled children in the classroom is promoted, in particular, by the support teachers.

It should be noted, however, that the aforementioned laws have drawn a degree of criticism from psychologists and educators. According to Meazzini and Nisi (1985), the dogmatic core of Law 517 (i.e., total mainstreaming regardless of the degree and type of learning impairment) is its major limitation. Placing developmentally disabled children in regular classes may indeed foster socialization and prevent (to a certain extent) the effects of social stigma. On the other hand, these placements can have a detrimental effect on their cognitive development. According to Law 517, in school settings that have "normal" schedules (i.e., 24-hour/week schedules), for example, disabled children receive only 1 hour per day of individualized instruction. Consequently, the remediation generally does not adequately address the educational needs of most developmentally disabled children (cf. Meazzini & Nisi, 1985; Meazzini & Pagliaro, 1985). To address this point and other limitations of the new educational system, the community services, the *Unita' Socio-Sanitarie Locali* (ULSS), or other local authorities (e.g., regional school authorities) assign one or more socioeducational assistants to special education classes. These assistants provide supplementary physical and individualized instruction services for the more severely handicapped.

Because of their overlapping competencies, school professionals (i.e., regular teachers, support teachers, socioeducational assistants, psychologists, and *pedagogists* or education theorists) do not always work in a coordinated manner. Moreover, because of the idealistic and antipragmatic approach to special education promulgated by Italian educators, *global* goals such as personality development are selected over *specific* goals such as development of cognitive skills as targets of intervention. As a result, the impact of remedial interventions in the regular classroom is further weakened (Meazzini & Nisi, 1985).

The Training of Regular Teachers and Auxiliary Teachers

After the mandatory 8 years of schooling, students can continue their education by entering a higher secondary school (*Scuola Media Superiore*). They can also receive vocational training at local education centers. As evidenced in Table 2.1, higher secondary schools offer different areas of specialization. The two major subdivisions are the *liceés* (which offer specialties in classical, scientific, linguistic, and artistic areas of study) and the institutes (which offer specialties in commerce, technology, industry, agriculture and teacher training). The duration of most of these programs is 5 years. Teacher training institutes, on the other hand, offer a 4 year program, and diplomas from the institutes meet the minimal requirement for participation in national examinations that are designed to select elementary school teachers for public schools.

As shown in Table 2.2, the overall numbers of students enrolled and teachers employed are similar to the corresponding figures in lower secondary schools. Moreover, the ratio of teachers to students remains relatively low for the different programs of specialization despite the fact that secondary schooling is not mandatory.

The training of the elementary school teachers is largely theoretical. Their curriculum of studies includes general subjects such as literature, history, geography, and mathematics, as well as subjects more directly related to education such as psychology, pedagogy, and teaching methods. It should be noted that the number of practicum courses is limited (Boga, 1987). New teachers typically learn the applied aspects of their profession after they start teaching.

The training of secondary schools teachers, in contrast to the elementary schools, is specialized. Secondary school teachers, in fact, have university-level training in the subjects they teach. A university-conferred degree (for any specialization) is called *laurea* or *dottorato* and is based on a focused curriculum of studies (of 4 to 5 years duration) culminating with the presentation and defense of a thesis that is directly related to the area of specialization. Math teachers, for example, usually attain *laureas* in mathematics. Unfortunately, training in educational issues and teaching strategies is usually lacking for secondary school teachers.

The educational training of the support teachers for preschool, primary, and secondary schools, is rather comprehensive. After the passage of Law 517 in 1977, the Ministry of Public Instruction instituted a 2 year specialization program for support teachers. These courses integrate the preexisting curricula for educators, and are organized by universities or other educational institutions. The schedule of the program is intense, providing approximately 1,300 hours of training over a 2 year interval. The curriculum is based on psychology courses, intervention courses (e.g., training and teaching techniques for blind or deaf children), and medical courses. Finally, the specialized program mandates the successful completion of supervised school-based practica.

DEVELOPMENTAL PSYCHOLOGY AND SCHOOL PSYCHOLOGY IN ITALY: BACKGROUND AND CURRENT STATUS

The ideological basis of the field of education and special education in Italy is found in the writings and in the influence of philosophers who defined themselves as *pedagogists* or *education theorists*, such as Croce, Gentile, and Montessori. Historically, the role of pedagogists involved specifying the ideological tenets underlying the development and reform of school programs. Most of these philosopher–pedagogists ascribed to idealistic theories, often stemming from historically ancient traditions, and were not concerned with pragmatic approaches to education (cf. Croce, 1923; Gentile, 1912). The writings on education relating to this school of thought were usually based on personal views and speculations organized and presented in aesthetically attractive theories that lacked, unfortunately, empirical validation and practical application (Meazzini & Nisi, 1985). An exception to this antipragmatic/idealistic approach to education was provided by Maria Montessori, a pedagogist whose work and writings had a significant impact in the field of education both in Italy and in other countries (Montessori, 1912). Montessori's approach to education and school psychology was particularly innovative in that it emphasized the use of observational methods and psychological evaluations to design individual curricula and proposed methods of teaching tailored to the needs of different children (cf. Montessori, 1912).

The birth of Italian psychology must be seen in relation to the aforementioned ideological Zeitgeist. Among the personalities that were influential in bringing this field of study to the forefront was Father Gemelli, president of the Catholic University (*Universitá Cattolica*) in Milan. He created and taught the first course of psychology as an independent discipline. This course was called psychotechnique (*Psicotecnica*). The initial interests of psychologists in developmental issues were mostly related to cognitive assessment and testing. This approach to developmental psychology was later severely criticized on methodological and ideological grounds.

Critics argued that the use of normative tests, for example, reflected and imposed the ideological values of the establishment, and that the use of "labels" such as IQ classifications, stigmatized and alienated children without providing suggestions for remedial instruction (cf. Basaglia, 1968; Jervis, 1976). Through the years, this position regarding psychological evaluation gained wide acceptance and the testing approach came to be considered useless or destructive. Currently, psychological testing constitutes a very limited portion of psychological interventions in the schools (Adelman, Taylor, & Cornoldi, 1981). It is extremely rare, in fact, for teachers or parents to request a psychological evaluation of a child's learning abilities.

Other theoretical orientations that had an impact on the direction taken by developmental psychology and school psychology in Italy are those related to: (a) Piagetian theories of cognitive development, and (b) psychodynamic theories of psychosexual development. More recent influences are due to: (c) an eclectic approach to personality development based on French post-war educational philosophies known as *Psicomotricitá* (Psychomotricity); (d) systemic and family theories; (e) operant and social learning approaches to behavior management; and (f) neuropsychological approaches (Meazzini & Nisi, 1985).

The Piagetian model, referred to as *genetic epistemology* (*epistemologia genetica*), presenting a view of cognitive development that included both psychological and physiological maturation, was considered comprehensive and compatible with the Italian ideological approaches to the study of human behavior, and was, therefore, easily incorporated in the Italian psychological mainstream. Moreover, most Piagetian works were written in French, a language familiar to the Italian scientific community.

Although Piagetian and psychodynamic approaches to school psychology are still being widely accepted by Italian professionals, the dissemination of these ideas reached its climax during the 1960s and 1970s (cf. Meazzini & Nisi, 1985). During those years, psychoanalytic theories (and in particular those emerging from the works of analysts such as Reich, Fromm, Sapir, Sullivan) and Marxism formalized their existing relationship with an unexpected ideological marriage. A number of works was published that emphasized the similarities and ideological compatibilities between the two doctrines (e.g., Gente, 1971). The endorsement of psychoanalytic views by the Marxist intelligentsia induced a heavy reliance on psychoanalytic treatments by analysts who were often inadequately trained. Terms such as *wild psychoanalysis* were used to describe this phenomenon, which was sharply criticized by the more orthodox analysts (Jervis, 1976). By the end of the 1970s and the beginning of the 1980s, a gradual decline in the use of psychoanalysis became apparent. On the other hand, psychoanalytic procedures are still being used in many schools. These treatments typically stress diagnostic procedures that result in symbolic explanations for behavioral problems.

Toward the end of the 1970s, school psychology in Italy (especially in the preschool and primary school) was significantly affected by *psychomotricity*, a psychological approach that combines elements of psychodynamic, neuropsychological, and Piagetian theories (Lapierre & Aucouturier, 1971; Vayer & Destrooper, 1976). This movement emerged in France at the end of World War II to address the problems of children who had been physically and mentally affected by the war. The aim of this approach is to enhance the harmonic development of a child's personality and psychological adjustment to the environment (cf. Lapierre & Aucouturier, 1971; Vayer & Destrooper, 1976). These global (and vaguely defined) goals are addressed by emphasizing the study of the human body in its psychophysiological functions and in its rapport with spatial and temporal dimensions of reality. Intervention techniques are based on the use of physical exercises, gymnastics, music, and relaxation induction procedures, usually implemented in a group format. In the early 1980s, childhood problems, even learning difficulties, were generally treated with this approach. As we come to the end of this decade, psychomotricity has lost some of its glamour with school professionals due to a dearth of information pertaining to its effectiveness (cf. Meazzini & Nisi, 1985). It is noteworthy, however, that almost every elementary school in Italy has at least one psychomotrist. This role is usually assumed by a regular school teacher or a gymnastics teacher who has specialized in this area (but who is not usually a psychologist).

Systemic theories are currently gaining influence due to several active groups (e.g., Selvini Palazzoli in Milan). Central to this approach is the notion that childhood learning and behavioral problems are symptomatic of a relational dysfunction within the school environment or, even more importantly, within the family. The goal of the family therapist usually involves the restructuring of the interpersonal relationships in the child's family and/or in the school environment. Changes in communication patterns are usually primary targets for therapy (Selvini Palazzoli, Boscolo, Cecchin, & Prata, 1975). Systemic approaches, analogous to psychodynamic approaches, have primarily clinical goals and do not directly address learning difficulties in school-aged children.

Somewhat different is the impact of behavioral theories on school psychology. Operant and social learning models met with considerable resistance before being incorporated into Italian psychology. The scientific rigor of this orientation was interpreted by critics as ideological rigidness and its interest in problem specificity was interpreted as a "fragmentation" of the personality, carrying the intrinsic risk of "mechanization" of the human being (cf. Bagnara et al., 1975; Jervis, 1976; Meazzini, 1980).

At the end of the 1970s and at the beginning of the 1980s, a gradual appearance of the translated works of the major proponents of the behavioral movement (e.g., Dollard and Miller, Watson, Hull, Skinner, Wolpe, Eysenck, Rachman, and Staats), and the theoretical and experimental publications of Italian behaviorists (e.g., Meazzini, 1978, 1980, 1982a, 1982b, 1983, 1984, 1985; Nisi, 1980, 1982), provided psychologists and educators with direct information about the potential applications of the behavioral approach. Moreover, the creation of professional associations and journals of behavioral orientation promoted further dissemination of this theoretical orientation (for a review see Meazzini & Rovetto, 1983). Slowly, the Zeitgeist changed and professionals began to accept the behavioral views more readily (cf. Meazzini, in press; Vivian, O'Leary, & Nisi, 1986). Basic research on animal and human learning began in northern Italian universities, such as Padua, Milan, and Siena. Applied child clinical research conducted mostly at the University of Padua, focused both on cognitive learning processes underlying school achievement and rehabilitative educational processes in the classroom (e.g., Cornoldi 1979; Cornoldi & Pra Baldi, 1979; Cornoldi & Soresi, 1977; Longoni & Scalisi, 1979; Vivian, 1978). As in the case of the United States (cf. O'Leary, 1984), behavioral approaches in Italy have had their greatest impact on the field of school and educational psychology.

In reviewing the theoretical orientations underlying the field of school psychology in Italy it is noteworthy to mention the neuropsychological and biopsychological approaches to learning problems. Italy is culturally a very "medicalized" country: there are, in fact, more doctors in Italy than in any other country in Western Europe, and Italians consume more medication every year than most of their fellow Europeans (Meazzini & Nisi, 1985). Meazzini and Nisi (1985) have suggested that hypochondria may very well be one of the national "hobbies." Because of this, neuropsychological, psychophysiological, and biopsychological approaches to childhood problems coexist with behavioral and educational approaches.

In summary, during the last few years, idealistically oriented educators have moved toward the adoption of more pragmatic and applied positions (e.g., Ballanti, 1976; Pontecorvo, 1979; Titone, 1977). The works of Gagné (e.g., Gagné, 1970) are becoming more popular with these professionals. In a similar vein, experimental reports dealing with cognitive assessment, behavior modification in the classroom, and methods for classroom observation, are being positively accepted (Zambelli, 1984). For example, O'Leary, Vivian, and Cornoldi (1984), and Vivian, Nisi, and O'Leary (1986), surveyed northern Italian child clinical psychologists, pediatricians, and child neuropsychiatrists to determine how these professionals would assess and treat a child presenting with hyperactivity and learning problems. These investigations revealed that profound changes have taken place in the Italian psychological approach to learning problems and school psychology over the past several years. That is, professionals treating children in the schools are currently more likely to be familiar with, and use, assessment and treatment procedures for the management of childhood problems related to attention deficits and hyperactivity than they were several years earlier.

TRAINING AND EMPLOYMENT OF PSYCHOLOGISTS AND PEDAGOGISTS

The education of psychologists and pedagogists differs to a certain extent. The diploma attained through comprehensive examinations at the end of the secondary schools permits entry to all university specializations without any restriction.

According to a recent report by Sartoratti (1986), 53 Italian cities have university centers, and some cities have more than one university (e.g., Milan). Approximately 75% of the universities are publicly administered, whereas about 8% are administered by the Catholic Church (e.g., Universitá Cattolica di Milano) and the rest are administered on a secular basis. Although departments of pedagogy are found in most Italian universities, only the University of Padua and the University of Rome have departments of psychology providing applied training and a laurea in psychology. The degree has been considered comparable to a masters of arts in psychology (Fichter & Wittchen, 1980). Until 1985, the course of studies for a laurea in psychology lasted 4 years. Recent changes in curriculum and format added another year of studies to the program. The first 2 years of training are equivalent for all divisions of psychology. From the third year on, students can specialize in different areas of psychology. Among the specializations, the division of developmental and educational psychology provides directive training for school-based interventions. In this curriculum, students take courses such as developmental psychology, educational psychology, methods of research for developmental psychology, assessment and intervention in the schools, and child psychopathology. Graduates of this program often continue their training by enrolling in 4-year specialization courses that are privately organized by Italian psychological associations. These courses generally emphasize applied intervention and offer supervised practica in schools and research centers.

The possibilities for employment for psychologists or pedagogists are limited almost exclusively to those provided by the National Health Services. Medical services in Italy are socialized and free for all the citizens. The coordination and the distribution of any health-related service is regulated by the Local Socio-Sanitary Units (ULSS). Every ULSS has one or more teams of professionals that deal with childhood and school-related problems. The coordinator of these teams is usually a physician (typically a neurologist or a neuropsychiatrist). The remaining two or three members of the team are usually psychologists or, very rarely, pedagogists. ULSS teams are in direct contact with schools, and regular classroom teachers or parents can make direct referrals to them. According to estimates provided by two northern Italian ULSS, the case load of a team ranges from 200 to 300 children per year (ULSS #65, Region: Lombardia, and ULSS #26, Region: Veneto, personal communication, April, 1987).

The type and the quality of intervention provided by the ULSS team varies, depending on the particular training of the professionals and the ratio of professionals to children treated. In southern Italy, for example, where the ULSS units have only recently been created, the operational effectiveness of the teams is limited by the overwhelming number of cases that are referred for treatment. When the number of cases to be treated is too large for individual treatment by the team, the intervention usually shifts from the child to the teachers and parents, who, through meetings and training workshops, are usually provided with information about behavior management. In all situations, these services are free as are other specialized interventions provided by other ULSS teams, such as speech therapy and physiotherapy. However, if parents choose to bring their children to private practitioners, they are directly responsible for the fees that incur. Obviously, this system does not encourage the growth of services outside the ULSS network.

Finally, due to a complicated sequence of legislative changes in school policies, some primary and lower secondary schools have recently adopted an additional professional figure, the psycho-pedagogist. Psycho-pedagogists have specific training in school teaching and a laurea in pedagogy; their role is to provide the teachers with help for educational problems and individualized curriculum changes.

CONTRIBUTIONS

The antidiagnostic and antipragmatic attitudes, pervasive in the Italian psychology of the 1970s, did not favor the adaptation or the design of cognitive batteries or rating scales for use with school-aged children. Until recently, very few tests or questionnaires were available for school-based assessments. In view of this, researchers in the United States and Italy have developed an Italian adaptation and standardization of the Conners Teacher Rating Scale (TRS) (Conners, 1969). In so doing, O'Leary, Vivian, and Nisi (1985), and Vivian, O'Leary, Nisi, and Ceccarani (1986) sampled over 2,000 children from the northern, central, and southern regions of Italy. By using cut-off scores obtained with American children, a higher prevalence of hyperactive children was evident in Italy as compared with the United States. Although further investigations should be conducted to assess the psychometric properties of the translated TRS, the Italian adaptation of this measure can be easily used as a preliminary screening index for attention deficit disorder.

CONCLUSIONS

The review on school psychology in Italy presented in this chapter suggests the following conclusions:

1. School psychology, as known in Anglo-Saxon countries, is not a part of the Italian educational system and culture. Only recently have the pragmatic conceptualizations underlying this discipline had an impact on Italian educators and psychologists.

2. During the past decade, the legislative status of the school system, and that of public instruction in general, has been continuously changing. Significant changes have been those related to: (a) the total abolition of special schools; (b) the mainstreaming of handicapped children into the regular school; (c) the formation of the ULSS units and teams; (d) the restructuring of university programs to include first, training in psychology as a separate discipline (in 1971), and second, specialization in developmental-educational psychology (in 1985); and (e) the instituting of private postgraduate programs for applied specializations in the field of child clinical psychology.

3. Finally, research is needed to evaluate the effectiveness of the model of mainstreaming implemented in Italian schools.

The role of school psychology in Italy is currently very fluid and reflects continuous changes at both theoretical and practical levels of intervention. New educational reforms are being considered by the Ministry of Education and the resulting status of school psychology in Italy may significantly change within the next decade.

ACKNOWLEDGMENTS

The authors wish to thank Philip Saigh, Daniel O'Leary, Susan O'Leary, Evelyn Sandeen, and David Smith who provided helpful theoretical and editorial feedback on this chapter. The support given by the research center *Lega Del Filo D'Oro* (Osimo, Italy) and by Patrizia Ceccarani, a coordinator for research in that center, is similarly appreciated.

REFERENCES

Adelman, H. S., Taylor, L. L., & Cornoldi, C. (1981). La diagnosi delle difficoltá di apprendimento [The diagnosis of learning disabilities]. *Psicologia e Scuola, 6*, 42–45.

Bagnara, S., Castelfranchi, T., Legrenzi, P., Linguzzi, C., Misipi, R., & Parisi, D. (1975). Per una discussione sulla situazione della psicologia in Italia [Discussion on the situation of the Italian psychology]. *Giornale Italiano di Psicologia, 2*(2), 285–325.

Ballanti, G. (1976). *Il comportamento dell'insegnante* [The teacher's behavior]. Roma: Armando.

Basaglia, F. (1968). *L'Istituzione negata* [The unfit institution]. Torino: Einaudi.

Basaglia, F. (1971). *La maggioranza deviante* [The deviant majority]. Torino: Einaudi.

Boga, C. (1987). *La scelta della Scuola Media Superiore* [The choice of the higher secondary school]. Milano: Pirola.

Centro Studi Investimenti Sociali (CENSIS). (1986). *XX Rapporto sulla situazione sociale del paese* [XX Report on the social situation of the country]. Roma: Franco Angeli.
Comassi, M. (1979). *Per l'inserimento degli handicappati nella scuola* [The mainstreaming of handicapped (children) in the school]. Pisa: Dal Cerro.
Conners, C. K. (1969). A teacher rating scale for use in drug studies with children. *American Journal of Psychiatry, 126,* 152–156.
Cooper, D. G. (Ed.). (1969). *Dialettica della liberazione*. Proceedings of the congress "Dialectics of Liberation," London, 1967. Torino: Einaudi.
Cornoldi, C. (1979). Dal laboratorio alla ricerca applicata: Alcune considerazioni [From the laboratory to applied research: Some considerations]. *AP- Rivista di Applicazioni Psicologiche, 1*(1), 7–17.
Cornoldi, C. & Pra Baldi, A. (1979). Funzioni mnestiche, percettive e linguistiche implicate nei primi apprendimenti scolastici: Un' indagine su alcuni strumenti predittivi [Mnemonic, perceptual and linguistic functions underlying early school achievements: An investigation of predictive instruments]. *AP- Rivista di Applicazioni Psicologiche, 1*(4), 732–769.
Cornoldi, C., & Soresi, S. (1977). Diagnosi dei deficit di memoria nei bambini con difficoltá di apprendimento. [Diagnoses related to memory deficiencies in children with learning disabilities]. *Formazione e Cambiamento, 2,* 29–75.
Croce, B. (1923). *Problemi di estetica e contributi alla storia dell'estetica italiana* [Problems of aesthetics and contributions to the Italian history of aesthetics]. Bari: Laterza & Figli.
Europa Year Book (Vol 1). (1986). London, England: Europa Publications Limited.
Fichter, M. M. & Wittchen, H-U. (1980). *American Psychologist, 35,* 16–25.
Gagné, R. M. (1970). *The conditions of learning*. New York Holt, Reinhart & Winston.
Gazzetta Ufficiale della Repubblica Italiana (1928, February 5). Testo Unico 577 [Law #577]. Roma: Government Printing Office.
Gazzetta Ufficiale della Repubblica Italiana (1976, May 13). Legge 180 [Law 180]. Roma: Government Printing Office.
Gazzetta Ufficiale della Repubblica Italiana (1977, August 4). Legge 517 [Law 517]. Roma: Government Printing Office.
Gazzetta Ufficiale della Repubblica Italiana (1985, September 3). Circolare 250 a firma Franca Falcucci [Regulation #250 by Franca Falcucci]. Roma: Government Printing Office.
Gente, H.P. (Ed.). (1971). *Marxismus psychoanalyse sexpolitik* [Marxism psychoanalysis sexual-politics] Vol. 1. Frankfurt: Fischer.
Gentile, G. (1912). *Sommario di pedagogia come scienza filosofica* [Compendium of pedagogy as a philosophical science]. Firenze.
Goffman, E. (1961). *Asylum*. New York: Doubleday.
Jervis, G. (1976). *Manuale critico di psichiatria* [Critical handbook of psychiatry]. Milano: Feltrinelli.
Jones, M. (1968). *Social psychiatry in practice*. London: Penguin Books.
Laing, R. (1969). *The self and others*. New York: Pantheon Books.
Lapierre, A., & Aucouturier, B. (1971). *La symbolique du mouvement* [The symbolism of movement]. Paris: E.P.I.S.A.
Longoni, A. M., & Scalisi, T. G. (1979). Considerazioni relative ai processi percettivi e ai processi di memorizzazione in bambini con difficoltá di lettura [Considerations related to perceptual and mnemonic processes in children with reading disabilities]. *AP- Rivista di Applicazioni Psicologiche, 1,* 2, 315–330.
Meazzini, P. (1978). *La conduzione della classe* [The management of the classroom]. Firenze: Giunti-Barbera.
Meazzini, P. (1980) *Il comportamentismo: Una Storia culturale* [Behaviorism: A cultural history]. Pordenone: ERIP.
Meazzini, P. (1982a). La terapia e modificazione del comportamento [Therapy and behavior modification]. In M. Bosinelli (Ed.), *I metodi della psicologia clinica* (pp. 67–85). Bologna: Il Mulino.
Meazzini, P. (1982b). Psicoterapia? [Psychotherapy?] *Giornale Italiano di Psicologia, 9,* 17–27.

Meazzini, P. (1983, March). *Mainstreaming handicapped students*. Paper presented at the First European Symposium on Scientific Studies in Mental Retardation, Oxford, England.

Meazzini, P. (1984). Mainstreaming handicapped students. In J. Dobbing (Ed.), *Scientific studies in mental retardation* (pp. 527–540). London: MacMillan.

Meazzini, P. (1985). *Handicappato: Passi verso l'autonomia* [The handicapped: Steps toward autonomy]. Firenze: Giunti-Barbera.

Meazzini, P. (Ed.). (in press). *Proceedings from the Congress Disabilitá di apprendimento e problemi emozionali* [Learning disabilities and emotional problems]. Brescia: Regione Lombardia.

Meazzini, P., & Nisi, A. (1985). Behavior modification for developmentally disabled children: The state of art in Italy. *Analysis and Interventions in Developmental Disabilities, 5*, 211–221.

Meazzini, P., & Pagliaro, D. (1985). Per un'integrazione integrata: Filosofia e metodologia dell'integrazione nella scuola dell'allievo portatore di handicap [An integrated mainstreaming: Philosophy and methodology of the mainstreaming of the handicapped student in the school]. *HD- Handdicap and Disability, 6*, 3–10.

Meazzini, P., & Rovetto, F. (1983). Behavior therapy: The Italian way. *Journal of Behavior Therapy and Experimental Psychiatry, 14*, 1, 5–9.

Meazzini, P., & Soresi, S. (1983). Dislessia: Malattia del secolo o lapsus? [Dyslexia: Illness of the century or lapse?]. *Psicologia contemporanea, 57*, 9–13.

Montessori, M. (1912). *The Montessori method.* Toronto: William Briggs.

Nisi, A. (1980). L'approccio comportamentale ai problemi del bambino con handicap mentale grave illustrato attraverso il caso di un non-vedente pluriminorato [The behavioral approach to the problems of children with severe mental handicaps illustrated through the case of a blind and multiple handicapped child]. *Giornale Italiano di Analisi e Modificazione del Comportamento, 3–4*, 110–119.

Nisi, A. (1982). Il programma Kozloff: Un approccio sistematico ai problemi del bambino handicappato [Kozloff's program: A systematic approach to the problems of the handicapped child]. *Psicologia e Scuola, 7*, 30–39.

O'Leary, K. D. (1984). The image of behavior therapy: It is time to take a stand. *Behavior Therapy, 15*, 219–233.

O'Leary, K. D., Vivian, D., & Cornoldi, C. (1984). Assessment and treatment of "Hyperactivity" in Italy and the United States. *Journal of Clinical Child Psychology, 13*(1), 56–60.

O'Leary, K. D., Vivian, D., & Nisi, A. (1985). Hyperactivity in Italy. *Journal of Abnormal Child Psychology, 13*(4), 485–500.

Pontecorvo, G. (1979). *Psicologia dell'educazione* [Psychology of education]. Teramo: Lisciani-Zampetti.

Sartoratti, G. (1986). *Una scelta per l'universitá* [A choice for the university]. Padova: Liviana Editrice.

Selvini Palazzoli, M., Boscolo, L., Cecchin, & Prata, G. (1975). *Paradosso e contro-paradosso* [Paradox and counter-paradox]. Milano: Feltrinelli.

Szasz, T. S. (1961). *The myth of mental illness.* New York: Harper & Row.

Titone, R. (1977). *Modelli psicopedagogici dell'apprendimento* [Psycho-pedagogic models of learning]. Roma: Armando.

Vayer, P., & Destrooper, J. (1976). *La dynamique de l'action educative chez les enfants inadaptes* [The dynamics of movement education in settings for handicapped children). Paris: Doen.

Vivian, D. (1978). *Diagnosi e intervento in bambini con difficoltá di apprendimento: Problemi inerenti a specifici deficit di memoria* [Diagnosis and intervention with learning disabled children: Problems related to specific memory deficiencies]. Unpublished laurea thesis, Department of Psychology, University of Padua, Padua, Italy.

Vivian, D., Nisi, A., & O'Leary, K. D. (1986, September). *A comparison of assessments and treatments of "Hyperactivity" in Italy and the United States and a five-year follow-up with Italian professionals.* Paper presented at the 16th Congress of the European Association for Behavior Therapy, Lausanne, Switzerland.

Vivian, D., O'Leary, K. D., Nisi, A., & Ceccarani, P. (1986, September). *Prevalence of hyperac-*

tivity in Italy. Paper presented at the 16th Congress of the European Association for Behavior Therapy, Lausanne, Switzerland.

Zambelli, F. (1984). *L'osservazione e l'analisi del comportamento in classe* [The observation and the analysis of classroom behavior]. Veneto & Venezia, Italy: Istituto Regionale Ricerca Sperimentazione Aggiornamento Educativi (IRRSAE).

Chapter Three
School Psychology in France

J.C. Guillemard
Dourdan (France) Public Schools

THE FRENCH EDUCATIONAL SYSTEM

The educational system under the responsibility of the Ministry of Education is divided into three levels. The primary level includes pre-elementary and elementary schools for children ages 2 to 11. The secondary level includes "colleges" (e.g., junior high schools) for ages 12 to 15 as well as professional college and general and technical "lycees" (e.g., senior high schools) for ages 16 to 18. The tertiary level includes preparatory classes, schools for engineers, and universities. Although most classes and schools for special education are integrated in elementary and secondary schools, some are separate schools provided for by the Ministry of Health.

Students

The number of students ages 2 to 22 increased from 9.8 million in 1961 to 13 million in 1985. There were 11 million students in public schools and 2 million in private schools. Pre-elementary schools are especially developed in France. All children age 4 and above attend school; 92% of the children age 3 and 31% of those age 2 attend school. Among the 13 million students, 73,000 pupils are educated in special classes and schools at the elementary level and 126,000 at the secondary level.

Teachers

In 1985 there were about 900,000 teachers working in French schools; 63% were women and 9% worked part time. In pre-elementary and elementary schools there were 300,000 teachers, 74% of whom were women. Fourteen thousand teachers worked in special classes and special schools. In addition, 5,000 specialists worked in G.A.P.P. (school failure prevention teams) in cooperation with about 2,700 school psychologists.

Cost of Education[1]

In 1982, the total amount dedicated to education in France was FF245,902 millions (≃U.S. $40 million); this constitutes 6.9% of the country's gross national product. The sources of revenues include the following: the government (i.e., Ministry of Education): FF 170,075 millions (≃U.S. $28 million); local education authorities: FF35,745 millions (≃U.S. $5,950 million); other administrative authorities: FF954 millions (≃U.S. $159 million); firms and companies: FF13,611 millions (≃U.S. $2,260 million); and families: FF25,517 millions (≃U.S. $4,250 million).

HISTORY OF SCHOOL PSYCHOLOGY IN FRANCE[2]

The need for preparing qualified psychologists for service in French schools appeared just after World War II. After a successful trial period in 1945 in Grenoble involving the appointment of Bernard Andrey as the first school psychologist, a team of school psychologists began work in Paris in 1947 with Professor Henri Wallon (Andrey & Le Men, 1968).

However, applications of psychology in schools actually began years before. As early as 1894, Alfred Binet, who rightly may be considered as the grandfather of school psychology, created the "Free Society for the Psychological Study of the Child." In 1897 he wrote a paper (Binet & Vaschide, 1897) describing psychology in primary schools. In 1899, along with Pierre Vaney, a teacher, he opened a pedagogical and psychological laboratory in a Parisian primary school. In 1905, Binet was asked by the Ministry of Education to study problems exhibited by children who could not follow the normal school curriculum. The Binet–Simon test was used to detect mentally retarded children and to direct them toward special classes. The first special classes for mentally retarded children opened in Lyon in 1906; the following year, five special classes opened in Paris. In 1909, Marcel Foucault opened a laboratory of school psychology in Montpelliers, and in the same year the first vocational guidance service was created (Foucault, 1923).

Although Professor Henri Wallon first opened a laboratory of child psycholo-

[1]All of these statistics come from: *Ministere de Education Nationale: Reperes et references statistiques sur les enseignements et la formation*, 1986.

[2]Persons desiring more information on school psychology in France are encouraged to consult Guillemard (1980a, 1980b, 1984, 1985).

gy in a primary school near Paris in 1923, he was not able to expand the project involving school psychological service linked to a new democratic system of education until after World War II. According to Wallon, school psychology's mission was to help all children. Its aim was not to discriminate or, by selection, to deny children the benefits of a culture that must belong to everybody. Instead, school psychologists were to study methods and techniques so as to promote the growth of the child and to promote the educational milieu. In 1948, some school psychologists were appointed in secondary schools. The number of practitioners was large enough to warrant holding the first national convention at Sevres (near Paris) in 1949 and the second in Grenoble the following year.

In 1951, the Ministry of Education described the functions of school psychologists. This text (Wall, 1958) was used as the basis for discussion at the First International School Psychology Colloquium organized by UNESCO in Hamburg in November/December 1952 (Wall, 1958) and at the Second Colloquium in April 1954 also in Hamburg (Wall, 1958). At the very moment when French school psychology seemed to have an important part to play in the future development of school psychology on the international stage, their training and appointment in France were stopped and school psychologists were sent to primary schools as teachers.

However, the need for school psychologists increased substantially during the 1950s, chiefly due to an increase in the number of pupils and the accompanied increase in the maladjusted children. For these reasons, the Ministry of Education resumed training school psychologists for the main aim of identifying handicapped children in order to educate them in special classes and schools. As a result, the training initially focused on uses of psychometric tests and psychopathological theories.

In 1960, a degree in school psychology was created and four training centers opened in universities at Paris, Bordeaux, Grenoble, and Besançon. However, the new school psychologists were appointed only in primary schools. In secondary schools, vocational counselors endeavored to maintain control over psychological services.

During this period and especially after 1968, much attention focused on the significance of the school failure rate effecting about 50% of all pupils between the first and the fifth years at primary school levels. The general belief held that prevention was better than attempts to cure problems following school failure (*Les Groupes d'Aide Psycho-Pedagogique et la prevention*, 1970, 1976). The subsequent success of educational programs supported this belief. Thus, in 1970, the first prevention teams were established. Called G.A.P.P for *Groupe d'Aide Psycho-Pedagogique* (Psycho-Pedagogic Aid Group), they were in theory composed of a team consisting of one specialist in school psychology, one in psychoeducation, and one in psychomotor development. Each G.A.P.P. was intended to serve between 800 and 1,000 pupils and, although based in one school, often had to work in several schools within a prescribed area. Moreover, school psychologists had to devote one third of their time outside the G.A.P.P. area in assessing maladjusted children for special classes and schools. Since 1970, most school psychologists appointed in schools were G.A.P.P. based.

Preparation of School Psychologists

School psychologists are selected exclusively from teachers. Preparation in school psychology is added on to teacher training and experience.[3] Typically, 200 teachers have been selected yearly for school psychology training in training centers.[4] Although main trends in training are similar among the five programs, notable differences exist between them. Some centers emphasize clinical psychology, whereas others stress developmental or social psychology—depending on the scientific orientation of the program's director and the teaching team. To illustrate this point, the programs of two school psychology training centers are presented: the largest at Paris (*Universite Rene Descartes*) and the smallest at Besancon. Students in these centers follow the general program in the department of psychology (first, second, or third cycle depending on their initial level in psychology) and simultaneously the specialized program in school psychology.

In Paris, students take courses in the department of psychology. The program of the first cycle degree[5] consists of 15 to 18 hours a week in general, experimental, developmental, abnormal, and social psychology; mathematics; biology; English; and psychopedagogy. In addition, the school psychology program consists of lectures as well as technical and practical work in laboratories and schools. During 1985–1986 the first-year program included the following. Lectures were presented on child growth and development from birth to 3 years and then from 3 to 6 years. Methodology courses included applied statistics and psychometry, psychological interviewing, and psychological assessment. Practical field work focused on interviewing and assessing children in schools (under supervision). At the end of the first year students took a comprehensive examination that, if they passed, allowed them to begin the second program.

This program during 1985–1986 included the following. Lectures were presented on social psychology in schools, learning difficulties, and affective and emotional disturbances in children. Methodology courses stressed methods and techniques for psychological assessment. Specialized topics discussed children's

---

[3]Since 1985, teacher training for elementary and pre-elementary schools has consisted of a 2-year program at the end of which is awarded the university general studies degree and then another 2-year program in a college for education.

[4]In 1986, this number was reduced by one half and in 1987 there was no selection due to the reorganization of new training programs.

[5]University studies are divided into three cycles; the first cycle leads to the general studies degree (DEUG) in human sciences during a 2-year program. The second cycle leads to a licence degree (third year) and then a *maitrise* degree (fourth year). The third cycle leads to professional degrees (DESS) and doctorate. Although teachers traditionally did not have degrees in psychology, their level is now being raised and it is not unusual to meet students in school psychology preparing for a second or third cycle degree.

physical, sensory, and intellectual handicaps. Practical field work again emphasized interviews and psychological assessment of children in schools. Workshops and specialized seminars also were held. During the second year, students worked with a prevention team (G.A.P.P.) and/or in a child guidance center under the supervision of a certified school psychologist (4 weeks in September–October and then 1 day a week) where they conducted their own research.

At Besancon, about 25 students enroll yearly in a 2-year program that is divided into two sections: a theoretical or academic section taught in the department of psychology (in common with the other students in psychology), and a vocational section taught in the School Psychology Training Center. During 1985–1986, the academic program for the first year consisted of five courses: introduction to human sciences, general psychology, biology and physiology, mathematics and statistics, and English. Students select an additional elective course, usually educational psychology. During the second year, the academic program consisted of four required courses and one elective course; these are selected from developmental, social and abnormal psychology, and methodology and statistics. Each course consisted of 3 hours of weekly lectures.

The vocational program involves the following components during the first year: major trends and methods in school psychology; educational agencies and institutions; regular and special schools; psychological technology; analysis and interpretation of tests and other techniques; and planning and methodology for one's research. During the second year, each of these themes is studied in greater depth together with courses in applied statistics and personality approaches. Students also work for 1 week in a G.A.P.P. under the supervision of a certified school psychologist.

The School Psychology Centers at Aix en Provence, Grenoble, Paris and Besancon require students, at a minimum, to successfully complete the general studies degree simultaneously with the school psychology degree. This is not true at Bordeaux where the thesis is held to be more important when evaluating the students' work. Even though the time required by this training is rather extensive (with over 30 hours a week of lectures, technical and practical work), the preparation generally is considered to be insufficient to prepare one for all the practical and theoretical problems of the profession. Thus, most school psychologists subsequently study for higher degrees to improve their professional competence. They are allowed to utilize 6 work hours a week toward advanced training the year following their initial school psychology degree. This is possible only for those who work relatively near to a university with a psychology department.

Official in-service training has been organized for some years by training centers. The training consists of a 1- or 2-week session yearly that is attended by about 50 school psychologists. In 1985, the Ministry of Education provided more effective support and incentives for in-service training by making money available for this purpose. Professional organizations initiated training sessions. In 1986, the French Association of School Psychologists organized more than

100 in-service sessions throughout the country. A national Summer University program was organized in 1985 through 1987 in Paris attended by about 60 school psychologists.

Although their competence was increased, their pay remained the same. All school psychologists have contracts similar to those of specialized teachers. They must have worked as teachers for at least 5 years. In 1987, the minimum beginning salary was about FF 6,000 (i.e., U.S. $1,000) a month with a maximum career salary of about FF 10,000 a month (i.e., U.S. $1,800) with taxes not deducted. The legal retirement age both for teachers and school psychologists in primary schools is between 55 and 60 and between 60 and 65 for teachers in secondary schools and vocational counselors. They receive a pension of 75% of their last salary at retirement. They work an average of 24 hours weekly. Primary school teachers work 27 hours weekly, whereas those in secondary schools work 18 to 21 hours weekly. Holidays are the same for students, teachers, and school psychologists: 8 weeks in summer; 1 week in November; and 2 weeks for Christmas, in February, and again for Easter.

Professional Practices in School Psychology

In contrast to the practices in many countries, organized school psychological services do not exist in France. School psychologists formerly were appointed to a school by the education authority. From 1960 until 1976 appointments were made by the Department of Special Education. Now the administrative status of school psychologists is similar to that of special teachers; they mostly are appointed to a school in which a G.A.P.P. is based. As previously indicated, G.A.P.P. teams are devoted to preventing school failures among pre-elementary and elementary-age pupils (ages 2 to 12). They direct their attention primary toward the youngest children (ages 3 to 7). The psycho-pedagogist is the most specialized in learning problems, whereas the psychometrician is most specialized in behavior problems. School psychologists devote a part of their time to observing children in classrooms and conducting assessment when necessary. They typically assess emotionally maladjusted, behaviorally disturbed, and learning-disabled children for possible placement in special schools and in special classes that are integrated in ordinary schools. Some serve as consultants to teachers and parents. Those working in sprawling rural areas and in populated suburban areas devote much time to orientation assessment (see following for a description). There were about 3,000 school psychologists in France in 1986. Most work with G.A.P.P., a few work in child guidance centers and special schools, whereas a smaller number are involved in teaching, research, or administration. As previously indicated, no school psychologists work in secondary schools. Psychological work, when needed there, is performed by vocational counselors whose training consists of an extensive program in educational psychology.[6] The vocational counselor also may refer adolescents and their families to clinical psychologists who work at child guidance centers.

Main Trends in School Psychology Practices

In France, in the 1980s, school psychology practices have been directed by three main trends as defined by the Ministry of Education: orientation, prevention, and integration.

Orientation. Orientation involves considering issues and evaluating information in order to determine a student's eligibility for special services and to guide the student's subsequent development. It was considered the major if not the only function of school psychologists. School psychologists are not directly involved in decisions made either by teachers (if the child was maintained in normal classes or was directed into special classes or schools). However, in the first example, teachers and/or families might ask advice from school psychologists. In the second example, school psychologists must be consulted by the commission. Considered as experts, the school psychologists are asked to make diagnoses and to evaluate children's learning abilities, social and emotional adjustment, personal autonomy, and other relevant characteristics. During the psychological assessment for orientation, pychometric tests together with other techniques are used.

Prevention. Prevention was strongly emphasized among school psychologists during the 1970s. However, the concept of prevention was used somewhat ambiguously. It would be more correct to describe the activities as early assessment, screening, or early observation. One must question if true prevention of handicaps should not involve more directly medicine, social work, and educational politics than special education and school psychology. According to the prevention policy as defined by the Ministry of Education (*Les Groupes d'Aide Psycho-Pedagogique et la prevention*, 1970, 1976), school psychologists were to observe children as soon as they entered school (at 2 or 3 years of age) in order to improve those behaviors that suggest learning or behavioral problems and to prevent the development of these and other difficulties. School psychologists often helped teachers plan and execute special programs for children or asked a member of the G.A.P.P. to organize a special program to promote the development of a small group of children who exhibit similar difficulties in or outside the class-

[6]The psychologically oriented work of vocational counselors in France helps to explain why their professional organizations are members of the National Association of Psychologists' Organizations (ANOP) and are in the working group of educational psychology within school psychologists' organizations.

room. In some cases, school psychologists might intervene directly with children and their families.

Integration. Integration (i.e., mainstreaming children in regular education programs) became an official policy of the Ministry of Education in 1981 although many attempts to integrate handicapped children had been made previously. According to this view, the function of the school psychologist is to prepare regular education for the special needs of a child by informing teachers and pupils together with preparing the handicapped child and family. The school psychologist also serves as a liaison between the regular and special schools.

The profession as defined through only these three functions is very restricted. School psychologists perform various other functions depending on local needs and interests, specific needs in a population, and their personal interests and competences. A project by the Educational Psychology Working Group prepared by professional organizations together with the level of training required by law have opened new perspectives for the future of school psychology (National Association of Psychological Organizations, 1987).

SCHOOL PSYCHOLOGY: PRESENT AND FUTURE TIMES

Since 1980, under the leadership of the French Psychological Society, most of the professional organizations (representing two-thirds of the country's 15,000 psychologists) have joined together to form the National Association of Psychologists' Organizations (ANOP). ANOP's political activities have been effective; in July, 1985 the French Parliament passed legislation legally recognizing the profession L.nº87, 772, 25/07/85). Under this law, the title *psychologist* for professional use is exclusively reserved to persons who have earned a university degree in psychology. These include degrees involving academic and professional courses in a 5-year-minimum program. Persons who illegally use the title *psychologist* professionally can be prosecuted (French Penal Code art. 259). The law encompasses all categories of psychologists and should have important consequences for the profession of school psychologist—especially on training. The present level of training, as previously described, is likely to increase, thus effecting employment, selection, and salaries.[7] However, a transitory period allows state agencies employing psychologists to modify the conditions of employment.

[7]As of October, 1988 the Ministry of Education had not decided which procedures should be used to start this important change in the organization of the profession.

A Project Involving Professional Organizations of Psychologists

In 1985, five organizations that are members of ANOP[8] established a working group in order to define the profession of educational psychologist in France. Three areas have been considered: the functions of an educational psychologist working from the pre-elementary school to the university; training corresponding to these functions; and the organization of psychological services. Each of these is reviewed here. Functions of educational psychologist are described as belonging to an educational agency (public or private) that pays them. Their activities are designed to enhance educational goals and to encompass all children and youth in schools, not only those with special needs. As is typical in the practice of psychology, educational psychologists respond to the needs of their clients, but their actions involve different approaches. Educational psychologists consider the psychological reality of children while helping them to develop all aspects of their personality; parents, teachers, and other persons involved in the educational process are included as partners in the intervention process. Educational psychologists who help children fit into the social environment may not agree with all school and family standards. In some cases, their actions serve to change these standards. The services performed by educational psychologists are directed toward individuals, groups, and institutions and generally have the following goals: to prevent school failure, to promote social learning, to enhance the integration (mainstreaming) of handicapped children, to provide support for academic and vocational development of students, and to enhance the training of teachers, social workers, administrators, and others in education.

Educational psychologists do not work in the abstract but with children and youths who live in a collective context in which they are expected to acquire knowledge and knowhow in more or less uniform ways. Consequently, educational psychologists cannot satisfy themselves by merely performing an individual and punctual intervention. Their work must consider a larger context that takes into account pedagogical constraints, educative standards, and the cooperativeness of other professionals (e.g., teachers, school counselors, headmasters, inspectors, social workers). Educational psychologists who are inexperienced as teachers must acquire a knowledge of schools before entering the profession.

Academic and Vocational Training of Educational Psychologists

The Working Group has built a training program in cooperation with several university departments of psychology. This program has been discussed and adopt-

---

[8]The French Association of School Psychologists, The French Association of Vocational Counselors, The Union of School Psychologists, The Union of Vocational Counselors, and The Association of Educational Psychologists in Catholic schools.

ed (with some changes depending on local possibilities) by several universities (Paris V, Bordeaux, Toulouse, Aix en Provence). The program is opened to students who have graduated from a 4-year university program in psychology (*maitrise degree*) and have taken a number of courses in educational psychology. The program is composed of the following three sections: studies in child and adolescent psychology, psychological approaches to education and training, and psychosociological approach of educational agencies in their economic and social context. The yearly program consists of more than 500 hours in lectures, practical and technical work, and specialized seminars. An additional 180 hours of work occurs in psychological service under supervision. During the sixth year, students are appointed to a school psychological service unit as assistant psychologists and write theses that are submitted to an examining board at the end of the year.

Reorganization of School Psychological Services

In contrast to most countries, France has not developed psychological services for its school psychologists who were appointed in schools with integrated G.A.P.P. On the contrary, vocational counselors in high schools historically have worked in vocational counseling services. The project established by the professional organizations recognizes the need to create psychological services in which school psychologists and vocational counselors should work together as educational psychologists (with vocational counseling being considered as a psychological function). This service should serve a geographic area that includes a general (and/or technical) senior high school, a professional high school, several junior high schools, elementary and pre-elementary schools and possibly special education schools. The basic idea is that such services should be able to cope more effectively with various needs of pupils at various ages. This reorganization initiates great changes for school psychologists and vocational counselors and strongly impacts relationships among practitioners, headmasters, and inspectors.

The centralized and hierarchical French school system generally is reluctant to consider any changes that could give more autonomy to personnel and structures. Consequently, if one expects that the law will be applied and that in the near future school psychologists will be prepared at a doctoral level, one cannot expect great changes in the general organization and the status of professionals before some time. However, internal influences (e.g., professional organizations, clients) and external influences (e.g., development of E.E.C. policy in the field of education) could change things faster than now imagined.

FUTURE TRENDS IN SCHOOL PSYCHOLOGY

French school psychology has been guided for years by a small number of theoretical references. Working under the banner of psychoanalysis, many school psychologists have worked in schools as though they were clinical psychologists and were unaware of many nonpsychoanalytical practices. Only recently have other theories (e.g., cognitive, psychosomatic, ethological, systemic, behavioural, ecological) and approaches become known to practitioners.

Research in psychophysiology, cerebral functions, perception, language development, the treatment of mental disorders, cognitive learning, and personality processes are likely to produce important modifications in the importance of theoretical references considered to be important to school psychology. A better knowledge of learning processes together with the development of computerized education probably will have major consequences on the practices of school psychologists in the coming years. One can expect that educational technology will enable schooling to become more effective and that school psychology will be more involved in actions that effect the ecology of learning and the systems of education; this stands in sharp contrast to prevailing practices that emphasize dyadic relationships. School psychologists also will be more involved in providing therapy and counseling and less involved in assessing children for special education services.

However, the future of school psychology, as with other human endeavors, depend on the nature of the evolution of our broader society and will be strongly influenced by the major economic, social, political, and ideologic trends that influence schools. One such trend is a demographic population shift that affects France as well as many other Western countries. On the whole, there are fewer elementary school pupils. Although this phenomenon could improve the pupil-school psychologist ratio, education authorities instead are not appointing new school psychologists when others are retiring.

The French economic background does not favor the development of services that are considered to be unneeded by school administrators. The challenge for school psychologists lies in convincing political leaders that education will be a strong asset to the nation in the coming years and that the needed improvements of school performances for all the children can be achieved through better use of educational psychology services, including research, teachers' training, and providing guidance to parents and children about needed psychological services.

REFERENCES

Andrey, B., & Le Men, J. (1968). *La psychologie l'école—Paris* [Psychology at school]. Paris: Presses Universitaires de France.

Binet, A., & Vaschide, N. (1897). La psychologie a l'école primaire [Psychology in primary schools]. *L'Annee Psychologique, 4,* 1–14.

Foucault, M. (1923). *Observations et experiences de psychologie scolaire* [Observations and experiences in school psychology]. Paris: Presses Universitaires de France.

Guillemard, J. C. (1980a). School psychology in France. *School Psychology International, 1*(5), 8-9.

Guillemard, J. C. (1980b). School psychology and prevention of failure in French schools. The Third International School Psychology Colloquium: Psychology for children today and tomorrow. *A.E.P. Journal*, *5*(4), 29.
Guillemard, J. C. (1984). The future of school psychology in France. *School Psychology International*, *5*(1), 21–26.
Guillemard, J. C. (1985). Training of school psychologists in France. *School Psychology International*, *6*(2), 69–71.
Les Groupes d'Aide Psycho-Pedagogique et la prevention. (1970). Official Bulletin of the Ministry of Education (No. 8).
Les Groupes d'Aide Psycho-Pedagogique et la prevention. (1976). Official Bulletin of the Ministry of Education (No. 22).
National Association of Psychological Organizations. (1987). Groupe Psychologie de l'education: *La profession de psychologue de l'education et de la formation—Paris* [The profession of educational psychologist] (a report by the Educational Psychology Division of NAPO).
Wall, W. D. (1958). *La psychologie au service de l'école* [Psychology for schools]. Paris: Bourrelier.

Chapter Four
School Psychology Services in Ireland

James Chamberlain
University College Dublin

Although school psychology in Ireland is of relatively recent origin (the Department of Education's school psychological service was established in 1965), the Irish educational system has a long and complex tradition that reaches back to the 7th and 8th centuries. To appreciate this complexity, two factors must be borne in mind. First, for centuries Irish schools served as a vehicle for the preservation of the country's culture and sense of national identity before national independence was achieved in 1922. Second, 95% of the population is Roman Catholic. For historical reasons most schools are denominational and private rather than secular or state-owned. This means that although the schools are almost totally financed by the state, they remain "private" in the sense that the land and buildings remain the property of the particular religious denomination that operates the schools. Ireland has a population of 3.5 million, approximately 50% of which is below the age of 25. This statistic helps to explain the unusually high rate of participation in full-time education, which is 23% of the total population (more than 800,000), giving the country one of the most highly developed educational systems in the world (Tussing, 1978).

THE EDUCATIONAL SYSTEM

Like most educational systems, the Irish structure comprises three levels: primary, second-level, and third-level schools. The first level consists of 3,550 primary schools (4.3% of which are private) that have about 570,000 children ranging in age from 4 to 13 years and employ roughly 20,000 teachers. In accordance with Article 44.4 of the Constitution, the state is obliged to provide free primary education. All teachers in the nonprivate (or *national* schools as they are called) are fully qualified and since 1974 are required to have received a university degree on completion of a 3-year full-time training course at one of the four main colleges of education.

The primary school is child centered and involves a program that ensures attention to both the cognitive and the affective development of the child (O'Brolachain, 1983). Pedagogical practice emphasizes individual and small-group learning through activity and discovery. For each, national school boards of management were established in 1975 that have responsibility for the day-to-day administration of the school and the appointment of teachers. The Department of Education, however, determines the program of instruction, prescribes the qualifications of the teachers, and assesses their performance through the use of an inspection system. Provision is made for handicapped and disadvantaged children within the overall framework of primary education. Handicapped children attend special schools or special classes within ordinary schools. In addition to their basic teaching qualification, their teachers must receive specialized certification such as a diploma in special education or teaching diploma for hearing-impaired children.

Postprimary education in Ireland comprises three main types of schools—secondary, vocational, and comprehensive/community. Secondary schools provide an academic education with a verbal and literary emphasis similar to that of the British grammar school (Chamberlain & Delaney, 1977). A tiny minority of primary schools incorporate what is known as a *secondary top*, classes in which their pupils may take part of the secondary school program. Secondary schools dominated Irish education until the mid-1960s, when comprehensive schools were introduced to offset what was thought to be their excessive educational and social influence (O'Connor, 1968). More specifically, the traditional secondary school syllabus was thought to emphasize the technological dimension insufficiently and to be overly biased in favor of material of particular interest to the middle classes (O'Connor, 1968). About 88% of secondary schools in Ireland are owned and controlled by Catholic religious institutions; 6% belong to other denominations, and the remaining 6% are owned by lay Catholics (et al., 1983). Given the extent of state subsidy, the question of whether the financing of secondary schools is public or private becomes particularly complex. The state traditionally has provided aid in the form of grants to secondary schools and has paid the greater part of the teachers' salaries. Since 1967, about 90% of secondary schools have joined what is known as the Free Education Scheme, whereby schools are provided with direct state grants equal to the amounts that had been raised by fees in previous years (Hannan et al., 1983).

The age of secondary school pupils ranges between 12 and 17 years. Their curriculum follows a 5-year course of study, involving a junior and senior cycle, that leads to the Leaving Certificate Examination. The importance of this examination for the students cannot be overstated; it has far-reaching vocational implications, as the results obtained determine whether the young people can enter a third-level institution and in the case of universities, the courses to which they are admitted.

Vocational schools are public institutions owned and run by Vocational Education Committees (VECs). They were established in 1930 and exist throughout the country. From the point of view of social class, vocational schools tend to attract pupils from a working-class or small-farm background and to include a disproportionate number of students with educational disabilities (Hannan et al., 1983). Initially vocational schools were intended to provide continuation and technical education for children leaving primary school. *Continuation* education was an extension of the subjects taught at primary school and *technical* education consisted of work-oriented courses geared to the needs of the young boys and girls entering the local labor market. The latter involved apprenticeship training for many of the skilled trades. On the completion of a 2-year program the students sat for an examination known as the Group Certificate. Since the 1960s, however, the scope of the vocational program has been considerably widened to include courses leading to the Leaving Certificate. Moreover, the VECs currently offer third-level education through the regional technical colleges.

Comprehensive schools were initiated in 1963 and correspond broadly in character to the comprehensive schools in Great Britain. They were intended to offer both secondary and vocational-type courses and to provide a meaningful educational experience for the children who would be affected by the raising of the compulsory school attendance age from 14 to 15 years in 1967. Since the early 1970s, comprehensive schools have been superseded by community schools, which are intended to combine the resources of the local secondary and vocational schools while retaining the comprehensive idea. Ownership of these schools rests with the Department of Education, but the administration is handled by a Board of Management representing the VEC, the relevant religious congregation, the parents, and the teachers.

Specialist qualification are required for certain categories of postprimary teaching, but a university degree in the subject being taught is the general requirement. In secondary schools, one also needs a teacher-training qualification or an acceptable qualification in one's specialized subject area in order to satisfy the registration council. Certification is not required in the vocational or community school sectors but teachers are usually required to hold a university degree in their subject area. Table 4.1 presents a breakdown of the schools in the postprimary sector together with the number of pupils and teachers in each category.

SCHOOL PSYCHOLOGY

School psychology effectively began in Ireland in the mid-1960s when the Department of Education initiated a school psychological service, one of the main functions of which was to oversee the development of guidance and counseling in

TABLE 4.1
Number of Postprimary Schools, Pupils, and Teachers in Ireland 1980/1981 by Category of Schools

Category	Schools	Pupils	Teachers
Secondary	524	200,000	11,500
Vocational	242	69,000	5,500
Comprehensive	15	8,000	500
Community	34	19,000	1,000
Secondary tops	3	500	–
Total	818	296,500	18,500

Note: From O'Donnell (1983).

postprimary schools. In a sense, this was less of a bold innovation than a response to a number of significant developments that had begun to take place in Ireland and abroad. In Great Britain a shift toward comprehensive education had already begun and a number of British universities, such as Reading and Keele, had introduced courses in school counseling. Moreover, one Irish VEC (Dublin City) had established a school psychological service in 1963 that was increasingly seen to be serving a felt need (O'Doherty & Chamberlain, 1969). By introducing a centralized school psychological service, the Department of Education preempted similar initiatives by other VECs, and today Dublin City's VEC remains the only committee with its own service. The wisdom of centralizing the service in this fashion has been questioned by the Psychological Society of Ireland (PSI), which would prefer a regionalized structure affording greater sensitivity to local needs (PSI, 1974).

University College Dublin introduced a full-time 1-year guidance and counseling graduate program in 1967. Although there is a degree of overlap between the functions of the school counselor and the school psychologist they nevertheless are separate and distinct roles, each represented by its own professional association. The majority of school counselors are classroom teachers who are assigned a set number of hours during the week to guidance and counseling work. The amount of time given to counseling is determined by the number of pupils attending the school. No matter how great the number, however, the counselor is required by Department of Education regulations to engage in at least 3 hours of ordinary classroom teaching each week. The Department of Education's psychologists do not themselves work within the schools; rather they supervise and act as consultants both to the school counselors and to remedial teachers. During 1967 the Department of Education also organized a series of 3-week crash courses that were intended to qualify serving postprimary teachers as competent guidance teachers. This initiative provoked a strong reaction from Irish educators and after a 2-year period of intermittent debate the department finally established an Advisory Committee on Pupil Guidance. Although the Advisory Committee's 1971 report was never published, its conclusions represented a major advance for school counseling: It recommended no less than a year's full-time training for teachers who are to assume the guidance and counseling role. At present there are more than 400 school counselors employed in postprimary schools.

There is little doubt that the foregoing factors have been partly responsible for the sluggish development of school psychology in the Irish educational system (Chamberlain & Delaney, 1977). Now, more than a quarter of a century after the introduction of applied psychology in Ireland, the Department of Education employs no more than 26 educational psychologists whose activities are mainly concerned with servicing school counselors at the postprimary level. In the Irish educational system neither primary nor postprimary schools employ school psychologists. The psychological needs of primary school children are left to voluntary nonstate agencies and educational research tends for the most part to be conducted elsewhere.

Questions relating to the identification and treatment of emotionally disturbed or mentally handicapped children in primary schools were first raised by the St. John of God Brothers (a religious order with a special concern for the mentally handicapped). In conjunction with the World Health Organization they established the first child guidance clinic in Dublin in 1955. Child guidance clinics now are established throughout the country, and children are referred to these clinics through the school medical service. There are 118 special national schools for the handicapped with 8,455 children and 852 teachers (O'Fiachra, 1983). Table 4.2 summarizes the provision of special schools for the various categories of handicapped children at the primary level.

Scope of Services

The Department of Education's school psychologists introduced courses in remedial education for second-level school teachers in 1970. This initiative enabled them to work more closely with, and complement the activity of, the child guidance clinics, which cater mainly to primary school children. Nevertheless, the post-

TABLE 4.2
Number of Special National Schools for the Handicapped, Pupils and Teachers by Type of Handicap

Type of Handicap	*Schools*	*Pupils*	*Teachers*
Mentally handicapped	65	5712	501
Children with impaired hearing	5	811	138
Blind and partially sighted	2	155	22
Physically handicapped	15	692	58
Emotionally disturbed	15	473	65
Other special schools	16	612	68
Totals	118	8455	852

Note: From O'Fiachra (1983).

primary sector remains the focus of their professional activity and even here their interaction with the children is largely indirect. This contrasts with the typical role of the school psychologist in countries such as Great Britain, where services are usually located in the community and are directly concerned with facilitating the development of individual children within the school environment (Thompson & Lindsay, 1982).

The role of the Department of Education psychologists has been influenced by the need to spread their resources as widely as possible. As a result they have concentrated on developing an intervention model that emphasizes a classroom–staffroom orientation. Within these limitations they serve as consultants to postprimary teachers and offer advice on a variety of issues concerning school pupils (e.g., individual differences, maladjustment, facilitating the learning process, and assisting with vocational choice).

It is difficult to understand the reluctance of the Department of Education to provide a psychological service for primary school children, where the need is patently greatest (Department of Education, 1962; PSI, 1974; Tussing, 1978). Indeed, even the limited functioning of its psychological service at the second level (i.e., monitoring the activities of guidance and remedial teachers) has been considerably circumscribed by the Department's financial cutbacks. The Minister for Education will permit only schools with an enrollment of 500 or more pupils to engage a guidance counselor outside the quota of teachers allowed to a school. Prior to January 1983, schools with 250 pupils were so permitted. In effect, the Minister's ruling meant that, whereas 68% of Irish postprimary schools had been entitled to engage a school counselor, now only 23% may do so (Chamberlain, 1983).

The Minister's decision had serious implications. First, it has already adversely affected guidance and counseling training programs. Enrollment of postprimary teachers in the University College Dublin course, which has existed since 1967 and has trained the majority of the Republic's school counselors, has dropped by more than 70%. Second, it set the stage for the eventual disappearance of the school counseling role itself. In January 1984 the Minister launched the Department's Programme for Action in Education 1984–1987. Although this represented a new and refreshing approach to Irish education, it gave relatively little space to school guidance and where it did, its intentions were unclear. For instance, one of the program's proposals involved allocating school counselors on the basis of "school needs" (Department of Education, 1984, p. 23) rather than in accordance with the previous quota system. Its intention to consider factors other than number of students was welcome. Yet, in the absence of any meaningful criteria by which school needs were to be assessed, this could only mean a further erosion of the practitioners' role. A third implication of the Minister's ruling concerned its likely negative consequences for the Department's existing school psychological service, one of the main activities of which is the supervision of school counselors.

Administration and Training

As indicated earlier, the administration of school psychology programs is almost entirely within the jurisdiction of the Department of Education, apart from a small local service organized by the City of Dublin's Vocational Educational Committee, which employs four psychologists. The Dublin VEC service began in 1962 by developing a career guidance program within its schools and subsequently extended its service to include remedial education and curriculum development.

In order to be employed as an educational psychologist by the Department of Education, one must hold an honors degree in psychology and be eligible for membership in the PSI or the British Psychological Society. In addition, one must have a number of years of teaching experience. Following recruitment, psychologists are assigned to one of seven regional centers throughout the country and are answerable to the senior psychologists who administer the service.

There is no specific training for educational psychologists other than the basic training that they receive as part of their primary degree. Although this course program is reasonably comprehensive and includes a grounding in the theoretical and applied aspects of educational psychology, no graduate program is available in Ireland. The Psychological Society of Ireland's report *A Psychological Service to Schools* (1974) emphasized the importance of a graduate program and identified this lack as the greatest obstacle to ensuring a high level of competence. Without such a facility, the kind of specialization in which educational psychologists need to engage can never become a reality.

Primary degree courses in psychology are offered by each of the colleges of the National University of Ireland (i.e., Dublin, Cork, and Galway) and by Trinity College Dublin. Educational psychology constitutes a major part of these courses and typically includes units in educational theory, learning theory, psychometrics, research design, statistics, vocational psychology, and counseling theory. In the experience of the author, who served for several years on the PSI's Qualifications and Accreditation Board, the orientation of the courses tends to be eclectic, and the contributions of the dynamic and behavioral theorists are drawn upon equally. In the main, the courses combine an information-centered approach with interactive methods that focus on learning and experience.

Contributions

Because of the indirect intervention model on which the Department of Education's psychologists operate, they have little direct contact with the pupils. Most of their professional activity is concerned with advising remedial teachers or guidance counselors and with organizing in-service courses. To a lesser extent they also develop achievement tests for school use.

As a result of the centralized, bureaucratic organization of the school psychological service, school psychology in Ireland has experienced little imaginative, innovative, or significant changes. It is likely that this situation will not be remedied until the Department restructures its service in accordance with the regionalized model recommended by the PSI (1974). Until then, its psychologists will continue to be seen more as civil servants or administrators than as concerned professionals. But in the absence of restructuring they will not feel free to criticize the present system inasmuch as ministerial personnel are obliged to refrain from any public comment on department policy.

FUTURE TRENDS

Much of the pressure for change has tended to originate outside the Department of Education. The Psychological Society of Ireland, in particular, identified in 1974 the following major areas in which it anticipated that development would take place.

1. *Counseling/School Psychology*: The work of school psychologists should occur at three levels, that is, with teachers, guidance counselors, and individual children.
2. *Educational Retardation*: School psychologists have an important role to play in the treatment of mental, physical, and sensory handicap. Together with teachers and parents, they can alleviate many of the problems that children encounter in school.
3. *Preschool Children*: Psychologists should be directly concerned with the development of preschool services within the community.
4. *Teacher Education*: School psychologists should be involved in teacher education at three levels (basic training, in-service training, and special training).
5. *Curriculum Development and Evaluation*: Practitioners should have a role in the evaluation of educational procedures and methods.
6. *Pupil Assessment*: The role of the school psychologist in this area should preferably be advisory. The PSI recommends that the psychologist "leave to others as much as possible of the testing and psychometric work" (PSI, 1974, p. 5). Although it does not specify to whom, it presumably means teachers and guidance counselors.
7. *Educational Planning*: School psychologists should be involved in educational planning at central and local levels.
8. *Research*: Even at the local level individual psychologists may engage in subsidiary and specific research.

Unfortunately, no reorganization of the kind that would facilitate these developments has taken place. The president of the PSI, in a foreward to the report's second printing in 1981, noted with regret the lack of progress in the implementation of its recommendation. As a result, "Ireland, a full member of the European Community, still has virtually no educational psychological service available to some half-million children and 17,000 teachers in its primary schools" (Kealy, 1981). In anticipating the expansion of school psychology, the PSI favored the ratio of one psychologist for every 6,000 pupils as recommended by UNESCO (1956). This would imply a force of 125 school psychologists in Ireland, but as yet the number does not exceed 26.

The prospect of constructive development does not appear promising at present, primarily because of the constraints imposed by the economic recession. Nevertheless, some tentative steps have been initiated that may result in beneficial change. It is apparent, for instance, that school psychology, like other services, must become regionalized if it is to be effective, and some discussion has taken place with this goal in mind. Such a development may result in greater provision for the needs of primary school children. The establishment of graduate training programs at the master's level is a development that cannot be indefinitely postponed; some discussion has also taken place in this regard. Most necessary of all is a clear statement of policy from the Department of Education. The Department's Action Programme (1984) was a welcome initiative. It is unfortunate, however, that it leaves a great deal to be desired vis à vis the department's school psychological service and it is hoped that more progressive planning will be undertaken in the future.

ACKNOWLEDGMENT

Reprinted by permission of the *Journal of School Psychology*, *23*, 217–224, as published in 1985.

REFERENCES

Chamberlain, J. (1983). Guidance and counseling in the Republic of Ireland. *Personnel and Guidance Journal*, *61*, 479–482.

Chamberlain, J., & Delaney, O. (1977). Guidance and counselling in Irish schools. *British Journal of Guidance and Counselling*, *5*, 3–5.

Department of Education. (1962). *Investment in education*. Dublin: Stationery Office.

Department of Education. (1984). *Programme for action in education*. Dublin: Stationery Office.

Hannan, D., Breen, R., O'Higgins, K., Watson, D., Murray, B., & Hardiman, N. (1983). *Schooling and sex roles: Sex differences in subject provision and student choice in Irish post-primary schools* (Paper No. 113). Dublin: The Economic and Social Research Institute.

Kealy, S. (1981). *A psychological service to schools*. Dublin: The Psychological Society of Ireland.

O'Brolachain, D. (1983, May). *Primary education*. Paper presented at the EURYDICE Information Seminar, Dublin, Ireland.

O'Connor, S. (1968). Post-primary education: Now and in the future. *Studies*, *57*, 233–251.

O'Doherty, E. F., & Chamberlain, J. (1969). Vocational guidance. *Education and Training, 11*, 463–464.

O'Donnell, K. (1983, May). *Second level schools*. Paper presented at the EURYDICE Information Seminar, Dublin, Ireland.

O'Fiachra, S. (1983, May). *Special education in Ireland*. Paper presented at the EURYDICE Information Seminar, Dublin, Ireland.

Psychological Society of Ireland. (1974). *A psychological service to schools*. Dublin: Author (available from PSI, 4–5 Eustace St., Dublin 2).

Thompson, D., & Lindsay, G. (1982). Professional development of educational psychologists. *Bulletin of the British Psychological Society, 35*, 275–277.

Tussing, A. D. (1978). *Irish educational expenditures—past, present and future* (Paper No. 92). Dublin: The Economic and Social Research Institute.

UNESCO. (1956). *Psychological services for schools*. Hamburg: Author.

Chapter Five
Educational Psychology in the Schools of England and Wales

Geoff Lindsay
Psychological Service, Sheffield Local Education Authority, and University of Sheffield

LOCAL EDUCATION AUTHORITIES

In England and Wales the provision of education services is delegated to local education authorities (LEAs). These are areas based on metropolitan districts or county councils. The former cover some major cities including my own authority, Sheffield. They are characteristically metropolitan conurbations with perhaps some rural fringes. The counties, on the other hand, are usually geographically larger and mainly rural, although some include large towns and cities. For example, Nottinghamshire County Council incorporates the city of Nottingham.

The situation in the London area is more complex. Education is provided by the Inner London Education Authority (ILEA) for the boroughs that make up the center of London, which used to comprise the London County Council, and by 20 outer London boroughs.

Thus, education provided by the state is in fact administered by 104 separate and autonomous LEAs. There is legislation laying out the way education must be provided, but this tends to be of a general nature. The balance is now shifting toward greater direction from central government, with proposals for an agreed national curriculum. However, at present, LEAs have a great deal of autonomy in matters of staffing, types of schools provided, and support services, for example. The provision of psychological services is one such area in which LEAs vary.

SCHOOLS

Children are subject to compulsory education between the ages of 5 and 16. In many LEAs children are admitted to school at one of three times per year, depending on date of birth. These entry times coincide with the beginnings of the three school terms: September, January, and April. A common procedure is for children to enter school at the start of the term in which they will become 5 years old; consequently some children will be only just over 4 years old. In some cases, such young children will attend half-day sessions until nearly 5 years old.

LEAs are also able to provide nursery education. Provision of this service is optional, and consequently practice varies considerably. LEAs may afford pre-5 schooling in separate nursery schools, in nursery units attached to primary schools, or in reception classes in primary schools (as previously described). LEAs vary greatly in their provision of places for the pre-5s from 79% in the best to 12% in the worst provided LEA (1986 statistics are for England only). These figures refer to 3- and 4-year-olds.

From the age of 5 years children attend primary schools until about 11 or 12 years. Again there are several different systems, both between and even within LEAs. The traditional primary system comprises an infant (5–7) and a junior (7–11) school, sometimes combined in an all-through junior and infant school. But in addition, there are first schools, either for ages 5–8 or 5–9 years, and middle schools for either 8–12 or 9–13 years. In addition some first and middle stages will be within the same combined school.

Secondary education is consequently provided for different age ranges depending on the age of transfer from primary (i.e., 11, 12, or 13 years). Pupils must attend until 16 years, after which many choose to continue their education either in the same school, a college of further education, or a tertiary college. In the first case, they would normally stay until 17 or 18 years old. Colleges of further education contain a mixture of students who have just left secondary school and are continuing full-time education, young people at work on "day release" or other patterns of education, and students attending other training initiatives. Tertiary colleges are rare at present, but are designed as a combination of the other two systems.

Secondary education in England and Wales is now largely comprehensive; that is, entry is not on the basis of ability or attainment but normally on catchment (geographical) area and choice. Colleges of education and other post-16 education modalities vary. For example, some schools will limit staying on past 16 years to the more able pupils who will be studying for the General Certificate of Secondary Education at advanced level. Some LEAs still operate selection at 11 years by examination (the "11 plus") and others, urged by the present government against the express desires of the majority of educational organizations, are considering reintroducing such procedures.

In most of the country's primary and secondary schools, therefore, there will be the full range of normal ability, with less than 2% attending segregated special schools, and a small percentage of secondary pupils attending grammar schools for higher ability pupils.

There is, in addition, a private sector of education operating throughout the age range. Nationally this takes only a small percentage of pupils but in particular areas, for example, London, it can have a more significant effect on the educational system. In general, private schools tend to cater to high-ability children, and some are renowned for their selection of the very able.

TEACHERS

Teachers are employed by the LEA (unless working for a private school) but on salary scales negotiated nationally. The pupil:teacher ratios will vary from one LEA to another as will the precise terms of contract. A typical junior school for about 200 pupils would have eight teachers, including the deputy principal, plus the principal, who would not have a direct teaching commitment. Larger secondary schools, which often contain about 1,000 pupils, and sometimes 1,500–2,000 (rarely more), would have three assistant principals and a number of year tutors (responsible for students of specific grades) or other posts who would have oversight of the academic and personal development of the pupils.

Statistics for 1986 reveal that in England the overall pupil:teacher ratio for primary schools was 22.2, with a range 17.1 for the best-provided to 24.9 for the worst-provided LEA. In secondary schools the overall ratio was 16.1, with a range of 12.3 to 17.8 (in all cases the numbers of teachers includes nonteaching principals).

SUPPORT PERSONNEL

In addition to educational psychologists, the main school support personnel employed by the LEA are educational advisers, careers officers, and educational welfare officers. Educational advisers normally are experienced teachers who have a general responsibility for a number of schools and either a stage (e.g., primary) or a subject (e.g., mathematics). They advise schools on matters of policy, advise the LEA on practice in schools, are involved in appointment of staff, and also have an inspectorial role on behalf of the LEA—indeed in some LEAs they are termed *inspectors*. Another major aspect of their role is providing in-service education for teachers.

Careers officers are employed to advise pupils about careers and educational opportunities once they leave school. Education welfare officers have traditionally been involved in ensuring attendance: the "school bobby" (policeman) role. More recently they have tried to develop a greater social work orientation and in some areas are indeed called *education social workers* (Craig, 1984).

LEAs also normally employ a number of teachers who help support children with special educational needs in mainstream schools. These have various titles and differing job descriptions ranging from a focus on direct teaching to one on advising other teachers. They are not on the staff of a school but are either attached to and work from a special school or work from a central base in the LEA.

These services have recently expanded following recommendations made in the Warnock Report (Department of Education and Science, 1978), which argued for an increase in the proportion of children with special educational needs who should be integrated, with support, into mainstream schools.

Finally, there are Her Majesty's Inspectors, who form an independent inspectorate to advise the secretary of state for education. They undertake inspection of schools and of LEAs and report directly to the minister. Like LEA advisers and inspectors they also provide some in-service education for teachers, but such programs are normally for teachers from a number of different LEAs.

GOVERNMENT OF SCHOOLS

Every school has its own governing body that reflects a range of interests and operates under an article of government prepared by the LEA and approved by the secretary of state. Since 1988 there has been a standard constitution of governing bodies, although the number of representatives from different groups varies with the size of the school.

There are five constituencies from which governors must be drawn. As an example, a school with between 300 and 599 pupils will have as its governing body four parent governors, four governors appointed by the LEA (usually political appointees), two teacher governors (from the school), the principal, and five co-opted governors. Before the Education (No. 2) Act of 1986, which instituted this model constitution, LEAs varied greatly in their arrangements. This legislation is an advance for some areas and reflects the government's wish to bring parents into governing bodies. However, this was already the norm in some LEAs and indeed the new legislation is more restricting for authorities including Sheffield, which previously included nonteaching staff and pupil representatives (the latter for secondary schools only).

The governing body is responsible for the general management of the school, although the day-to-day decisions are normally delegated to the principal, who has traditionally enjoyed a great deal of autonomy. Governing bodies operate within the general framework of the LEA's policies, which are decided by the education committee of the county council. This comprises elected representatives (councillors), teacher representatives, and other interests. Ultimately the education committee, through the council must act within the general framework laid down by national legislation.

There is, therefore, a dynamic tension in the running of the education service between on the one hand, national legislation and "advice," via Circulars that do not have the force of law and, on the other hand, LEA policies, governing bodies' views, and the views and practices of the staff in the schools. At the present time, there is concern that this equilibrium is being upset and that the present government is trying to centralize decision making and power. For example, although education services are paid for by the LEAs, the government provides about half this money through grants. Over recent years it has gradually reduced this amount of financing, urging LEAs to cut costs (i.e., reduce services). Some LEAs have, instead, increased local taxes (rates), which has led to government "fines" (a process known as *rate-capping*). This limitation of LEA autonomy is a subject of great concern to members of all political parties at the local level.

PSYCHOLOGICAL SERVICES

Prevalence of Educational Psychologists

Psychological services are provided by LEAs and as such are subject to variation in terms of provision. They are not mandatory, but every LEA now has a psychological service. Also, with the passing of the 1981 Education Act, LEAs must take advice from an educational psychologist employed by themselves, either full time or for the purpose of the assessment.[1] In effect, therefore, an LEA must have a psychological service.

In England and Wales, educational psychologists are the professionals most comparable to school psychologists in the United States. However, there are in addition a number of clinical psychologists who also work with children, often as a minority aspect of their work, and whose role overlaps with that of the educational psychologist (Lindsay & Cogill, 1983; Wedell & Lambourne, 1980). In the summer of 1983, a survey by the Association of Educational Psychologists[2] of 101 of the 104 LEAs in England and Wales revealed the wide variation in provision.

Inspection of Table 5.1 reveals that the range in provision of psychological services by LEAs varies between 3,750 and 18,667 pupils to our educational psychologist. The ILEA has a slightly better overall ratio but acts as a regional resource to other services. The relative number of educational psychologists available is one obvious constraint on the type and amount of work that can be done. Compare the ratios in Table 5.1, for example, with those in Scotland (Conochie, 1984).

Development of Psychological Services

Psychological services as they exist today have their roots in several different bases. First there is educational psychology, which can be traced back to Sir Cyril Burt, the first educational psychologist (EP; Hearnshaw, 1979). Burt was em-

[1]Education (Special Educational Needs) Regulations, 1983. Statutory Instrument No. 29.

[2]Association of Educational Psychologists Survey of Staffing at 1st July 1983 (3 Sunderland Road, Durham, England).

ployed as the London County Council's (LCC) psychologist from 1913 to advise on providing individual educational treatment, and to advise the LCC on educational policy from his experience as a psychologist. Aspects of this role included research, psychometrics, and work with schools.

A separate strand of development derives from the child guidance system imported from the United States (Sampson, 1980). The first child guidance clinic opened in London in 1927; by 1935 there were 18 clinics throughout the country, by 1945 there were 424 (Sampson, 1980). Work in the clinics was carried out by the *trinity*, as Sampson terms it, of educational psychologist, child psychiatrist, and social worker. Aspects of the role that developed from this base include clinical and multidisciplinary teamwork, a focus on maladjustment and underachievement, and work with parents.

The third strand was that of teaching. Educational psychologists have tended to have been teachers, in schools, at some stage during their training (see section on Training). This influence brought with it a strong educational component, working with teachers on problems they have identified, and improving teachers' skills. Indeed, until recently many educational psychologists would leave the profession to become involved in the initial training of teachers.

By the 1960s, these strains had produced a small profession whose work was divided between that in a child guidance clinic, and that in a school psychological service. The extent to which these two services were integrated, in respect to delivery, varied considerably. In 1968, a government committee investigated the provision of psychological services and recommended a major expansion of training and posts (Department of Education and Science, 1968). In the 1970s and 1980s the profession saw a rapid increase in the numbers of educational psychologists in service from the equivalent of 354 full-time employees in 1966 to over 1,400 in 1988.

In addition to this increase in the number of educational psychologists, several other major factors shaped services as they are today. First, evaluation of the child guidance model (Tizard, 1973) led to a growing dissatisfaction with this pattern of work. Second, the "giving psychology away" philosophy prevalent

TABLE 5.1
Range in Provision of Psychological Services in England and Wales: Ratio of Number of Educational Psychologists to Number of Children Served

LEAs	*n*	*Lowest*	*Highest*	*Overall*
English counties	39	1:5,253	1:13,889	1:8,079
Welsh counties	7	1:6,667	1:10,100	1:9,017
Metropolitan districts	35	1:4,500	1:18,667	1:6,220
London boroughs	19	1:3,750	1:10,750	1:5,476
ILEA	1			1:3,636[a]

[a]This conceals work carried out on behalf of other services.

in the 1970s spurred educational psychologists to work with others (primarily parents and teachers) in a training capacity (Bushell, Miller, & Robson, 1982; Pugh, 1981). Third, the increase in numbers of well-qualified EPs altered the balance in special education procedures away from medical to psychoeducational influence. Whereas up until the 1970s, school medical officers made many of the assessments of children with special educational needs and recommended future placements, by 1975 this role was undertaken by the EP acting in collaboration with teachers but often having control of the procedures and decision making (Cornwall & Spicer, 1982).

Fourth, and related to this, was the development of the role of *consultant* to schools on matters of policy and on individual children, and away from simply working with referred children.

Fifth, there was a growing disenchantment with normative assessment techniques, especially tests of intelligence, and a growing interest in criterion-referenced approaches and those based on task analysis and curriculum-related assessments. Finally, methods of intervention with individual children broadened from those prevalent in child guidance clinics, normally based in psychoanalytic frameworks, to encompass a wide range of humanistic and behavioral therapies.

Present-Day Services

As there is no "typical" educational psychology service, I provide an example of one service and describe how others may vary.

Sheffield is an industrial city in the heart of England, famous for special steels. Recently, this industrial base has diminished and there are now more white- than blue-collar workers in the city, which is about 500,000 in population. The LEA has about 200 primary, 35 secondary, and 19 special schools and separate provisions for children with special educational needs. There are about 79,000 children of all ages attending school (based on 1987 figures).

The psychological service comprises the equivalent of 16.1 full-time educational psychologists: 1 principal, 4.6 seniors, and 8.5 basic grade posts. One senior, myself, has responsibility for training and has a joint appointment with the university for 40% of time to train EPs. The EPs provide a service to all the schools in the LEA and also accept referrals from any other source that provides the parents' consent (e.g., family doctors, social workers). Many parents refer their own children, often through the school.

The work of the service is divided between that which it carries out with individual clients (i.e., children and families) and the provision of an advisory service, primarily to schools. The former comprises both assessment and intervention procedures with the full range of children with special personal or educational needs. The latter includes in-service training projects (Cox & Lavelle, 1982) and LEA-based research (Galloway, Ball, Blomfield, & Seyd, 1982; Harrison, 1983;

Lindsay, 1981a). The service budgets about 40% of its time on these activities, which it terms *projects*, and until recently has produced a brochure on its activities each year.[3]

Work in schools is generally organized on a time allocation basis whereby schools are given regular visits to permit consultation. Psychologists generally have a geographical area of the city to service for this aspect of work, and the typical workload is 4 secondary schools of about 1,000 pupils each, 20–25 primary schools, and several special schools and units. At this time the service is changing to a system of age-sector teams, for secondary, primary, and preschool work. There is also a small team of two part-time psychologists and the principal, who conduct clinic-based therapy, including family therapy.

This pattern of working reflects the development of services generally. Although the Sheffield service has been regarded as a leader in this development, it is now far from atypical. Many other services also allocate time in the way described here, although there is still a good deal of practice around the country that is more traditional—that is, clinic- rather than community-based.

Administration

Psychological services are provided by LEAs and vary according to the policies of the individual authority, as noted previously. At this time, there is no requirement by law that the EPs an LEA employs must be qualified by a program of study recognized by the British Psychological Society. There are, indeed, a small number of people who entered this profession 10 or more years ago who are not fully trained. However, such an event would be unlikely now.

There is now a certification system for different kinds of psychologists. This situation has been under investigation by the British Psychological Society, whose working party on registration proposed the general format of a process of certification ("chartering") followed by registration, which was agreed upon at the 1984 annual general meeting of the society. A new charter and statutes were passed by the 1985 annual general meeting and the Privy Council agreed to the Society's proposals for the development of chartering. In December 1987 the Privy Council granted leave for the Society's Royal Charter to be amended in order that the Society might maintain a register of chartered psychologists. Only suitably qualified psychologists will be eligible for chartered status, although at present inclusion on the register will be voluntary. It is expected that an act of parliament for the legal registration of psychologists will follow once the Society's register has been in operation for a few years.

The most recent comprehensive survey of educational psychologists was undertaken by the Division of Educational and Child Psychology (DECP) in 1977 and reported by Wedell and Lambourne (1980). In total, 310 questionnaires were

[3]"Projects of the Psychological Service," Nos. 1-3. Sheffield Psychological Service.

returned by EPs, a response rate of about one third. However, the demographic data matched the results of a 1977 survey by the Association of Educational Psychologists, which included data on 90% of EPs. Table 5.2 shows the age distribution of the profession at that time, as compared with that for a sample of school psychologists in the United States, described by Lacayo, Sherwood, and Morris (1981). It can be seen that the age structures were similar and that the two professions are relatively young, with just over half of the DECP sample being 35 years old or younger. Furthermore, 39% of the EPs were women, 61% men. Subsequently this ratio will have altered, as trainees over the past 7–8 years have been predominantly women, in a ratio of about 2:1. Those EPs with 10 years or less experience constituted 83% of field workers and 65% of principals. Of the sample, 89% had teaching experience (mean 3 years, median 4 years) compared with 55% of the U.S. sample (mean 8 years, median 5 years), whereas 94% had postgraduate qualifications, a figure similar to the 99% of the U.S. sample of Lacayo, Sherwood, and Morris (1981).

Training Facilities

Educational psychologists are trained in 12 centers: 1 in Wales and 11 in England. Of the 12 programs, 10 are situated in universities, 1 in a polytechnic, and 1 in a specialist center: The Tavistock Clinic. On completing training, graduates from the universities and polytechnics receive a masters degree, while those from the specialist clinic receive a certificate of that center. All programs are of 1 full calendar year, except two university programs that are 2 years in length.

The basic preparation for educational psychology is as follows: first degree in psychology, teaching qualification, at least 2 years teaching experience with children, postgraduate qualification from 1 of the 12 centers. Thus the minimum period of preparation following a first degree is 4 years. However, there is a strong alternative tradition of people entering the profession from a first experience of teaching, subsequently taking degrees in psychology and then the postgraduate qualification. Such people, and indeed many of the former group as well, have longer teaching experience than the minimum requirement. In addition, many

TABLE 5.2
Age Distribution (% of total) of a Sample of Educational Psychologists in England and Wales and School Psychologists in the United States

	Under 25	*26–29*	*30–34*	*35–39*	*40–49*	*50–59*	*60+*
DECP study[a]	0.6	19.5	32.2	13.7	21.5	11.1	1.3
U.S.[b]	3.9	19.7	22.4	10.7	21.7	16.7	4.5

[a]Division of Educational and Child Psychology study (Wedell & Lambourne, 1980). Data from Wedell and Lambourne (1980).

[b]Data from Lacayo, Sherwood, and Morris (1981).

trainees have other relevant precourse experience as social workers, youth workers, and the like, prior to entering the EP training program.

Evaluation of the postgraduate training programs is carried out by the British Psychological Society, through the Training Committee of the Division of Educational and Child Psychology, which has recently produced a new paper setting out its criteria (DECP, 1984). All programs are expected to have a major practical component that comprises about half of the course time. Practical work is carried out in field situations supervised either by local EPs or by training staff from the program. The theoretical curricula are wide ranging and include child development; methods of assessment and intervention with children, parents, and institutions; other allied services; and children with special needs. Each program is expected to cover a wide range of theoretical and practical components, but it is also expected that each will develop a particular specialized orientation. This may be, for example, in terms of a theoretical basis (e.g., behaviorist, personal construct theory, psychodynamics) or of focus of intervention, (e.g., child, family, or school orientation).

Contributions

The work of the EP in England and Wales is very wide-ranging. The following summary can only be a very limited overview.

Children and Families

Some work is carried out by clinical psychologists working within the National Health Service and by the very small number of private psychologists, but by far the greatest amount is done by educational psychologists working within LEA psychological services. They have a statutory responsibility to assess children who are considered to have special educational needs, and for whom assessment is requested under Section 5 of the 1981 Education Act,[4] and to advise the LEA on such children's educational needs. In addition they see children in regard to a wide variety of developmental problems including those of learning, behavior, and emotional development. The DECP survey (Wedell & Lambourne, 1980) reveals that, at that time, the major problems dealt with were poor school attainments, behavior problems, and mild intellectual handicap, but included a wide range of other difficulties (Table 5.3).

[4]The 1981 Education Act came into operation in England and Wales in April 1983. Under this act any child who is considered to have special educational needs may be assessed. This assessment must include advice from an educational psychologist, in addition to medical and educational advice. The local education authority must determine, on the basis of this advice, whether a child does indeed have special educational needs, in which case the child must be the subject of an official statement that includes both the advice concerning the needs and a declaration of the provision the LEA will make to meet those needs.

TABLE 5.3
Percentage of Time Spent With Various Groups of Children by Educational Psychologists in England and Wales

Type of Problem	*Percentage of Time*
Poor school attainment	20
Behavior problems	20
Mild handicap	10
Poor school attendance	8
Offenders	6
Communication disorders	6
Severe mental handicap	6
Habit disorders (e.g., enuresis)	5
Speech problems	5
Motor impairment	4
Auditory handicap	3
Physically ill (e.g., cardiac, accident)	3
Psychotic and autistic	1
Visual handicap	1
Gifted and outstanding	1
Other	1

From Wedell and R. Lambourne (1980; Copyright by the British Psychological Society. Reprinted by permission.)

Techniques of assessment have been changing away from a reliance on psychometrics to a greater use of observation and miniexperiments. Intervention programs with individual children are generally based on either a counseling approach, or one involving behavioral methods, although the use of psychodynamic approaches is still to be found with a minority of practitioners. More recently, family therapy and hypnotherapy have developed to a significant degree, although such intensive, clinical methods are still relatively uncommon.

Schools

A major development over the past 10 years or so has been the increase in the amount of work with schools. This varies from serving the school as client (Harrison, 1983) to helping teachers to develop programs of parental involvement with reading (e.g., Bushell et al., 1982). The use of "systems" work has been seen to be a more efficient use of psychologists' time and has become popular, with increasing evidence of efficacy (Gillham, 1978, 1981). The two aspects of systems work that distinguish it from much clinic-based work is the recognition that the school as a system can be both a casual factor in a problem situation and a suitable focus for intervention (Lindsay, 1981b).

Other Clients

In addition, EPs also contribute to the child-care system and may help to assess the needs of children taken into care by the local authority, including delinquents. In such cases, the major role is undertaken by social workers, but the EP may act as an adviser, or may assess the child's psychological and educational needs. The scope of psychologists work in social service settings has recently been the subject of an investigation by the British Psychological Society Professional Affairs Board (1983).

Educational psychologists also often work in health settings, particularly pediatric and psychiatric clinics, but normally this is on a part-time basis. For further details of the range of services see Wedell and Lambourne (1980).

Special Problems

Historically the two major problems for EPs were shortage of numbers and conflicts with medical colleagues over primacy of authority. The former problem has been eased by the trebling of the profession's practitioners in less than 20 years, but, of course, more work has been found as new, successful patterns of intervention are developed. Conflicts with medical colleagues now are rare as EPs are working from different bases and in a "network" relationship with autonomous decision making, as recommended by a government Circular in 1974.[5] However, as the number of educational psychologists in LEAs has grown, new sources of conflict have developed with the administrators and educational advisers, as role overlap now exists with these professionals rather than medical practitioners. The growth of advisory teacher services has also been the source of problems, as these often have developed without consideration of their integration with the work of EPs. However, there are several examples of joint work of EPs and advisory staff (Cox & Lavelle, 1982; Lindsay, 1980).

The reduction in the use of normative, particularly cognitive, tests has reduced the need for concern about the validity of U.S. tests. In addition, the production of the British Ability Scales (Elliott, Murray, & Pearson, 1983) has provided a British test of cognitive abilities.[6]

Future Trends

The most immediate problem facing educational psychologists at this time is the implementation of the 1981 Education Act. The history of the effect of PL 94-142 on school psychologists in the United States appears apposite to EPs in this country (Brown, 1980; Kehle & Guidubaldi, 1980).

Despite the good intentions of the act, to be a safeguard for children and to increase the involvement of parents in decision making, there is a danger that

[5]Circular 3/74, "Child Guidance."

[6]The British Ability Scales can be purchased from the NFER-Nelson Publishing Co., Darville House, 2 Oxford Road East, Windsor, Berks, SL4 1DF, U.K.

the major result will be a massive increase in bureaucracy. In addition, there are fears that the act will demand an increase in the proportion of EP time spent on individual assessments, with a decrease in the time available for preventative and systems work. We may have a scenario in which the development of the profession is reversed by unfortunate legislation. A recent research project by the Department of Education and Science, based at the Institute of Education, London, was intended to investigate these and other aspects of the act's implementation. This is as yet unpublished, but preliminary reports confirm the fears expressed here.

There are several other potential problems to be faced in the next 5–10 years. First, the profession is becoming increasingly aware of the lack of members of minority ethnic groups within its ranks. The increase in the numbers of young people from such groups, and particularly of those for whom English is a second language, has impressed on the profession the need to actively seek EPs from among minority groups.

Second, the structure of the society is changing in this country, with a massive increase in the amount of unemployment, particularly among the young just as they leave school. The unlikelihood of a job has reduced the effectiveness of using the passing of public examinations as a motivating force, which has implications for the curriculum and for control of behavior in schools. For example, only 1 in 10 of 16-year-olds in Sheffield now enter full-time jobs. Some continue their education but most join government training schemes. At the same time, owing to the fall in the birth rate, the school population is declining, with a concomitant decrease in the numbers of teachers. School rolls are dropping generally 30%–40%, with an impact on curriculum range: In some cases schools are being closed and teachers redeployed.

Third, on a more positive note, there is likely to be a significant increase in evaluation studies of EP services. During the 1970s, many EPs sought to break away from the traditional role of tester in a clinic. The profession's journals of this period (in particular *Educational and Child Psychology*, previously the *Occasional Papers of the Division of Educational Psychology of the British Psychological Society*, and *Educational Psychology in Practice*, the journal of the Association of Educational Psychologists) have many articles describing new initiatives and pilot projects. The effectiveness of these ways of working is now being evaluated and these results should guide the manner of consolidation and further development of the 1980s and 1990s.

CONCLUSIONS

Educational psychologists in England and Wales are currently at a watershed. They have developed many exciting new initiatives during the past decade to supplement or replace the patterns of working of the 1960s and earlier. They have increased their work as consultants to schools and as providers of further training for teachers, often in school-based and school-focused programs. Their methods of assessment have changed, with a reduction in the degree of reliance on normative measures and an increase in curriculum-based assessment. Methods of intervention have also changed (e.g., through teachers and parents). But there are fears that the 1981 Education Act will reverse this trend and force EPs back into the role of testers.

In my view, this latter perspective is overly pessimistic. I do not consider that the gains of the past decade will be so easily lost, particularly as the usefulness of these ways of working is recognized by our clients and employers. Rather I suggest that we must now build on these past successes and seek to develop further those elements of our practice that are demonstrably useful.

ACKNOWLEDGMENT

Reprinted by permission of the *Journal of School Psychology, 23*, 305–317, as published in 1985.

REFERENCES

British Psychological Society, Professional Affairs Board. (1983). *Psychological services in social services departments*. Leicester, England: Author.

Brown, R. T. (1980). A closer examination of the Education for All Handicapped Children Act: A guide for the 1980s. *Psychology in the Schools, 17*, 355–360.

Bushell, R., Miller, A., & Robson, D. (1982). Parents as remedial teachers. *Association of Educational Psychologists Journal, 5*(9), 7–13.

Cornwall, K., & Spicer, J. (1982). DECP Enquiry: The role of the educational psychologist in the discovery and assessment of children requiring special education. *Occasional Papers of the Division of Educational and Child Psychology, 6*(2), 3–30.

Cox, K., & Lavelle, M. (1982). Experiential workshop on gaining techniques for use in school Inset work. *Occasional Papers of the Division of Educational Child Psychology, 6*(3), 58–63.

Craig, B. (1984). The school social worker. In G. Lindsay (Ed.), *Screening for children with special needs* (pp. 134–152). London: Croom Helm.

Division of Educational and Child Psychology, British Psychological Society. (1984). *Criteria for the evaluation of training courses in educational psychology*. Leicester, England: Author.

Department of Education and Science. (1968). *Psychologists in the education services*. London: HMSO.

Department of Education and Science. (1978). *Special educational needs*. London: HMSO.

Elliott, C., Murray, D., & Pearson, L. (1983). *The British Ability Scales*. Windsor: NFER-Nelson.

Galloway, D., Ball, T., Blomfield, D., & Seyd, R. (1982). *Schools and disruptive pupils*. London: Longman.

Gillham, B. (Ed.). (1978). *Reconstructing educational psychology*. London: Crom Helm.

Gillham, B. (Ed.). (1981). *Problem behaviour in the secondary school*. London: Croom Helm.

Harrison, B. (1983). 'Vandalism' in schools. In G. Lindsay (Ed.), *Problems of adolescence in the secondary school* (pp. 209–230). London: Croom Helm.

Hearnshaw, L. (1979). *Cyril Burt: Psychologist*. London: Hodder & Stoughton.

Kehle, T., & Guidubaldi, J. (1980). Do too many cooks spoil the broth? *Journal of Learning Disabilities, 13*, 552–556.

Lacayo, N., Sherwood, G., & Morris, J. (1981). Daily activities of school psychologists: A national survey. *Psychology in the schools, 18*, 184–190.

Lindsay, G. (1980). Monitoring children's learning: An in-service approach. *British Journal of In-Service Education, 6*(3), 189–191.

Lindsay, G. (1981a). *The Infant Rating Scale*. Sevenoaks: Hodder & Stoughton.

Lindsay, G. (1981b). Getting it out of your system. *Association of Educational Psychologists Journal, 5*(5), 33–36.

Lindsay, G., & Cogill, S. (1983). Psychological services for children: Grass roots opinion. *Bulletin of the British Psychological Society, 36*, 155–158.

Pugh, G. (1981). *Parents as partners*. London: National Childrens Bureau.

Sampson, O. (1980). *Child guidance: Its history, provenance and future*. Leicester, England: British Psychological Society.

Tizard, J. (1973). *Maladjusted children in the Child Guidance Service*. London Educational Review, 2(2), 22–37.

Wedell, K., & Lambourne, R. (1980). Psychological services for children in England and Wales. *Occasional Papers of the Division of Educational and Child Psychology, 4*(1, 2).

Chapter Six
School Psychology in the U.S.S.R.

Hagop S. Pambookian
Elizabeth City, North Carolina
Ivan Z. Holowinsky
Rutgers University

Although school psychology as an organized or separate discipline does not currently exist in the Union of Soviet Socialist Republics, Soviet psychologists have studied problems relating to children, schools, and learning. In fact, the formulation of new instructional programs, learning strategies, and curricula has occurred because of psychological research within the schools. Psychologists, primarily prepared in educational and developmental areas, are actively investigating various dimensions of the teaching–learning process in an effort to improve the total development of learners. This chapter presents an overview of the Soviet educational system, discusses the training of psychologists and psychological services provided for school children, and describes the increasing concern and need for the establishment of school psychology as a profession.

SOVIET GENERAL EDUCATION AND SCHOOLING

The schools in the U.S.S.R. are public, and the educational system is characterized by continuity, uniformity of requirements, and centralism in planning and administration. However, some provisions are made for local decisions regarding native language and literature in each of the 15 Union republics.

General education is compulsory. Children typically have started school at the age of 7 and attended classes for 5 or 6 hours a day, 6 days a week for 10 years. As of 1986, the duration of general education schools was changed to 11 years, with children starting school at 6 years of age. However, these changes and other educational reforms described in the Soviet *Guidelines for Reform of General and Vocational Schools* will be gradually implemented and become uniformly effective in 1990 (*Guidelines*, 1984). The school year is divided into four quarters with vacation following each quarter.

Generally, the mandatory weekly classwork is 24 periods lasting 45 minutes for children in the first four grades and is 30 periods of 45 minutes for pupils in Grades 5–10. Students have some electives, ranging from 2 hours a week in the seventh grade to 6 hours in the 10th grade or senior year (Malkova, 1981). However, these requirements may vary slightly for students in nonRussian republics. The Armenian youngsters, for instance, study more subjects in the Armenian Republic schools than do the Russian pupils in the Russian Federated Republic schools. Homework is mandatory for school children in each class.

The main tasks of general education are clearly spelled out in the Legal Foundations of Education of the U.S.S.R. and the Union republics, as adopted by the Supreme Soviet of the U.S.S.R. on July 19, 1973. In part, they call for

> The implementation of general education of children and youth, conforming with contemporary requirements of social, scientific and technological progress, the inculcation of a solid knowledge of the bases of science, the encouragement of the striving for continuing improvement of knowledge and of the ability for self-improvement as well as of skills in practice. (Zimin, 1977, p. 42)

Education also calls for the information of a materialistic outlook, communist convictions, and a communist attitude toward work. Children also should acquire a spirit of collectivism, friendship, internationalism, and mutual aid based on socialist ideology and humanism (Kairov, 1963; Zimin, 1977).

In order to promote total development of each youngster, Soviet education offers courses and experiences in mathematics, natural sciences, social sciences, humanities, workshop training, art, music, and physical education. Sciences and foreign languages, however, hold a significant place in the curriculum, as do polytechnical training and labor education. Moreover, education is closely linked to life and work. This is in line with Lenin's conviction that "we could not believe in teaching, training and education if they are restricted only to the schoolroom and divorced from the ferment of life" (Zimin, 1977, p. 41).

During the 1980–1981 academic year, 44.3 million pupils were enrolled in 145,000 general education schools (elementary, incomplete secondary, secondary, evening, and correspondence). In addition, nearly 3.7 million students were studying in 7,242 vocational–technical institutions, 4.6 million in 4,383 specialized secondary schools, and over 5 million men and women in 883 institutes and universities (Panachin, 1982). There is a chain of well-established preschools, and over 129,000 nurseries and kindergartens accommodate 12 million young children. There are also special-emphasis schools (e.g., physics, English), boarding and special schools for the gifted and handicapped, and extended-day schools for children who remain in school after regular classes in order to take part in supervised extracurricular activities and classwork.

Education has apparently a high priority for the Soviet Communist Party and the Government. Of the total 1979 funds budgeted for education, health and physical culture, social security, state social insurance, and aid to single mothers and to mothers with many children, a 41% share (15.73 billion rubles, nearly $23.438 billion at the official rate of $1.49 per ruble) was spent on the general education and upbringing of children and adolescents, and on work involving adults (Hutchings, 1983). Another 8.465 billion rubles ($12.613 billion) was provided for the education and training of students in vocational-technical and specialized secondary schools, and in higher educational institutions (Panachin, 1982). The state in 1977 spent an average of 160 rubles ($238) a year per pupil in general education schools (Scherer, 1978). However, the cost of instruction and support services per student in extended-day schools, specialized secondary schools, and boarding schools is appreciably higher.

TEACHER TRAINING AND STATUS

In order to study at one of the 883 higher education institutions, including universities and pedagogical institutes (see Panachin, 1982, for the 1981 data), students must complete secondary school and pass national examinations in (a) subjects closest to their intended specializations, (b) Russian language and literature (or native language and literature), and (c) one foreign language. Attendance at institutes and universities is tuition free. Moreover, students are offered free dormitory facilities if they cannot commute, nursery–kindergarten services, free medical care, and a system of stipends of about 50 rubles ($74.50) a month, and 100 rubles ($149) when they are on Lenin or Karl Marx scholarships for exemplary and excellent accomplishments (Pambookian, 1982a). Of the 2.7 million day students in 1977, 77% received monthly stipends (Scherer, 1978).

For students attending institutions of higher education, the academic year consists of two semesters (September 1 through January 23 and February 7 through June 30) with month-long exams scheduled at the end of each. Class attendance is mandatory and the students' weekly (6-day) workload of compulsory studies generally ranges from 24–36 semester hours. The course of study lasts 4–5 years (5 years at a university; 4 years at a pedagogical institute for students majoring in one subject, and 5 years for those with a double major). Irrespective of areas of specialization, all students must study several required courses such as Marxist–Leninist philosophy, history of the Communist Party of the Soviet Union (C.P.S.U.), scientific communism, political economy, scientific atheism, Marxist–Leninist ethics and esthetics, and a foreign language.

Usually, kindergarten and elementary school teachers are trained in pedagogical schools, whereas secondary school teachers are trained in pedagogical institutes and universities. In 1980 there were 426 pedagogical schools, 200 pedagogical institutes, and 68 universities (Panachin, 1982). The pedagogical school curriculum consists of general education and specialized subjects (e.g., teaching methodology in elementary school, school hygiene, psychology). After completing all the requirements, including student teaching and other practical work, the graduating students are examined and, if successful, receive their diplomas. Teachers in training for elementary and kindergarten positions must learn to play a musical instrument (Pambookian, 1982a).

The secondary school teachers' training curriculum includes sociopolitical, psychoeducational, specialized, and secondary school-related courses. At the end of their courses of study, students must pass state examinations in several areas (e.g., major subjects, education, the fundamentals of scientific communism, methodology of teaching the subject matter) in order to be certified to teach one or two subjects in a general education secondary school. Obviously, Soviet students can specialize in Russian language and literature (as well as in the language and literature of a republic or a major ethnic group), mathematics, biology, history, physics, geography, and chemistry at both pedagogical institutes and universities. However, they must attend a pedagogical institute to major in foreign languages, elementary school pedagogy and psychology, music and singing, defectology (i.e., special education), drawing, and general-technical disciplines (Aleksandrov, 1978). Moreover, only universities offer courses in the Romance and Germanic languages and literatures. The three popular specializations or subjects in great demand in the mid-1970s, judged by total enrollment and the number of graduating teachers, were Russian language and literature, mathematics, and foreign languages.

Once every 5 years, the 2.5 million teachers employed in general education schools must complete the required in-service training at one of the Institutes for the Improvement of Teacher Qualification. These institutes as well as the Scientific Methodological Centers and Houses of Education Workers operate in order to (a) develop and improve programs and curricula, (b) provide teachers technical and methodological assistance, (c) promote study of teaching and training strategies, (d) disseminate information about teaching styles, (e) raise the level of professional commitment and ideological–political knowledge and, of course, (f) improve the skills of educators and other professional personnel.

Teaching seemingly is held in high esteem in the U.S.S.R., and teachers are generally respected for their work (Malkova, 1981; Pambookian, 1982a). Mikhail A. Prokofiev, the Minister of Education, in a 1978 interview by *Uchitelskaya Gazeta* (Teachers' Gazette), perceived the teacher as a "fighter on the front of ideas" realizing through dedication and hard work "the Communist Party line and precepts" (Pambookian, 1982a). Indicative of the Soviet leadership's high regard for teachers is the observance of Teachers' Day, the first Sunday of October, as a national holiday. (In the 1984 *Guidelines for Reform of Schools*, the commitment to quality teaching and teachers was reiterated by Soviet leaders, who declared September 1 "The Day of Knowledge," as a national holiday to be oberved annually.) Moreover, teachers are awarded various honorary titles, lapel pins, and medals for their outstanding work in the upbringing of a new generation. In the fall of 1977, for instance, 290,000 teachers were awarded U.S.S.R. Orders and Medals, 35,000 were honored as Honored Schoolteachers, and another 125 were declared Heroes of Socialist Labor (Panachin, 1982).

PROFESSIONAL PREPARATION OF SOVIET PSYCHOLOGISTS

Degree-granting faculties in psychology were officially established at Moscow State University and Leningrad State University in 1966. The first psychology degrees were awarded in 1968. In addition to these two programs, psychologists are being trained in psychology departments at the universities of Kharkov, Kiev, Rostov, Saratov, Tartu, Tashkent, Tbilisi, Yaroslavl, Yerevan, and Vilnius. Psychologists and researchers also are trained at scientific research institutes such as the Institute of Psychology of the U.S.S.R. Academy of Sciences, the Institute of General and Pedagogical Psychology of the U.S.S.R. Academy of Pedagogical Sciences, the D.N. Uznadze Institue of Psychology of the Georgian Academy of Sciences, and the Institute of Psychology of the Ukrainian Ministry of Education (Ivannikov, 1978; Lomov, 1982; Pambookian, 1982b). Students can pursue advanced degrees in psychology, preschool pedagogy and psychology, and defectology at several pedagogical institutes and research institutes as well.

Psychological training consists of specialized preparation in psychology and in sciences, including instruction in social sciences, mathematics, biology, and foreign languages. Independent of their specialization, Soviet psychology students complete a wide range of course offerings.

In order to be admitted into a graduate program in psychology, interested students (with diplomas from an institute or a university) whose age does not exceed 45 years must pass the psychology examinations as well as foreign language and C.P.S.U. history exams. Only after passing these tests can the applicants be considered and classified as *aspirants* (i.e., graduate students). The graduate student's course of study for the ensuing 3 years (usually, the accepted term of study) is planned with the major adviser. At the end of the 3-year term, students sit for "candidate's minimum" qualifying examinations in dialectical materialism, a foreign language, and psychology. The successful "doctoral" students then submit their dissertations for defense; only after their studies are published as monographs or articles in professional journals do they obtain the *Candidate of Psychological Sciences* (CPS) degrees (comparable to an American or British PhD). This first degree, as well as the more advanced (and prestigious) *Doctor of Psychological Sciences* (DPS) degrees and other academic ranks and titles, are approved and confirmed by the Supreme Certifying Commission in Moscow. The Commission confirmed a total of only 287 CPS and DPS degrees during the 4 years following approval of the granting of advanced degrees in psychology in the U.S.S.R. (Volkov, Panov, & Kolmakov, 1975).

Several journals and reviews contribute to the academic and professional training and development of Soviet psychologists. Besides the *Voprosy Psikhologii* (Problems of Psychology) published by the U.S.S.R. Academy of Pedagogical Sciences and the Academy of Sciences' *Psikhologichenski Zhurnal* (Psychological Journal), psychologists publish articles on the teaching of psychology, and on theory and research in psychology, learning, and the education and upbringing of children in *Novye Issledovaniya v Psikhologii* (New Research in Psychology), *Semya i Shkola* (Family and School), and *Sovietskaya Pedagogika* (Soviet Pedagogy). For the dissemination of their research findings, professional knowledge, and views, psychologists also make use of other journals issued by various ministries in each republic and the Union.

Employed as instructors by universities and pedagogical institutes, and as researchers by scientific research institutes and ministries, Soviet psychologists teach and do research in an environment shaped by the country's sociopolitical and economic factors. These factors are intended to guide students' development and learning in and for the collective good of the nation. Mental health issues and problems are not the professional concern of psychologists. Mental and behavioral problems as such are treated in outpatient clinics, hospitals, and psychiatric research institutes by psychiatrists, psychotherapists, and neuropathologists.

THE PRACTICE OF SCHOOL PSYCHOLOGY

The practice of Soviet school psychology seems to fall within the scope of the doctoral-level specialty in school psychology that Bardon (1983) described—one emphasizing schooling and education, educational attainment (rather than mental health), and educational psychology as a knowledge base for practice. In line with this, educational and developmental psychology are inseparably linked to the educational process in the U.S.S.R. Therefore, teaching, learning, and the cognitive development of youngsters as well as curricula, content, and methods of instruction have been influenced by "natural experiments" and research conducted by psychologists in applied settings. On the other hand, quantitative psychological measurement or nationally standardized assessment is not typical of Soviet research. In lieu of this, attention is focused on those factors that they perceive to most strongly influence the development and behavior of students in the process of learning. In addition, other "qualitative" techniques (e.g., observation, interview, analysis of learner's work, autobiographical sketch) are used to gather data for informed psychoeducational generalizations and instructional recommendations.

The use of intelligence testing and other forms of standardized tests and questionnaires was abolished by the July 4, 1936, decree "On Pedological Distortions in the System of People's Commissariat of Education" (Menchinskaya, 1969; Petrovskii, 1978; Shore, 1947). *Pedology,* whose purpose was to identify and assess individual differences in cognitive skills and to develop a "science of education," was seen to be a pseudoscience, taking over the role of "Marxist science of children" in the 1920s and 1930s and downplaying the importance of pedagogy in the upbringing of children. According to Petrovskii (1978), pedology, with ideological and mechanistic orientations, viewed psychology as the study of what was subjective, and "was excessively infatuated with scientifically unfounded tests which determined the intelligence quotients of pupils and students" (p. 386).

However, in the past 10 years the attitudes of Soviet psychologists toward diagnosis have changed to a considerable degree. Indicative of this are a number of symposia and conferences organized on the topic of psychodiagnosis. Yassman (1975) described such a symposium at which those in attendance decided to petition the Executive Council of Soviet Psychological Society and the U.S.S.R. Academy of Pedagogical Sciences for permission to develop theoretical and practical approaches to psychodiagnosis. The major objective of subsequent symposia also dealt with the issue of psychodiagnosis in schools (Bogoyavlenskaya, 1980).

More attention has been recently paid to the assessment of exceptional children. In collaboration with the Institute of Pedagogy, the Institute of Psychology in Kiev published a work entitled *Principles of Assessment and Education of Atypical Children*. Likewise, in a 1978 book Bleykher and Burlachuk (cited in Rozhdestvenskaya, 1979) described psychological diagnosis of intelligence and personality.

An example of the sort of assessment practiced by psychologists in the U.S.S.R. can be gained from a study, published in 1977, by Umanskaya, who provided a description of the intellectual assessment of preschool children with delayed speech development. She addressed herself to the differential diagnosis between oligophrenia (the term *oligophrenia*, as used in the Soviet Union, describes mental deficiency) and delayed intellectual development related to retarded speech development.

Umanskaya's sample included 200 preschoolers diagnosed as either oligophrenic or aphasic (alalic). In her battery of tests she used Seguin Form Board and a variety of tasks such as (a) classification of objects according to form, size, and color; (b) discrimination of minor pictorial details; (c) object assembly, and (d) construction of figures by using matches or small sticks. She also observed how children selected and used toys, and attended to and terminated play during free-play situations. Such an approach that focuses more upon a process rather than a product of problem solving has been described as qualitative assessment (Holowinsky, 1980). There have also been a number of attempts to develop tests of cognitive abilities. One such test (see Zambatsavichene, 1984), designed for children 7–9 years of age, has 107 verbal items grouped into four subjects that are supposed to measure such clusters of abilities as (a) recognition of essential features, (b) recognition of dissimilar concepts, (c) logical relations, and (d) generalizations.

Recent developments since 1980 reflect occasional references, infrequent but noticeable, to the use of traditional and widely known standardized intelligence tests. For example, Novakova (1983) discussed the use of the Stanford–Binet with learning-disabled children and suggested that it is a valuable instrument for the purpose of cognitive assessment. Panasiuk utilized an adaptation of the Wechsler Intelligence Scale for Children (WISC) as an index of intellectual development (Zambatsavichene, 1984). Moreover, Anastasi's (1982) *Psychological Testing* has been translated into Russian and published in two volumes in Moscow. Her text was also reviewed in a 1983 issue of *Voprosy Psikhologii* (Antsiferova, Kartseva, & Rousalov, 1983).

PSYCHOLOGICAL RESEARCH AND CONTRIBUTION

Soviet psychologists play a significant role in the educational process and, therefore, serve children and support school practices. Over the years, they have made appreciable contributions to the educational system and the upbringing and education of youngsters (Davydov, 1981) through the modification and improvement of teaching strategies, school curricula, textbooks, and the establishment of "scientifically based" educational practice and learning environments (Bozhovich, 1978). Differences in emphasis in the psychology of learning nothwithstanding, it appears that psychologists in the U.S.S.R. attempt "to develop the psychological foundations for developmental teaching that form the personality of school pupils in accordance with the demands of our life, and the building of a Communist Society" (Menchinskaya, 1981, p. 214).

Moreover, educational psychologists have stressed the importance of the teacher's role in facilitating the total development of children, adolescents, and adults. In fact, the relationship between teaching and intellectual development is consistent with the view on the unity of consciousness and activity as conceptualized by Rubinshtein (see Petrovskii, 1982). Since consciousness or personality is formed during activity (i.e., play, study, or work), that activity must be analyzed because consciousness, as Lomov (1982) put it, "is formed by, developed through, and modified in human activity" (p. 582). Therefore, any change in the latter will affect the learners who are, themselves, active participants in the educational process and are developed while being taught, educated, and trained. This is best illustrated, for instance, by Markova (1981), who noted that

> Learning motivation is considered one aspect of a child's active relationship with school subject matter, an important aspect of his own orientation to a given subject, and one of the criteria for molding of a child in the course of teaching activity. (p. 218)

Soviet psychologists have also studied memory, creative thinking, and motivation for schoolwork (Davydov, 1981; Menchinskaya, 1981; Petrovskii, 1982;

Zaporozhets, 1975). Interest in educational practices is further exemplified by psychological research involving the upbringing and education of children in kindergartens and elementary schools, as well as by research relating to the communication of preschoolers, school failure, self-appraisal, and intellectual development.

CONCERN FOR AND FUTURE DEVELOPMENTS IN SCHOOL PSYCHOLOGICAL SERVICES

Soviet psychologists do contribute to classroom instruction and the upbringing of children. However, they are not assigned administratively to a particular school nor are they employed for the purpose of diagnostic screening of children or educational intervention. Moreover, the adversely pervasive attitude toward assessment (e.g., of cognitive skills) and the Communist Party's control and direction of all aspects of life do not seem to hinder the psychologists' understanding of psychoeducational practices or limit their usefulness in providing psychological services for schools and children.

Despite the significant contributions of Soviet psychology to school practices, there has been a keen interest in expanding its functions as well as the furtherance of assessment (e.g., Bozhovich, 1983; Davydov, 1981). "It is therefore necessary," wrote Davydov (1981), "to set up a system of psychological services in schools. This already exists in a number of countries, and the time is now ripe in our country as well" (p. 195). For the establishment and success of such a system, Davydov felt that the question of its scope and content, the methods of organization, and the theoretical duties of psychologists should be addressed. Similarly, Bozhovich (1983) suggested that a number of problems still have to be corrected before school psychology can emerge as a separate profession. She indicated that at least three areas need special and immediate attention: (a) initiation and coordination of the psychoeducational efforts of practitioners in psychology and education; (b) undertaking of more investigations in order to clarify the impact of psychological research upon educational practice; and (c) development of increased and better communication between psychologists and educators. The lack of communication was ascribed to the fact that teachers are inadequately trained in psychology and psychologists are inadequately trained in education.

A much needed impetus to the emerging interest in school psychology was the organization of two roundtable discussions in 1982 that explored several issues related to the establishment of school psychology services at the elementary and secondary school levels. These discussions focused on the preparation and role of school psychologists (cf. Agaphanova, 1982; Ivannikov, 1982; Talyzyna, Sapharov, & Ivannikov, 1982). Ivannikov (1982) suggested that such services should be established at regional- or district-level centers. Ivannikov further proposed that a center should employ 8–10 psychologists with expertise in developmental, educational, and social psychology. However, stressing the need of school psychological services, Talyzyna et al. (1982) felt that the lack of consensus regarding the functions of psychologists in the schools was a serious obstacle. Furthermore, they suggested that an important goal involved the training of psychologist-educators who are well versed in educational practice and psychological intervention. A similar view was expressed by Harasymova (1982), who indicated that until a number of school psychologists were trained as professional psychologists, their functions could be performed by faculty members of university education departments.

In order to function effectively in applied settings, Agaphanova (1982) emphasized that school psychologists should (a) be familiar with specific issues within the areas of developmental psychology and general education, (b) show awareness of current issues in the field of special education, (c) demonstrate adequate guidance counseling skills, and (d) have knowledge of abnormal psychology. She further suggested that school psychologists should have studied family dynamics and be familiar with school law, rules, and regulations.

As for the main functions of school psychology services, Matyushkin (1982) argued that they should involve psychodiagnosis, prognosis,and the study of human learning and communication. Markova (1982), on the other hand, referred to consultation, diagnosis, and therapy as the primary functions. However, Dubrovyna and Prikhozhan (1982) indicated that schools primarily expect school psychologists to provide individualized assistance to students with academic problems.

The 1982 roundtable participants also suggested that school psychologists should not serve more than two schools (Zakharov, 1982). It was also felt that they should have the authority to monitor parental obligations towards schools in order to assist psychologists in fulfilling their responsibilities (Cherpanova, 1982) and that coordinating centers for psychological services should be set up at various adminstrative levels (Agaphanova, 1982). Tsybenova (1982) recommened a rather comprehensive list of responsibilities for school psychologists and their involvement in (a) promoting psychological knowledge and its introduction into school practices, (b) providing psychoeducational seminars for teachers, (c) providing consultation for parents and teachers, and (d) supplying practical help to students in resolving their personal problems.

Several major changes are needed for the adequate training and functioning of psychologists in the U.S.S.R. Of paramount importance are (a) the availability of more educational facilities for students in psychology, inasmuch as only a dozen or so institutions of higher education have programs in psychology; and (b) the acquisition of psychology books (and journals) in Russian and nonRussian languages by universities and pedagogical and research institutes. Moreover, barring restrictions in the name of ideological purity and reform, future developments in Soviet psychology will likely include: (a) greater input through research and publications by nonRussian psychologists in Union republics, (b) a renewed interest in and use of various intelligence tests, personality inventories, and other psychometric instruments, (c) introduction of general psychology into the curriculum of general education schools and the provision of psychology as an elective in the senior year, and (d) regular psychological exchanges and collaborative research between psychologists in the U.S.S.R. and in nonsocialist countries.

ACKNOWLEDGMENT

Reprinted by permission of the *Journal of School Psychology, 25,* 209–222, as published in 1987. Pambookian is now on the psychology faculty of Shawnee State University, Portsmouth, Ohio.

REFERENCES

Agaphanova, K. V. (1982). Psychological service in the school (roundtable). *Voprosy Psikhologii, 3,* 62–93.

Aleksandrov, N. V. (1978). Pedagogical education. In M. L. Waxman (Ed.), *Great Soviet encyclopedia* (Vol. 19, pp. 373–374). New York: Macmillan.

Anastasi, A. (1982). *Psychological testing* (5th ed.). New York: Macmillan.

Antsiferova, L. I., Kartseva, T. V., & Rousalov, V. M. (1983). Urgent problems in psychodiagnosis. *Voprosy Psikhologii, 5,* 157–159.

Bardon, J. I. (1983). Psychology applied to education: A speciality in search of an identity. *American Psychologist, 38,* 185–196.

Bogoyavlenskaya, D. B. (1980). Psychodiagnosis and school. *Voprosy Psikhologii, 4,* 184–186.

Bozhovich, E. D. (1983). Experimental organization of psychological-pedagogical consultation in school. *Voprosy Psikhologii, 6,* 81–88.

Bozhovich, L. I. (1978). Educational psychology. In M. L. Waxman (Ed.), *Great Soviet encyclopedia* (Vol. 19, p. 42). New York: Macmillan.

Cherpanova, E. M. (1982). Psychological service in the school (roundtable). *Voprosy Psikhologii, 3,* 62–93.

Davydov, V. V. (1981). Psychological problems in the education and upbringing of the rising generation. In B. R. Tabachnick, T. S. Popkewitz, & B. B. Szekely (Eds.), *Studying teaching and learning: Trends in Soviet and American research* (pp. 183–199). New York: Praeger.

Dubrovyna, I. V., & Prikhozhan, A. M. (1982) Psychological service in the school (roundtable). *Voprosy Psikhologii, 3,* 62–93.

Guidelines for reform of general and vocational schools. (1984, May 27). *Moscow News,* No. 21 (Suppl.).

Harasymova, V. S. (1982). Psychological service in the school (roundtable). *Voprosy Psikhologii, 3,* 62–93

Holowinsky, I. Z. (1980). Qualitative assessment of cognitive skills. *Journal of Special Education, 14,* 155–163.

Hutchings, R. (1983). *The Soviet budget.* Albany, NY: State University of New York Press.

Ivannikov, V.A. (1978). Psychology education. In M. L. Wasman (Ed.), *Great Soviet encyclopedia* (Vol. 21, pp. 324–325). New York: Macmillan.

Ivannikov, V. A. (1982). Psychological service in the school (roundtable). *Voprosy Psikhologii, 4,* 75–103.

Kairov, L. A. (1963). The new CPSU program and the tasks of pedagogical science. *Soviet Pedagogy, 3*, 3–16.
Lomov, B. F. (1982). Soviet psychology: Its historical origins and contemporary status. *American Psychologist, 37*, 580–586.
Malkova, Z. (1981). *L'Union Soviétique aujourd'hui et demain: L'instruction* [The Soviet Union today and tomorrow: Education]. Moscov: Editions de l'Agence de Presse Novosti.
Markova, A. K. (1981). Psychological factors in the formation of school pupils' learning motivation. In B. R. Tabachnick, T. S. Popkewitz, & B. B. Szekely (Eds.), *Studying teaching and learning: Trends in Soviet and American research* (pp. 218–221). New York: Praeger.
Markova, A. K. (1982). Psychological service in the school (roundtable). *Voprosy Psikhologii, 3*, 62–93.
Matyushkin, A. M. (1982). Psychological service in the school (roundtable). *Voprosy Psikhologii, 3*, 62–93.
Menchinskaya, N. A. (1969). Fifty years of the Soviet psychology of learning. In F. Ablin (Ed.), *Contemporary Soviet education: A collection of readings from Soviet journals* (pp. 29–44). White Plains, NY: International Arts and Sciences Press.
Menchinskaya, N. A. (1981). Some aspects of the development of the Soviet psychology of learning. In B. R. Tabachnick, T. S. Popkewitz, & B. B. Szekely (Eds.), *Studying teaching and learning: Trends in Soviet and American research* (pp. 200–217). New York: Praeger.
Novakova, K. (1983). Interrelation of different forms of thought activity as a diagnostic criterion of mental development impairments. *Defectology, 4*, 275–285.
Pambookian, H., S. (1982a). Teachers and teaching in the Soviet Union. *International Psychologist, 23*(1), 18–19.
Pambookian, H. S. (1982b). *Notes on Soviet psychology: Past and present.* Unpublished manuscript.
Panachin, F. G. (1982). Education. In M. L. Waxman (Ed.), *Great Soviet encyclopedia* (Vol. 31, pp. 446–455). New York: Macmillan.
Petrovskii, A. V. (1978). Pedology. In M. L. Waxman Ed., *Great Soviet encyclopedia* (Vol. 19, p. 386). New York: Macmillan.
Petrovskii, A. V. (1982). Social sciences: Psychology. In M. L. Waxman (Ed.), *Great Soviet encyclopedia* (Vol. 31, pp. 403–404). New York: Macmillan.
Rozhdestvenskaya, M. (1979). Psychological diagnosis of intelligence and personality. *Defectology, 5*, 89–90.
Scherer, J. L. (Ed.). (1978). *USSR facts and figures annual* (Vol. 2). Gulf Breeze, FL: Academic International.
Shore, M. (1947). *Soviet education: Its psychology and philosophy.* New York: Philosophical Library.
Talyzyna, N. F., Sapharov, N. S. & Ivannikov, V. A. (1982). Psychological service in the school (roundtable). *Voprosy Psikhologii, 4*, 75–103.
Tsybenova, N. Ch. (1982). Psychological service in the school (roundtable). *Voprosy Psikhologii, 3*, 62–93.
Umanskaya, N. M. (1977). Techniques of the assessment of intelligence in preschool children with delayed speech development. *Defectology, 2*, 64–72.
Volkov, M. N., Panov, V. G., & Kolmakov, P. K. (1975). Dissertation. In M. L. Waxman (Ed.), *Great Soviet encyclopedia* (Vol. 8, pp. 304–305). New York: Macmillan.
Yassman, L. (1975). New developments in psychodiagnostic methods. *Defectology, 2*, 89–94.
Zakharov, A. I. (1982). Psychological service in the school (roundtable). *Voprosy Psikhologii, 3*, 62–93.
Zambatsavichene, E. F. (1984). Preparation of a standarized test for rating level of mental development in normal and deficient children. *Defectology, 1*, 28–34.
Zaporozhets, A. V. (1975). Child psychology. In M. L. Waxman (Ed.), *Great Soviet encyclopedia* (Vol. 8, pp. 23-25). New York: Macmillan.
Zimin, P. V. (1977). The Soviet school system. In N. Kuzin & M. Kondakov (Eds.), *Education in the USSR* (pp. 40–80). Moscow: Progress Publishers.

Chapter Seven
School Psychology in Spain

Isabel Caro, Ma A. Miralles
University of Valencia

Spanish education is compulsory and free for children between the age of 6 and 14 years. The basic purpose of the compulsory education program is to provide students with the requisite skills that are needed for later specialization *(Nuevas Orientaciones,* 1977). Examined within this context, elementary school students are taught in self-contained classes until they complete the basic education sequence. Following this, students who wish to continue their studies may pursue one of two options. The first option involves attending a *Bachillerato Unificado Polivalente* (BUP) program that is similar to American high school programs. The BUP program presents a 3-year sequence of courses that are intended to prepare students for university study. The second basic option for compulsory education graduates involves enrolling in a professional training school. These schools offer a 2-year assistant technician degree that may be followed by 3 additional years of vocational study that culminate in a technical specialist diploma. Higher education is currently available for qualified candidates at 20 state universities, an open university, 3 polytechnics, 2 independent universities, and 8 technical schools (Europa Year Book, 1987).

Examined quantitatively, 30% of Spain's schools are privately owned and operated by the Catholic Church and the remaining 70% are founded and administered by the Government (Europa Year Book, 1987). It should be noted in this regard that public enrollment slightly exceeds private enrollment in urban areas and significantly exceeds private enrollment in rural sections of the country (Europa Year Book, 1987). Taken collectively, Table 7.1 presents a comprehensive summary of the national enrollment figures.

PSYCHOLOGICAL TRAINING

Professional training in psychology is provided at almost all of the state universi-

Table 7.1
Number of Institutions, Pupils, and Teachers Across Levels of Education

	Number		
Level	*Institutions*	*Pupils*	*Teachers*
Pre-school	37,001[a]	1,197,897	36,846
Elementary	178,845	5,629,874	214,391
Secondary	2,488[b]	1,124,329	67,931
Vocational	2,323[b]	619,090	40,190
University	244	414,473	24,761

[a]Classes
[b]Centers
Source: Europa Year Book *(1987)*

ties. Although program requirements differ to a certain extent, the basic core requirements (i.e., developmental, educational, and clinical psychology as well as statistics, psychometrics, and psychotherapy) are consistent across programs. Students who successfully complete 5 years of graduate study are awarded master's degrees and are eligible to provide services on a professional basis. Graduates who wish to earn a doctorate must complete 2 more years of graduate study and write a dissertation. At this time, Spanish universities do not offer specific majors (e.g., school psychology or clinical psychology). Students may, however, elect to secure a degree of expertise in a particular concentration by enrolling in courses that are indicative of a particular specialty during the later stages of their graduate training.

Unfortunately, not all Spanish universities offer practicum or internship experiences for students. On the other hand, universities are generally quite research oriented and this orientation can provide students with a degree of applied skills. Viewed along these lines, applied training opportunities generally occur when students assist faculty in investigation in educational of clinical settings. Interested students may also receive supervised training through the auspices of established practitioners.

SCHOOL PSYCHOLOGY SERVICES

In considering the role of school psychology in Spain, it is important to distinguish between the functions of educational and school psychologists. The former generally focus on questions relating to educational research, whereas the latter generally provide applied intervention services (Genovard, Geotzens, Montané, 1981).

With this in mind, the Ministry of Education established the School Vocational Counseling Service in 1977 (*Actividades,* 1982). The principal function of this body involves the coordination of provision or mental health services to meet the diagnostic, counseling, and instructional needs of elementary school students, teachers, and parents. Examined within these parameters, practitioners conduct psychoeducational assessments and provide counseling as well as applied interventions.

By Royal Order, the Ministry of Education also established Institutes of Educational and Professional Counseling in 1980. The primary function of this unit is to provide assessment and counseling services to secondary school students. In addition, the ministry also created the Parental Training Program in nine Spanish provinces in 1982. This program generally provides psychological counseling to elementary students. Exceptional children also receive services through the Ministry of Education's National Institute for Special Education. Viewed within this context, multiprofessional teams of school psychologists, physicians, counselors, teachers, and social workers combine their expertise in providing treatment services and preventive information (*Composicion,* 1982).

Regrettably, the Ministry of Education's extant school psychology services are limited to the public sector. Moreover their services frequently do not address the needs of students with exceptional needs on a case by case basis. In view of this, a number of Spanish cities (e.g., Madrid and Valencia) independently established publicly financed Council Health Centers and Council Health Promotion Centers. These groups strive to meet student needs through the provision of assessments, counseling, and intervention as well as teacher–parent consultations (Tierno Jimenez, 1984). In addition to the aforementioned provisions, school psychology services are likely provided by private practitioners within the parochial schools.

Problems

Examined comprehensively, it is apparent that a number of factors are exerting a negative influence on the scope and quality of psychological services. Initially, a dearth of standardized psychoeducational measures has made it difficult to formulate accurate diagnosis in instances involving suspected learning disabilities. Moreover, a heavy demand for psychological services coupled with a shortage of adequately trained practitioners has compelled the majority of psychologists to devote most of their time to the provision of direct services at the expense of preventive work. Moreover, the theoretical orientations of Spain's graduate psychology programs has not helped matters inasmuch as recent university graduates frequently require on the job training in their field. It is also unfortunate to note that the instructional methods within the schools are quite traditional and that innovative techniques such as mastery learning or self-paced instruction are not utilized. Finally, a number of established school administrators and teachers tend to view the practice of school psychology in a negative way and their attitudes have on occasion made it difficult to provide services in the schools.

FUTURE DEVELOPMENTS

It is expected that the Ministry of Education will decentralize its school psychology-related programs in the future. In doing so, more authority and resources will be allocated to mental health units at the regional level. This in effect will result in a more even distribution of services. In conjunction with this, it is expected that investigators and practitioners will develop and validate norm-referenced measures to facilitate the diagnostic efforts of school-based practitioners. Moreover, it is anticipated that university psychology programs will initiate applied training courses to meet the increased demand for psychological services in the schools. Taken collectively, these developments are expected to facilitate the scope and quality of psychological services throughout the country.

REFERENCES

Actividades de los servicios de orientación escolar (1982). (Activities from the school and vocational counseling services). *Papeles del Colegio, 4–5,* 83–87.

Composición y funciones de los equipos multiprofesionales del I.N.E.E. (1982). (Composition and functions of the I.N.E.E. multiprofessional teams). *Papeles del Colegio, 6,* 53.

Europa Year Book (1987). *Spain.* London: Europa Publications Limited.

Genovard, C., Geotzens, C., & Montané, J. (1981). *Psicología de la Educación.* Barcelona: Ed. Ceac.

Nuevas Orientaciones pedagógicas. (1977). (New pedagogical approaches). *Escuela Española Editores.* Madrid.

Tierno Jimenez, B. (1984). *El fracaso escolar.* Barcelona: Ed. Plaza and Janés.

Chapter Eight
School Psychology in Turkey[1]

Nevin Dölek
Derya Inceoglu
Foundation of Education and Culture, Istanbul, Turkey
Neylan Ozdemir
Robert College, Istanbul, Turkey

Psychological services in Turkish schools began about 30 years ago. An understanding of this history, current status, and future directions of these services requires some understanding of more general characteristics of the Turkish society and its school systems. Information in these areas is outlined briefly here.

THE PRESENT TURKISH EDUCATIONAL SYSTEM

The Turkish population was 52,845,000 in 1987. About 38% of this population consists of 0–14-year-olds and 28% consists of 15–29-year-olds (Ana Britannica, Comparative National Statistics, 1986). Thus, more than 50% of the Turkish population can be expected to be involved in some kind of an educational program.

At the primary and secondary education levels, 10,117,347 students were being educated in 58,717 schools by 381,616 teachers in 1986 (*Günes* Pocket Library 3, 1987). Table 8.1 shows the distribution of students, teachers, and schools at different educational levels in 1986.

As inferred from Table 8.1, among the 6,635,858 students in primary education about 53% continue their education at the secondary level. Among the 3,511,489 students at the secondary level, about 11% enter universities or colleges. The rates of schooling are about 82% for ages 7–12, 47% for ages 13–15, and 18% for ages 16–18.

[1]Little information exists about psychological services in schools in the rural areas of Turkey. Much of the information discussed in this chapter applies most directly to Turkey's two major cities, Istanbul and Ankara.

TABLE 8.1
The Numbers of Students, Teachers, and Schools at Different Educational Levels in 1986

Level of Education	*Number of Students*	*Number of Teachers*	*Student/ Teacher Ratio*	*Number of Schools*
Primary education	6,635,858	212,717	31:19	49,097
General secondary education (junior and senior high schools)	2,887,826	129,710	22:26	7,726
Vocational education (secondary level)	623,663	34,184	15:91	1,894
Total	10,147,347	376,611	26:94	58,717

In Turkey, primary education is compulsory and normally requires 5 years. Education normally requires 6 years at the secondary level, the first 3 years of which are referred to as junior high school education, whereas the next 3 years are called senior high school education.

Most schools in Turkey are public; less than 1% are private. All aspects of schooling, including educational programs, curriculum, selection of teachers and resources are supervised by the Ministry of National Education, Youth, and Sports.

As a major focus of this chapter is on the guidance and counseling services personnel in Istanbul, more specific citations on the numbers of students, teachers, and schools in Istanbul are useful (Table 8.2).

Istanbul is a cosmopolitan city with a continuous migration of people from various provinces within Turkey. With its population of nearly 6 million, the city also has the most schools, students, and teachers compared to other cities in Turkey. In Instanbul, 58% of the students attend primary schools, 35% attend at the secondary level, and 7% attend vocational schools. Although 12% of the students who reside in Turkey's largest 67 cities live in Istanbul, Istanbul has only 3% of its schools. Most schools in Istanbul are very crowded; classes of 50 to 70 students are common. Thus, the school facilities do not meet the needs of students.

HISTORY OF SCHOOL PSYCHOLOGICAL SERVICES IN TURKEY

Psychological services in the schools of Turkey started in the early 1950s. The necessity of such services within the educational system was formally recognized

TABLE 8.2
The Numbers of Students, Teachers, and Schools in Istanbul, 1986[a]

Levels of Education	*Student/ Teacher Ratios*	*Numbers of*		
		Students	*Teachers*	*Schools*
Primary education	37:98	707,220	18,618	987
General secondary education (junior and senior high school)	30:67	436,642	14,236	576
Vocational education (secondary level)	19:45	80,891	4,157	150
Total	33:09	1,224,753	37,011	1,713

[a]Adapted from The Educational Reports on the Province of Istanbul by The Republic of Turkey, The Ministry of National Education, Youth and Sports, 1986.

by a decree of the Ministry of Education in 1953, which resulted in establishing the first center for school psychological services in Ankara in 1955. Later in 1958, a by-law of the Ministry of National Education was issued, changing the names of "Psychological Services Center" to "Guidance and Research Center," in order to specifically emphasize the need for guidance and research (Öner, 1977).

The period between 1955 and 1960 marked the beginning of guidance and counseling services in Turkey and thus the establishment of psychological services in its schools. Within the framework of this movement, psychological services in schools were defined by the functions of those employed by the Ministry of Education at the Guidance and Research Centers.

The impact of the testing movement constituted a second force in the growth of psychological services. Group tests of mental and educational abilities were initiated in guidance centers and in schools; individual tests of mental and personality characteristics quickly became standard procedures in psychiatry or mental health clinics (Öner, 1977).

By 1986–1987, 56 Guidance and Research Centers had been established in 27 of the 67 major cities in Turkey; some cities had more than one center; 320 specialists worked in these centers (The Ministry of National Education, Youth, and Sports, 1987).

The establishment of guidance and counseling services in junior and senior high schools was mentioned in the Second Five Years-Developmental Plan that was to have been implemented between 1968 and 1972 (State Planning Institute, 1967). In the Third Five Years-Developmental Plan, covering 1973 to 1977, the importance of guidance in education was further emphasized (State Planning Institute, 1973). In the Basic Law of National Education, guidance and counseling services were deemed necessary in schools. Item 6 of this law states that, in educating individuals, their interests and abilities should be considered. Furthermore, these functions must utilize guidance and counseling services (Journal of Legislation 14 574, 1973). In accordance with the decisions taken at the meeting of the Ninth National Council of Education in 1974, a 2-hour weekly guidance program was included in the curriculum of junior and senior high schools (The Ministry of National Education, Youth, and Sports, 1975).

The academic year of 1970–1971 was a turning point for the introduction of systematic and programmed guidance activities in secondary schools. Guidance and counseling services were started in schools during this academic year. This number increased to 577 by the end of the 1986–1987 academic year. During the 1986–1987 academic year, 648 specialists worked in the guidance and counseling services in the secondary schools (The Ministry of National Education, Youth, and Sports, 1987). The ratio between students and guidance counselors was approximately 10,000:1.

THE TRAINING OF SCHOOL PSYCHOLOGICAL SERVICES PERSONNEL IN TURKEY

In the beginning, services in the Guidance and Research Centers were rendered by experienced and interested teachers who were briefly trained in guidance and educational testing. Some were sent abroad by the Ministry of Education for graduate training in measurement, psychometrics, guidance, and counseling. However, upon their return, very few stayed with the ministry and sought employment elsewhere in positions offering more prestige and better salaries (Öner, 1977). After 1965, as new universities were established, service professionals with degrees in psychology or education from Turkish universities began to fill positions in these centers.

Turkey has five universities that provide educational preparation in psychology at the undergraduate level: University of Ankara, Bosphorus University, Ege University, University of Istanbul, and Middle East Technical University. Neither the quantity or quality of education in these existing undergraduate programs can be considered adequate to meet present demands (Öner, 1982). Seven universities offer 4-year undergraduate programs specifically in guidance and counseling: University of Ankara Bosphorus University, Gazi University, Hacettepe University, Karadeniz University, Marmara University, and Middle East Technical University.

A 2-year master's program for guidance counseling is offered by the Hacettepe University's Department of Education and by the University of Ankara's School of Education. In Istanbul, similar master's degree programs are offered by two universities, the Bosphorus University's Faculty of Education and the University of Marmara's Department of Education. Several doctoral programs in psychology are offered at the universities of Istanbul, Ankara, Hacettepe, and Marmara.

THE ORGANIZATION OF SCHOOL PSYCHOLOGICAL SERVICES IN TURKEY

School psychological services in Turkey are mainly performed by the guidance and counseling offices in junior and senior high schools and in the Guidance and Research Centers of the Ministry of National Education, Youth, and Sports. The organization of guidance and counseling services in the cities is as shown in Fig. 8.1.

As seen in Fig. 8.1, the head of the school guidance and counseling services is responsible for the planning, programming, coordinating, executing, and inspecting the guidance and counseling services as a whole within the city.

Guidance and Research Centers in Turkey

According to the Decree of Guidance and Counseling Services, Guidance and Research Centers were to be established in all city centers in Turkey (Journal of Announcements, Dec. 16, 1985. No: 2201). These centers are designed to coordinate the activities of guidance and counseling services in junior and senior high schools. The functions of these centers are as follows (The Journal of Announcements, Dec. 16, 1985. No: 2201):

1. To open and supervise special classes in regular elementary schools for students who are not academically successful due to low levels of intelli-

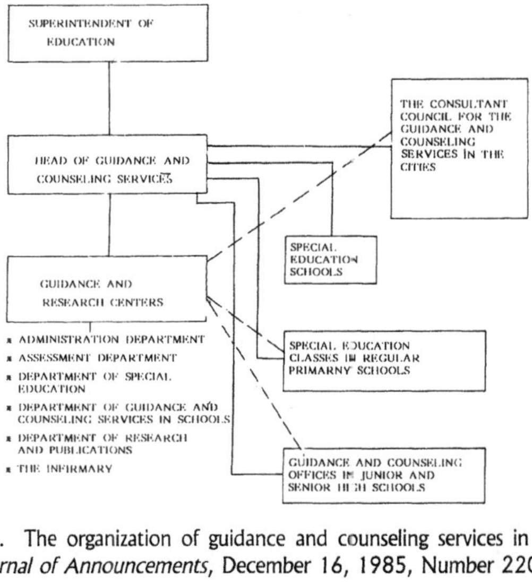

FIG. 8.1. The organization of guidance and counseling services in the cities (*The Journal of Announcements*, December 16, 1985, Number 2201)

gence; to select teachers; to provide in-service training for them, and to prepare the curricula for these classes.

2. To organize in-service training programs for school guidance counselors.
3. To conduct research for the purpose of developing better educational methods and strategies at schools; to supervise the yearly program for the school guidance and counseling services.
4. To render vocational guidance services at schools by administering general and special aptitude tests and interest inventories.
5. To study local problems in educational institutes and to submit reports about them to the authorities.

In carrying out their function of remediation of students with problems, the centers are expected to refer children with extreme problems to the medical centers located at nearby universities.

Guidance and Counseling Services in the Secondary Schools

The Ministry of Education issued a model for guidance services in the schools in 1985 (Fig. 8.2), (Journal of Announcements, Dec. 16, 1985. No: 2201). The model provided for a guidance-counseling office in every school; this model, however, has yet to be fully actualized.

In each school, the school principal is the primary person responsible for the execution of guidance and counseling services. The coordinating guidance counselor serves as a liaison between the school administration and the guidance-counseling office; this person also works as a counselor in the guidance-counseling office. All guidance counselors perform the following functions (Journal of Announcements, Dec. 16, 1985. No: 2201):

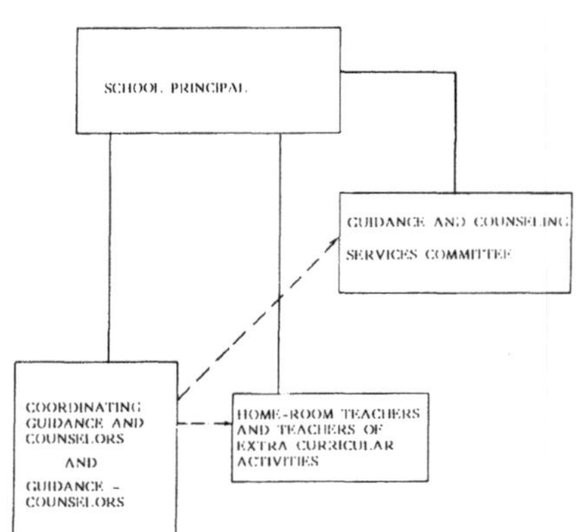

FIG. 8.2. The organization of school guidance services

1. to cooperate with the homeroom teachers in preparing the guidance-hour programs;
2. to administer various psychological tests, inventories, or questionnaires to students and to prepare students' personal files;
3. to assess and remediate students' psychological problems;
4. to provide vocational counseling;
5. to assess students with special abilities or superior intelligence and to submit a report on them to the school principal;
6. to assess the general needs of students;
7. to perform guidance services to the students (e.g., to orient them to the curriculum, to increase school achievement, and to remedy learning problems);
8. to assess the major problems affecting school achievement in order to prepare programs to increase the general achievement level while working in cooperation with teachers and school administrators;
9. to cooperate with parents in gathering information about the students' problems and their remediation;
10. to advise the disciplinary committee on discipline cases when consulted; and
11. to conduct follow-up studies of graduates and to analyze the information gathered from them.

Homeroom teachers, chosen among the full-time teachers at the beginning of each academic year, are responsible for carrying out the guidance-hour programs in their class. As just indicated, guidance-hour programs are developed jointly by the guidance counselors and homeroom teachers at the beginning of each academic year. Homeroom teachers are to consult the guidance counselors when they encounter problems during the application of these programs.

REVIEW OF STUDIES DONE ON THE SCHOOL PSYCHOLOGICAL SERVICES IN TURKEY

Few studies have examined the status of school psychological services, their roles, definitions, and concerns in Turkey. The results of studies examining these issues are reviewed here.

Kepçeoglu (1971, 1976, 1978) conducted a number of studies on the roles, functions, and concerns of school psychological services personnel in Ankara. In a study intending to follow-up and to evaluate the guidance and counseling services in 23 pilot secondary schools that had initiated guidance counseling offices in the 1970–1971 academic year, Kepçeoglu (1971) reported the major problems of the counseling offices to be a lack of training and a lack of consensus on the attitudes toward guidance and counseling services.

Kepçeoglu (1976) examined the professional problems of guidance counselors and found that the major problems were lack of financial resources, lack of cooperation with other school personnel, lack of necessary materials, inadequate professional training in the area of guidance counseling, and the rules and regulations governing the school system.

In order to better describe the school psychological services in Turkey, Öner (1977) administered a questionnaire to 55 psychologists, psychiatrists, counselors, and guidance teachers who were employed in the guidance research centers, private and public secondary schools, universities, and mental health clinics in order to elicit information on such topics as the definitions, goals, and functions of psychological services and the education and training of the psychological services personnel. The definition of psychological services generally included testing, guidance and counseling. The term *school psychologist* was either unknown or incorrectly conceived by people who defined it as being synonymous with guidance counselor. Other findings revealed that about 40% of the respondents had educational or pedagogical orientation and the rest a social or psychiatric orientation. Lack of job effectiveness, lack of job satisfaction, and feelings of inadequacy were indicated by a large number of respondents (Öner, 1977).

Gökhan (1979) surveyed 16 metropolitan Istanbul secondary schools that had guidance counseling offices in order to better understand their activities. The most crucial factor favoring the development of cooperation between the guidance counseling office and the other school personnel were positive attitudes among the school principals. Other factors contributing to the effectiveness of guidance-counseling services were the familiarity of the students and the teachers with the guidance-counseling services, their acceptance of the notion of guidance and counseling, the rapport between the students and the counselors, and the level of training of the counselors.

Common characteristics of the referrals to a guidance and research center in Istanbul were examined by Çakiroglu (1980). She found that 601 students were referred to this center over a 3-year period. The majority of referred students came from primary schools. She concluded that the functions of the center mainly were to assess students and place them in special classes in regular elementary schools or in special schools.

Current Information on School Psychological Services in Istanbul

Most of the research previously cited on school psychological services rendered in Turkey were conducted before 1980 and their samples were mainly limited to the school psychological services in Ankara. However, more than one fourth of guidance counselors in Turkey are employed in Istanbul. Thus, the need for more current information that examines the present status and problems of school psychological services in Istanbul is apparent. The following discussion reviews the results of a recent (1987) study that examines the present status, functions, and problems of the school psychological services in Istanbul. This information was obtained through a questionnaire developed by the authors and completed by 77 guidance and counselors employed in various public and private secondary schools and educational specialists employed in the Guidance and Research Centers of the Ministry of National Education, Youth, and Sports in Istanbul.

Demographic Characteristics. Almost 80% of the sample is female; their average age is 33. Their educational levels range from junior college through graduate level. About 80% have a BA degree, 21% have a MA degree, whereas 2% have attended only a 2-year junior college. Their undergraduate majors were in psychology (40%), pedagogy (27%), education (26%), and sociology (1%). Thirteen of the 16 people (81%) who attained a master's degree received their degree in educational psychology.

The majority of the professionals work in senior high schools (60%), whereas 23% work in junior high schools and 1% work in elementary schools. Others (14%) work in Guidance and Research Centers. Of the respondents who work in schools, 62% work in public schools and 23% work in private schools. The professionals average 7 years experience in providing psychological service. A plurality of respondents (42%) had 1 to 4 years of professional experience. Almost 70% work full time.

Services Rendered by the School Psychological Personnel. The following results were obtained when the respondents were asked to rank the services they performed.

The highest ranked service (55%) was information gathering about students. Other services include individual counseling (18% of the respondents) and organizing guidance periods and preparing the yearly guidance program (14%). Almost 45% reported that vocational counseling never constituted a part of their services, whereas 27% reported that they did not administer psychological tests.

The order of services from the most commonly performed to the least commonly performed by the professionals is as follows: information gathering about students and their problems, individual counseling, organizing guidance periods and preparing their programs, vocational counseling, group counseling, organizing extra curricular activities, testing, making family visits, consulting with parents, and consulting with teachers.

Common Problems Among School Psychological Services Personnel. The following constitute common problems among professionals providing school psychological services. Some problems relate to the professional training of the school psychological services personnel. Almost 58% of the respondents felt that their knowledge and education on guidance and psychological counseling was inadequate. Although 79% stated that they were able to conduct individual counseling, 53% did not think of themselves as competent to do group counseling. The majority of respondents (70%) thought that the number of higher education institutions offering professional preparation programs in guidance and counseling was too few. The quality of education offered by higher education institutes was thought to be low by 80%. The majority of respondents felt that books and other resources on guidance and psychological services in Turkish were inadequate both in quantity (66%) and in quality (67%).

Another set of problems relates to the recognition of guidance and counseling by the school administrators, teachers, students, and parents and the level of support received from these groups. Most respondents felt their roles and functions were not understood well by others; 64% are not well understood by school administrators, 70% by teachers, 69% by students, and 52% by parents. Most respondents report that they did not receive enough support from the teachers (66%), from the school administrators (45%), from parents (48%), or from students (44%).

Problems also exist relative to the amount of cooperation with colleagues and professionals in related areas. Although most (86%) report that the level of cooperation among their colleagues throughout Turkey was very low, 45% were satisfied with the level of cooperation they received from their colleagues with whom they work. However, 52% were not satisfied with their relationships with teachers. Only a few (1%) had a chance to associate with colleagues in other countries.

Problems also exist as to the amount of physical facilities available to the guidance and counseling personnel. About 70% had a room of their own to work in and were able to acquire the necessary secretarial help and office supplies. On the other hand, 80% did not have an adequate number of psychological tests and other information gathering instruments. The tests and information-gathering materials available to them were said to have inadequate reliability (65%) or validity (58%). The most commonly used assessment techniques were informal information gathering instruments such as sociometric instruments, problem checklists, autobiographies, and questionnaires.

The number of available school psychological services personnel working in the guidance-counseling offices at the schools and at the Guidance and Research Centers was found to be very low by most of the respondents (55%). About 32% work with 500 to 1,000 students and 23% work with between 1,000 to 2,000 students.

The majority (56%) chose this profession intentionally and still were satisfied with it. Only 9% of the respondents felt that their personalities were not suitable for this profession. Almost 50% complained of not having enough time for further professional development. Almost 40% felt they were unable to bring effective solutions to the problems of students and a majority (73%) stated they were unable to realize all of their yearly program goals. About 35% complained that their family and financial problems affected their professional efficiency.

CONCLUSION OF THE ISTANBUL STUDY

The majority of the school psychological services personnel in Istanbul are dissatisfied with their level of training. Neither the quantity nor the quality of the educational programs at the universities and available books and resources on the subject matter are adequate.

A majority of the school psychological services personnel think their role and functions are not understood well by the school administrators, the teachers, the students, or the parents, and that the levels of support received from these groups are inadequate.

The level of cooperation with the colleagues they work with is satisfactory whereas cooperation with other colleagues either on the national or international basis is very low.

The majority of the guidance counselors have their own rooms and adequate secretarial help and supplies but the ratio between school psychological personnel and students is too high to allow for efficient services. The quantity of available psychological tests with sound reliability and validity measures also is thought to be very low.

Yet, interest and motivation in the profession is high among the professionals. This is an important and positive factor favoring the continuing development of guidance and counseling in Turkey.

SUMMARY

A number of similarities exist between prior studies reported by Öner (1977) and Kepçeoglu (1976) almost a decade ago and our recent survey. Common problems stated by the school psychological services personnel include the following: The roles and functions of guidance counselors are not sufficiently clear, the support and cooperation they receive from school administrators and teachers are inadequate, school psychological professionals are not satisfied with their level of professional training, and few standardized psychological tests exist.

Although the number of universities that offer BA or MA degree programs in counseling has increased, there is still a need for more and better graduate programs on school psychology and counseling.

The quantity and quality of in-service training programs should be increased. Practitioners in the field should be encouraged to obtain graduate degrees.

The need is great for everyone involved in education (e.g., school administrators, teachers, students, and parents) to be informed about the advantage and the ways to cooperate with the school psychological services. Nevertheless, the best advertisement for school psychological services may be the results of the effective work performed by school psychological services personnel.

REFERENCES

Ana Britannica, (1986). *1986 comparative national statistics. Istanbul*: Encyclopedia Britannica, Inc.

Cakiroglu, F. (1980). *A survey of the students referred to Beyazit guidance and research center in the years 1976-77-78*, Unpublished master's thesis, Bogaziçi University, Istanbul.

Devlet Istatistik Enstitüsü (1987). *1986 Cep Yilligi* [1986 Pocket Yearbook]. In Günes Cep Kütüphanesi 3 (Günes Pocket Library 3), Istanbul.

Dokuzuncu Milli Egitim Surasi (Ninth National Council of Education). (1975). Istanbul: Milli Egitim Basimevi, Ankara.

Gökhan, M. (1979). *The current status of guidance services in Istanbul schools*. Unpublished master's thesis, Bogaziçi University, Istanbul.

Kepçeoglu, M. (1971). *Orta Dereceli Okullarda Rehberlik Anlayisi* [Counseling in Secondary Schools]. Ankara: Milli Egitim Bakanligi, Planlama ve Arastirma Dairesi.

Kepçeoglu, M. (1976). Okul Danismanlarinin Mesleki Problemleri [Professional Problems of Schools Counselors]. *Hacettepe Sosyal ve Beseri Bilimler Dergisi*, Mart-Ekim, 68–79.

Kepçeoglu, M. (1978). *Orta Dereceli Okullarda Rehberlik Uzmanlarinin Görevleri: Algilar ve Beklentiler* [Functions of Guidance Specialists in Secondary Schools: Perceptions and Exceptations]. Ankara: Hacettepe Universitesi Sosyal ve Idari Bilimler Fakültesi, Psikolojik ve Rehberlik Bölümü.

Öner, N. (1977). Psychology in the schools of Turkey. In C. D. Catterall (Ed.), *Psychology in schools in international perspective* (Vol. 2, pp. 90–102), Psychology Steering Committee.

N. (1982). *Setting up a school guidance counseling program: A naturalistic experiment in testing professional competence*. Paper presented at the 10th International Conference of The International Round Table For Advancement of Counseling, University of Lausanne, Switzerland.

T.C. Basbakanlik Devlet Planlama Teskilati (Republic of Turkey, Prime Ministry State Planning Institute). (1967). *Kalkinma Plani: Ikinci Bes Yil 1968–1972* [Developmental Plan: Second Five Year]. Ankara: Basbakanlik Devlet Matbaasi.

T.C. Basbakanlik Devlet Planlama Teskilati (Republic of Turkey, Prime Ministry State Planning Institute). (1973). Yeni Strateji ve Kalkinma Plani: Uçüncü Bes Yil [New Strategy and Developmental Plan: Third Five Year]. Ankara: Basbakanlik Devlet Matbaasi.

T.C. Milli Egitim Bakanligi (Republic of Turkey, Ministry of National Education). (1984). *Tanitma-I* (Introduction-I), 14-12-1983/01-09-1984 tarihleri arasinda Milli Egitim Gençlik ve Spor Bakanligi Faaliyetleri [Activities of Ministry of National Education, Youth, and Sports between dates 14-12-1983 and 01-09-1984]. Istanbul: Milli Egitim Basimevi.

T.C. Milli Egitim Bakanligi. (1985). Tebligler Dergisi [Republic of Turkey, Ministry of National Education, Journal of Announcements], Ankara: 16-12-1985. Cilt (Vol.): 48, Sayi (No): 2201.

T.C. Milli Egitim Bakanligi, (1986). Istanbul ili Egitim Inceleme Raporu (Republic of Turkey, Ministry of National Education, the Educational Reports on the Province of Istanbul).

Chapter Nine
School Psychology in the Republic of Cyprus

Philip A. Saigh
Graduate Center
City University of New York

Yola Ketchedjian
Nicosia, Cyprus

Cyprus, a 3,572 square mile island in the northeastern Mediterranean, lies approximately 70 miles off the Turkish coast (World Almanac, 1986). Before gaining independence from Great Britain, Cyprus was successively ruled by Phoenicians, Egyptians, Romans, Crusaders, and Turks (Luke, 1965; Munro & Khuri, 1984). Due to the proximity to Greece and Turkey, the population reflects the two ethnic groups. In 1983, it was estimated that there were 532,600 Greek Cypriots and 124,000 Turkish Cypriots on the island (Fisher, 1986).

In an effort to reach a formal union with Greece, the Cypriot National Guard staged a coup on July 15, 1974. Five days later, Turkish troops invaded the island (World Almanac, 1986). Since that time, the population has been divided along ethnic lines. On November 15, 1985, the Turkish Cypriots unilaterally established the Turkish Republic of Northern Cyprus (Fisher, 1986). As different systems of government serve the Greek and Turkish communities, this chapter is limited to the practice of school psychology in the Greek community's Republic of Cyprus.

SYSTEM OF EDUCATION

According to the Ministry of Education (1984), a four-stage system of education is in effect. Children may enter the system at the pre-primary stage (age range: 2.5–5.5 years) and proceed to the primary stage (age range: 5.6–11.5 years). Primary school graduates are eligible to enroll in secondary stage schools (age range: 11.6–16.5 years). Secondary students may pursue a general education in public *gymnasia* schools, vocational education in public technical schools or a Pedagogical Academy, vocational skills at the Higher Technical Institute, general nursing at the School of Nursing and Midwifery, psychiatric nursing at the School of Psychiatric Nursing, or hotel and restaurant management at the Hotel and Catering Institute of Labour (Ministry of Education, 1984). Although legislation to establish a national university was approved, the university has not been established and professionally oriented students are compelled to study abroad. Table 9.1 presents the Ministry of Education's general statistics for 1983. Examined along these lines it is apparent that the total ratios between students and teachers in the pre-primary, primary, secondary, third level, and special education schools are 26.23, 21.51, 15.25, 8.89, and 4.81, respectively.

Viewed from an administrative perspective, the Ministry of Education regulates the pre-primary, primary, and secondary schools (Ministry of Education, 1984). Free tuition is provided for public school students (Ministry of Education, 1984). Primary teachers are required to complete a teacher-training program at the Pedagogical Academy and secondary teachers must hold a university degree. Technical school teachers must be third-level technical school graduates who have completed a vocational teacher training program.

TABLE 9.1
Number of Schools, Pupils, and Teachers by Level of Education

Level of Education	*Number of Schools*	*Pupils*	*Teachers*
Pre-primary			
Public	188	7,086	289
Private	186	8,521	306
Total	374	15,607	595
Primary			
Public	380	45,331	2,091
Private	16	2,050	111
Total	396	47,381	2,202
Secondary			
Public	80	43,101	2,713
Private	25	5,651	482
Total	105	48,752	3,195
Third level			
Public	6	1,312	172
Private	9	1,268	118
Total	15	2,580	290
Special education			
Public	13	650	135
Private	0	0	0
Total	13	650	135

PSYCHOLOGICAL SERVICES

The Ministry of Education retains six psychologists on its staff (Thoma, personal communication, 1986). Five of these individuals hold master's degrees in clinical psychology and the sixth has a master's degree in educational psychology (Thoma, personal communication, 1986). Three master's level psychologists also provide services on a private basis in special education centers (Thoma, personal communication, 1986). Moreover, teacher-counselors provide general counseling services in the secondary schools (Thoma, personal communication, 1986).

Primary school referrals are initiated by regular teachers and forewarded to special education inspectors who may request services from the Ministry of Education's school psychologists. In a similar vein, secondary teachers refer students with academic and or behavior problems to teacher counselors who may request psychological services from the Ministry of Education. Once a referral is received, government psychologists visit the schools in order to discuss the designated problem with the referrants. Western mental ability tests are not in favor due to concerns about endemic validity (Thoma, personal communication, 1986). In exceptional cases (e.g., EMR diagnosis), the Wechsler and Binet scales have been used with reservation (Thoma, personal communication, 1986). In lieu of standardized testing, behavioral observations and nonstructured interviews are favored (Thoma, personal communication, 1986). Psychological services within special education facilities focus on the development of self-care skills and on integrating the more able students into the mainstream of society (Compos, personal communication, 1985). At the moment, there are no laws to regulate the practice of psychology within the private sector (Thoma, personal communication, 1986). On the other hand, the Ministry of Education closely reviews the qualifications of its psychologists and their professional conduct is monitored (Thoma, personal communication, 1986).

Problems

Given the number of qualified psychologists, it is apparent that these individuals cannot accommodate the treatment needs of the school-age population. To compound the situation, one of the six psychologists at Ministry of Education is an inspector (i.e., administrator) and three others work on yearly contracts that are subject to termination (Thoma, personal communication, 1986). In addition to heavy workloads, school psychologists must formulate difficult diagnostic and placement decisions in the absence of viable measures (Thoma, personal communication, 1986). Finally, many parents harbor misconceptions about psychology and these misconceptions have on occasion prevented the provision of services (Compos, personal communication, 1985).

Contributions

Despite the problems that confront school psychologists, a number of positive developments have occurred. School psychologists have been able to integrate physically disabled children into mainstream classes. Efforts have also been directed toward improving the general public's attitude toward the handicapped through activities at an annual special educational week (Compos, personal communication, 1985). The status of the profession was significantly advanced through the formation of a 60 member Psychological Association in 1980. This organization is working toward the promotion of professional psychology and a committee is looking into legal issues relating to practice (Thoma, personal communication, 1986). It is also interesting to observe that preliminary efforts have been made to redress the shortage of tests. In 1987, Saigh and Ellipos translated and validated the Conners Teacher Rating Scale (Conners, 1969). The Greek translation and normative tables are currently available for the 9 to 12 age range.

FUTURE DEVELOPMENTS

The future of Greek Cypriot school psychology is inextricably linked to the economic and political status of the island. In 1974, Turkish Cypriots annexed 38% of the island. Among other things, Greek Cypriots lost 70% of the island's productive resources, 60% of the tourist installations and the principal sea port (Fisher, 1986). Despite these losses, a sound fiscal policy coupled with massive drives to rebuild tourism and industry saw the 1983 Greek Cypriot gross national product exceed the entire island's 1973 gross national product by 12% (Fisher, 1986). It is also encouraging to note that Greek and Turkish Cypriot representatives have repeatedly met under United Nations auspices in an effort to reach an equitable accord (Bruce, 1985). Although these meetings have not led to a *reproachment*, hostilities between the two communities have not been evident since 1974.

Given the status of the economy and barring further military action, it is apparent that psychological services in the schools could be significantly upgraded. To do so would entail the realization of four basic recommendations. Initially, the Ministry of Education should enhance the professional skills of its teacher counselors through the provision of inservice workshops. More significantly, the Ministry of Education should retain more school psychologists and sponsor a research program to developed and/or cross validate psychodiagnostic tests. Finally, legal guidelines should be established to regulate the practice of psychology and to guard against the possibility of inexpedience in the future.

REFERENCES

Bruce, L. H. (1985). Cyprus: A last chance. *Foreign Policy, 58,* 113–115.

Conners, C. K. (1969). A teacher rating scale for use in drug studies with children. *American Journal of Psychiatry, 126,* 884–888.

Fisher, W. B. (1986). Cyprus. In *The Middle East and North Africa* (33 ed.). Rochester, United Kingdom: Europa Publications.

Luke, H. C. J. (1965). *Cyprus: A portrait and an apprepration.* London: Harrap.
Munro, J., & Khuri, Z. (1984). *Cyprus: Between Venus and Mars.* New York: Caravan Books.
Ministry of Education (1984). *Education in Cyprus 1981–83.* (Report for the 39th International Conference on Education) Geneva: Bureau of Education, UNESCO.
Saigh, P. A., & Ellipos, P. (1987). *Hyperactivity in the Republic of Cyprus.* Manuscript submitted for publication.
World Almanac (1986). *The world almanac and book of facts: 1987.* New York: Scripps Howard.

Chapter Ten
School Psychology in Israel

Amiram Raviv
Tel Aviv University

The beginnings of the Israeli educational system can be traced back to several decades preceding the establishment of the State of Israel in 1948. The foundations were laid by the Jewish settlement of Palestine at that time under the British Mandate government. The unique quality of the system derived from the fact that

> the Israeli school, from its very beginning was not merely an institution for the transmission of knowledge and the acquisition of skills. It was at the vanguard of creating a new society and culture . . . was looked upon as a major vehicle for materializing both general and particularistic aspirations for the future. (Benyamini & Klein, 1970, p. 211)

The pupil population in the pre-state period consisted predominantly of children from families of European origin. Following the establishment of the State of Israel in 1948, the school population changed radically in both its content and scope, as Israel absorbed waves of survivors of the Nazi camps and refugees from Moslem countries. The Israeli educational system had to accommodate increasing percentages of children from families of Middle Eastern and North African origin, many of whom presented what is currently considered the classical picture of cultural deprivation. In spite of limited resources, the educational system was assigned the task of assimilating this new population into the dominant culture and its values.

In 1949, the Israeli Parliament passed the Law of Compulsory Education, which mandated schooling for all children between the ages of 5 and 14, including 1 year of kindergarten and 8 years of elementary education. Four years later, the Law of State Education established the exclusive right of the state to provide official education including curricula, training, employment and assignment of teachers, supervision and inspection as well as financial and administrative control of the country's schools. In 1968, the age of mandatory education was raised to 16, and in 1978 free secondary education for all was affirmed by the parliament (Smilanski, Kashti, & Arieli, 1982).

The total population of Israel is about 4 million of whom 3,300,000 are Jewish. The Ministry of Education supplies separate services to the Arab and the Jewish populations except for several mixed schools in mixed population areas. Overall, there are 1,356,075 pupils in Israel, about 200,000 in the Arab education sector and about 1,150,000 in the Hebrew education section. The educational system includes kindergartens, primary schools (Grades 1–6 or 1–8), intermediate schools, and general and vocational secondary schools. There are 2,499 schools, of which 2,101 are in the Hebrew education sector. Table 10.1 presents the percentage distribution of pupils in the Hebrew education sector in the 1980/1981 school year. The primary schools section includes 1,316 regular and 208 special schools. The number of special schools has declined from 352 in 1960 owing to the trend of mainstreaming handicapped children into the regular primary school system. Today, about 60% of handicapped children are integrated into regular schools (Margalit, 1980). Special education frameworks include assistance to mildly handicapped children who otherwise continue to attend their home classes, special classes within the regular schools, and specialized separate schools. The average number of pupils per primary school is 358 in regular schools and 56 in schools for handicapped children. The average number of pupils per class is 27 in regular schools and 9 in special schools. The Hebrew schools are divided into state (75%), state religious (20%), and independent (5%). The latter belong to the ultraorthodox Agudat Israel trend and are not under the supervision of the Ministry of Education. There are no private schools in Israel. The school week is 6 days long and there are 15 weeks of holidays per year. Lessons are given in one continuous session, starting at 8 a.m. and lasting, depending on age and type of school, between 4 and 7 hours.

The national expenditure on education in 1980 was 8.8% of the GNP including the universities and 7.1% excluding the universities. In 1981 the national ex-

TABLE 10.1
Percentage Distribution of Pupils in Hebrew Education Sector in Kindergartens and Schools, by Type of School and Origin, 1980–1981

	Kindergartens	*Primary schools*	*Secondary schools*	*Special schools*
Born in Israel	37.9	23.6	19.8	9.2
Asian-African origin	39.7	52.1	52.0	74.5
European origin	22.4	24.3	28.2	16.3

penditure was 8.4% of the GNP. The GNP in that year was $20,748 million or $5,254 per person.[1]

In 1981–1982 the educational system employed 59,500 teachers in the Hebrew education sector and 8,500 in the Arab education sector. Some background characteristics of the teachers in the Hebrew schools are presented in Table 10.2. As in the case of European countries (Kleinberger, 1969), there are two groups of teachers in Israel: Most high school teachers hold an academic degree, whereas most primary school teachers are graduates of teacher training colleges, which until recently did not grant an academic degree. In recent years, there has been a trend to recognize some of these colleges as institutions of higher education.

SCOPE OF PSYCHOLOGICAL SERVICES

In the first years following the establishment of the State of Israel, the development of the school psychological services was slow and limited. The urgent financial and defense problems, the immense task of "in-gathering of the exiles," and the shortage of professional personnel limited the amount of attention assigned to the issue of mental health in the schools. In the 1960s few school psychological services were in operation in the large cities. These services concentrated primarily on diagnosing retarded children in need of special education and on providing educational and employment guidance to elementary school graduates. The majority of the school psychologists received their education in European and U.S. universities and some did not hold degrees in psychology. The first psychology department was established by the Hebrew University in Jerusalem in 1957, followed by Bar-Ilan University in 1958. Over 5 years elapsed until the graduates of these departments could be integrated into the educational system.

TABLE 10.2
Teachers in Hebrew Education Sector, by Level of Education and Various Characteristics, 1980–1981

	Total	*% of women*	*Median years of teaching*	*Median age*	*Academic degree (%) BA*	*MA & PhD*
Primary schools	37,700	85.4	10.0	33.3	10.6	3.2
Intermediate schools	9,800	69.0	9.8	34.9	40.5	10.0
Secondary schools	17,000	59.5	10.8	36.6	45.6	17.2

[1]Most of the statistical information about the educational system is based on the 1981–1982 report of the Israeli Central Bureau of Statistics, 1982. Statistical information about the number of schools and students and school and class size is based on the Israeli Central Bureau of Statistics, 1985.

An additional pool of locally trained manpower became available with the foundation of two additional psychology departments in Tel Aviv and Haifa Universities in 1966.

A major breakthrough came about in 1962 when the Ministry of Education and the Ministry of Labor jointly established the Institute for Guidance and Counseling. The range of activities undertaken by the institute included the establishment of school psychological services throughout the country, the preparation of tests and evaluation instruments suitable for local needs, the provision of in-service training programs and supervision to psychologists, and the sponsorship and promotion of university training programs. The institute fostered awareness in local municipalities of the contribution of school psychological services and encouraged the establishment of these services in numerous communities. In addition, the institute provided scholarships for promising candidates who made a commitment to work outside the large cities.

The results of these activities were soon evident: In 1970, 162 school psychologists were active in 32 centers across the country. Following 5 years of intensive activity, a separate Division of Psychology and Counseling Services (PCS) was established in the Ministry of Education, and the responsibility for the school psychology and counseling services was taken over by this division. Since 1970, the services have undergone a rapid expansion (Table 10.3). Today, about 840 school psychologists in about 500 positions function in 139 school psychological centers across the country. The practitioners are usually based in a clinic or center and make frequent visits to schools. Thus, the services are provided primarily within the schools, a practice that has fostered the school psychologists' acquaintance with an understanding of the school's operation and problems.

In marked contrast to their original concentration on diagnosis and vocational guidance, school psychologists presently carry out a wide variety of functions, by a variety of theoretical orientations. The variation in practice among the psychological services throughout the country is a function of numerous factors, such as the size of the locality, the number of psychologists in a given center, the ratio of children to child psychologists, the age group of children receiving the services, and the psychologists' personal qualities such as their experience, tenure, type of professional training, personal inclinations, the emphasis on the theoretical aspects of the practice, and so on.

A general picture of the time allocated by school psychologists among the various professional duties emerges from a recently conducted survey that involved

TABLE 10.3
Development of School Psychological Services in Israel, 1970–1986

	1970	*1973*	*1975*	*1978*	*1980*	*1983*	*1986*
No. of school psychological centers	32	65	81	98	113	125	139
No. of psychologists	160	290	350	567	705	835	840

most of the school psychological centers in the country (Raviv, Wiesner, & Bar-Tal, 1981). The psychologists were asked to report on the proportion of time they devoted to several work domains according to categories listed in the questionnaire. The following data, which of course are average results that do not reflect individual differences, were obtained: individual diagnosis, 16%; mental health consultation with teachers, 16%; parent counseling, 12%; family therapy, 3%; children psychotherapy, 6%; short-term counseling to pupils, 7%; classroom observation and group diagnosis, 6%; preparation of follow-up reports and other relevant documentation materials, 14%; staff meetings, 8%; meetings with other professionals, 4%; in-service training, 8%. (The survey included general categories without specifying the more detailed interventions. Thus, the category of teacher consultation included group work with teachers, organization development with school principals and their staff, consultation with individual teachers regarding discipline problems and interventions, curriculum development, and crisis intervention consultation.) In most centers, school psychologists perform all of the duties just listed and work with several age groups, although some centers specialize in distinct treatment techniques, such as "therapeutic teaching," usually depending on the age group of the children served or the types of problems encountered.

In recent years, there has been a growing trend to assist children through working with their teachers and parents. This trend is reflected in a relative decrease in individual diagnosis and an increase in primary and secondary prevention services. However, a significant proportion of time is still devoted to the classical task of individual diagnosis. This includes the diagnosis of pupils suspected of retardation or learning and behavior problems, as well as readiness testing of children referred by kindergarten teachers. Individual diagnosis is performed by means of a conventional diagnostic battery that includes in most cases the Wechsler Intelligence Scale for Children–Revised (WISC–R) or the Wechsler Preschool and Primary Scale of Intelligence (WIPPSI). The tests have been translated and standarized to meet local needs. An Arab version of WISC–R is also available for use in the Arab schools. Bender and Frostig tests as well as a variety of other visual–motor tests are commonly used. In addition, projection tests such as TAT, CAT, and Rorschach are employed, although to a lesser extent. It should be noted that the expansion of special education services, and the introduction of special education teachers and teacher-counselors to regular schools, have made possible the collection of valuable diagnostic material from these professionals without resort to the school psychologist's diagnosis, at least for pupils with relatively mild problems. However, the actual placement of children into special education programs cannot be carried out without a recommendation by a licensed school psychologist.

Since the 1973 war, there has been a growing recognition of the need to develop crisis intervention techniques, and increased attention has been directed toward problems encountered by the children and their families during times of crisis (Raviv, Klingman, & Horowitz, 1980). Special teaching aids have been developed and teachers have been trained to implement these aids. Each school holds an emergency kit (Ayalon, 1978) that provides a variety of techniques and instruments to be used by teachers at times of crisis. The general goal is to enhance the capacity of the school to deal with problems encountered in emergency situations, such as during preparation for war or prolonged stays in shelters, and to foster the development of effective coping skills by the children. Crisis intervention methods have been most extensively applied in border settlements, where the probability of emergency/war crisis is particularly high. Highly notable is the contribution of school psychologists at the northern border of Israel who, in a continuous effort to foster teachers' support skills (Lahad, 1981), designed a wide variety of simulation games, therapeutic teaching methods, creative writing, and so on. In numerous settlements, psychological service personnel fulfilled an important integrative role within the community, cooperating with the local authorities and other services in providing support to populations in crisis.

In general, school psychologists have become increasingly concerned with problems of personal and family crisis. Considerable effort is invested in increasing teachers' awareness of sensitivity to children's needs in times of crisis and in transforming the school into a support system for pupils and their families. Increasing proportions of parents turn to the school for counseling on issues related to death or illness in the family, divorce, and various transitional period crises.

The majority of school psychologists in Israel work with primary and intermediate schools and kindergartens. Psychological services in mother and child clinics as well as in high schools are recent developments and do not fulfill the existing needs. This distribution results from the fact that until 1978 psychological services were provided only for children aged 5–14, who were subject to compulsory education. The expansion of the services at present faces problems because of financial difficulties in all sectors of public services.

The heavy workload, the extensive demand for intervention activities, and probably the general attitude of the field practitioners have created a constellation in which very little time is devoted to systematic evaluation and follow-up research. Only a few large centers employ psychologists whose explicit function is to conduct research. Some additional research is performed by a small research unit with the PCS Division in the Ministry of Education. The bulk of research is carried out at the universities in collaboration with some school psychological centers, either as ongoing evaluation research or as research projects toward MA or PhD degrees. Doubtlessly, there is a shortage of basic research assessing the long-term efficiency and productivity of the various intervention and guidance approaches.

Administration

School psychological services are supplied by the local municipalities, which are the official employers of school psychologists. The services are the direct administrative responsibility of the director of the municipal department of education, who is responsibile for providing all the services (e.g., medical, social work) and facilities (e.g., buildings) to schools. The professional supervision is provided by the Ministry of Education's Psychological and Counseling Services Division, which includes the director general, his assistant, and the chief psychologist, who serves as an advisor to the director and other senior personnel in the Ministry of Education. In addition, the division includes district psychologists, who supervise psychological services in the six districts into which the Israeli educational system is divided, and psychologists in charge of special topics such as follow-up research, crisis intervention, special functions, and the editing of the *Israeli Journal of Psychology and Counseling in Education*, which is published twice a year by the division. The division's director general, the chief psychologist, and the district psychologists constitute the highest professional forum that defines the guidelines and the policy for the functioning of the psychological services within the educational system.

The functions of the division include professional supervision of the psychological services; personal and group guidance to school psychologists; organization of in-service training and further education for school psychologists; reception of reports on field activities and special requests for action within the ministry; confirmation of psychologists' employment by the local municipalities; follow-up research; preparation of evaluation instruments including translation, standardization for local needs, updating, and so on; and distribution of information on various topics of interest, including publication of the professional journal. Since 1984, the journal has been replaced by an annual report that summarizes various professional topics of interest for the field practitioners. In addition, the division issues a bimonthly report that circulates information on the division's policy and the decisions of the Ministry of Education, as well as field practitioners' reports on their activities, new projects, and other relevant topics.

The division also recommends the desired proportion of psychologists within various educational settings. For example, for regular education, one psychologist is recommended per 2,000 children, but in special education the recommended proportion is 1 per 800 children. Because in the past, most municipalities funded their psychological services locally, these recommendations were not compulsory. Consequently, in many settlements there is a discrepancy between the recommended and the actual number of school psychologists. This shortage is partially remedied by the 1,400 counseling teachers who serve in most schools. Like the school psychologists, these teachers are under the professional supervision of the PCS. However, in contrast to psychologists, they receive their salaries from the Ministry of Education and also perform part-time teaching duties.

In addition to school psychological services, the local municipality provides other mental health services, which are staffed by school medical personnel, probation officers (who deal with truancy and dropout problems), and social workers, whose main concern is to assist children with problems originating at home.

In recent years, social workers have increased their direct involvement with the educational system and the individual child rather than being solely concerned with families.

Although all of the aforementioned agencies provide services within the school, mental health services are available also outside the school. These services are jointly funded by the Ministry of Health and the Workers' Sick Fund and are provided by clinics in mental health centers and in general or psychiatric hospitals. They receive pupils through professional referrals (school psychologists, family physicians, social agencies) as well as by self-referral.

The consumption of private psychotherapeutic services, which was relatively rare up until 10 years ago, has grown considerably because of the general rise in the standard of living, the growing "psychological mindedness" of the public, and the increase in the number of private practitioners. However, the scope of the services provided by private practitioners is still limited and by no means replaces the public services. In fact, very few psychologists engage exclusively in private practice.

The subject of psychological practice was formalized and subjected to law only in 1977, when the parliament passed "The Psychologists' Law," which defines psychologists' functions and certification standards. The minimum requirement is an MA degree granted by a university psychology department. Four areas of specialization were defined: clinical psychology, school psychology, social industrial psychology, and rehabilitation psychology (Raviv, 1984). The school psychologist is required to complete specialization in an authorized educational psychological center for at least 2 years, in a full-time position, in the following areas: individual diagnosis of children and youth in a wide range of ages and problems; group diagnosis; child and family therapy; and psychological intervention in educational settings including kindergarten, primary, intermediate and high schools, and special education services. The specialization must be carried out under the supervision of an authorized supervisor, who is an experienced senior psychologist.

Over 75% of school psychologists are women and over 75% are aged 35 years or younger. Furthermore, over 50% hold a half-time position in the school psychological services. The implications of the demographic structure, the employment patterns, and the training background on the status of the profession have been discussed in detail elsewhere (Raviv & Wiesner, 1985).

Training Facilities

There are four universities in Israel that offer training in school psychology. Three of them—the Hebrew University, Bar-Ilan University, and Haifa University—have an educational psychology program within the framework of MA degree studies. Tel Aviv University offers a clinical child psychology program in which students receive training with clinical, community, and school orientations. A significant proportion of the graduates from this program enter the school psychological services.

The professional orientation of the Hebrew University training program is based on an organizational developmental approach with an emphasis on the school psychologist's role as a consultant and an agent of change. Graduates are provided with a wide variety of diagnostic tools and short-term treatment techniques. A highly similar approach characterizes the relatively new school psychology program of Haifa University. At the Bar-Ilan University, the emphasis is on diagnostic aspects and psychologists' work with the individual child and the class. The Tel Aviv University program is characterized by a more clinical orientation focused on providing diagnosis, treatment, and consultation while viewing the child in the constellation of his or her family, class, and community setting.

The theoretical orientation underlying the four programs is eclectic, although there is an emphasis on psychodynamic approaches. In recent years, behavioral and cognitive approaches have gained prominence. In general, the dominant theoretical approach is determined by the faculty members' inclinations. The general curriculum is similar across the four departments, although differences in emphasis may exist that reflect the degree of relevance assigned to various topics by the departments. The curriculum includes 40 semester credits, a thesis, and a final examination. A variety of courses are offered, covering the following subjects: diagnosis, psychopathological interview, school psychology, mental health consultation, various techniques of group treatment with children, teachers and parents, family therapy, treatment techniques based on a variety of theoretical approaches (psychodynamic, behaviorist, etc.), organizational development techniques, test construction, and school sociology. These specialized courses are supplemented by training in research methods and advanced statistics courses. The minimal duration of studies toward the MA degree is 2 years following a 3-year BA program. Each year, students participate in a 1-day-per-week practicum. At Tel Aviv University, for example, the first-year practicum is carried out in an educational setting in collaboration with school psychological services. The second-year practicum is conducted in a child clinic. In the Hebrew, Haifa, and Bar-Ilan Universities most practicums are carried out within various school and educational settings. Owing to the extensive curriculum demands, the average student requires an additional year or two to complete his or her MA studies, including the submission of a research thesis. (The average Israeli student is 2–3 years older than his or her counterparts in the Western countries because of the 2–3 years compulsory military service.) At the same time, however, the shortage of professional personnel has encouraged the employment of a large proportion of the MA students in school psychology centers prior to the official completion of their studies. The recent financial cuts and the consequent changes in employment policy will probably curtail this practice severely. Beginning in

1984, the Ministry of Education is sponsoring 20 scholarships for outstanding psychology students in order to make possible their specialization in school psychology in spite of the current policy to freeze the opening of new positions.

Because there is no formal internship system for school psychologists in Israel, specialization is acquired along with field practice, which is carried out for at least 2 years under individual and group supervision within the employing agency.

The Israeli universities do not offer specialized PhD programs (i.e., in school psychology, or clinical psychology, etc.). The doctoral studies are based on the European tradition that emphasizes a research dissertation with minimal course requirements. Some field practitioners complete their doctoral dissertation along with their work in the educational field.

Special Problems

The school psychology field is faced with several problems. The most conspicuous problem stems from the freezing of positions versus the relative population growth. Although the existing proportion of psychologists per pupil is satisfactory, the complex problems of an extremely heterogeneous population and the prolonged periods of tension sustained by the Israeli public create a growing demand for psychological services. In fact, a situation seemingly has been created whereby the more psychologists are active and available, the greater the number of individuals seeking their help. On the other hand, overloaded psychologists who infrequently visit the schools soon are perceived as inefficient and even unnecessary. In addition, and quite paradoxically, as more effort is invested by psychologists in primary prevention, less tangible evidence is available as to their "accomplishments." This in turn reduces public pressure and concern in face of the shortage of professional personnel.

Another problem area is that of recruitment, particularly in regard to sources of future practitioners. Although psychology is a highly popular field of study and a prestigious profession, most students seek to specialize in clinical psychology. Consequently, a danger exists that a somewhat less-talented group will eventually enter school psychological services. There is a need to enhance the prestige of the profession, primarily by extending professional responsibility, increasing existing job options, and devoting more resources to research (Raviv & Wiesner, 1985).

A further problem concerns the expectations held by schools as the consumers of psychological services. The school psychologist's tasks are still expected primarily to consist of diagnosis and screening of children for special education services. There is less openness to consultation services, organizational development, and work with the many levels of the school system, that is, pupils, teachers, and management (Benyamini, 1982). In general, primary prevention is not viewed as an issue of top priority and the demand for such services within the regular school system is relatively limited.

In recent years, the traditional task of allocating pupils to various special education services has generated some complications. The school psychologist, deeply concerned with the stigma associated with special education, seeks to retain the problem child within the natural setting of the regular classroom. However, regular schools lack the funds for assisting the handicapped population and exert pressure on the school psychologist to provide such funds from the special education sector. Although in the past, these funds were easily attainable, the recent cuts in the special education budgets have changed this generous allocation policy. The special education authorities, although supporting in principle the mainstreaming approach, seek to restrict their budgets to severely handicapped children and require that only those children who cannot be integrated within the regular school system be referred to special education. Thus, the school psychologist is often faced with a professional dilemma in determining whether to recommend the problem child for special education. On the one hand, in contrast to the regular schools, special education has the tools and resources necessary for assisting such a child. On the other hand, such a recommendation carries the attachment of stigma to the child and leads to confrontations with the special education people. The dilemma is further aggravated by the psychologist's recognition that, in the absence of proper special education services within the regular school, the problem child is likely eventually to be placed in a segregated special education unit.

In the context of these and related problems it has been argued that ancillary services in general and psychological services in particular remove the responsibility from the teachers and produce low esteem and an unwillingness on their part to cope with problems. It has also been argued that the funds given to the various ancillary services would be more effectively used by decreasing the workload in regular classes. Evaluation of the various considerations in favor and against this stand are beyond the scope of this manuscript. However, it is worthwhile to note the existing difficulties in recruitment to the teaching profession in general, and the problems associated with training teachers to accept mental health consultation services in particular.

In spite of these problems, school psychologists in Israel enjoy high prestige and influence in numerous communities. In this regard, one last problem should be mentioned. In spite of their high status and autonomy of action, school psychologists have relatively little influence in the policy-making forums of the Ministry of Education. The Israeli education system has not yet succeeded in fully utilizing the school psychologists' training and skills for introducing meaningful changes in teaching methods, training of teachers, school atmosphere, school-community relationships, and so on. The introduction of these changes and others is an important aspect of the future goals that school psychologists are striving to achieve. A step in this direction was made towards the end of the 1983 school year, when the director general of the Ministry of Education decided to meet on a monthly basis with national representatives of school psychologists. These meetings will be devoted to discussions and exchange of views on issues of interest to the general manager and the psychologists. It is hoped that this arrangement will enable psychologists to provide professional feedback and consultation to the most senior person within the educational system after the minister of education.

FUTURE TRENDS

The growing complexity of the problems facing the Israeli educational system in the areas of integration, educational gaps, and enrichment are bound to increase demands for professional assistance that will require multiple professional competencies. Consequently, the field of school psychology will face the need of extending its domains of specialization into areas such as organization development, effective instruction techniques, applied research, behavior modification, cognitive therapy, and so on. A more active participation will be necessary in the policy-making processes of Ministry of Education, particularly in fostering the competence of teachers to serve as mental health agents in the schools. In general, there will be a need to increase the involvement of the psychologist as well as the educational staff in the areas of primary prevention. Greater attempts must be given to developing school–community and school–parent relationships. More attention should be directed toward developing skills to cope with problems created by economic, political, and social pressures that seem to intensify in the country. Finally, the central problems that Israel will have to cope with in the future will stem from the internal interethnic tensions that still plague the nation. The educational system will need to become a central instrument for fostering the principles of tolerance and equality. An active participation in the solution of these problems will constitute a major challenge to the Israeli school psychologists of the future.

ACKNOWLEDGMENT

Reprinted by permission of the *Journal of School Psychology*, *22*, 323–333, as published in 1984.

REFERENCES

Ayalon, O. (1978). *Emergency kit: Help!* Haifa: Hahevra Leyisum, Haifa University.

Benyamini, K. (1982). The four clients of the school psychologist. *School Psychology International, 3*, 15–22.

Benyamini, K., & Klein, Z. (1970). The educational system and mental health. In A. Jarus, J. Marcus, & C. Rapoport (Eds.), *Children and families in Israel: Some mental health perspectives* (pp. 208–237). New York: Gordon & Breach.

Kleinberger, A. F. (1969). *Society, schools and progress in Israel*. Oxford: Pergamon Press.

Lahad, S. (1981). *A project for training teachers and pupils for emergency situations*. Kiriat-Shmone Municipality: Department of Education.

Margalit, M. (1980). The development of special education system in Tel Aviv. *Megamot, 4*, 495–499.

Raviv, A. (1984). Psychology in Israel. In R. J. Corsini (Ed.), *Wiley encyclopedia of psychology*. New York: Wiley.

Raviv, A., Klingman, A., & Horowitz, M. (Eds.). (1980). *Children under stress and in crisis*. Tel Aviv: Otsar Hamoreh.

Raviv, A., & Wiesner, E. (1985). School psychology in Israel: Some problems of the profession. *Journal of School Psychology, 23*, 113–119.

Raviv, A., Wiesner, E., & Bar-Tal, D. (1981). *A survey of psychologists in the school psychological services: Research report*. Jerusalem: Ministry of Education.

Smilanski, M., & Kashti, Y., & Arieli, M. (1982). *The residential education alternative*. Haifa: Ach Publishing House.

Chapter Eleven
School Psychology in Jordan

Narjes Hamdi, Nazih Hamdi
University of Jordan

Since programs were introduced 19 years ago, psychology has become an important factor in Jordanian schools. Counseling services operate throughout the system with special education services offered additionally in special schools. As a basis for the understanding and assessment of such programs, this chapter presents a description of the present status of these counseling services including special education, an analysis of the problems to be faced and dealt with, and an outline of some possible areas for future development.

JORDAN'S EDUCATIONAL SYSTEM

Students in Jordan pass through 12 years of schooling in three main stages. The elementary stage consists of 6 years, from primary one to primary six. Students start school in Jordan at the age of 5 years, 8 months. The preparatory stage consists of 3 years, from the first preparatory to the third preparatory class where compulsory education in Jordan ends. The secondary stage, the final stage, consists of 3 years and offers a choice between vocational and academic education. Academic education begins with 1 year of general education, and then offers either a literary or a scientific stream for the final 2 years of second and third secondary classes. Although most schools are not co-educational, there has been a trend toward opening more co-educational schools at the elementary stage with predominantly female staff.

For the academic year 1983–1984, 824,901 students were enrolled in the three stages. Of this number 431,818 (52%) were male students and 393,083 were female (Ministry of Education, 1984). These numbers show that education of girls is no less important than the education of boys in Jordanian society. The 1983–1984 statistics also indicate 2,937 schools with 25,366 classrooms (Ministry of Education, 1984). According to these statistics, the average number of students per classroom was 32. Education in Jordan is controlled by four sources: The Ministry of Education, other governmental authorities (e.g., the Ministry of Defense and the Ministry of Wakf and Islamic Affairs), United Nations Relief and Work Agency (UNRWA), and private educational trusts. The Ministry of Education in Jordan retains a major responsibility for education as shown by the fact that 70% of all students in Jordan were enrolled in its schools in 1981–1982 (Ministry of Education, 1982).

COUNSELING IN JORDANIAN SCHOOLS

In 1969 the Ministry of Education in Jordan started a school counseling program by appointing counselors to six schools in Amman, the capital of Jordan. The Ministry of Education gradually increased the number of these counseling centers and extended them to different areas in the Hashemite kingdom of Jordan. By 1984–1985 the number of counseling centers in schools had reached 218 (Department of Counseling, 1985).

In Amman there are 134 counseling centers; 97 (72%) of these are located in preparatory and secondary schools for girls (Amman School District, 1985). There are several reasons for this high proportion of female counseling services: Females in Jordanian society are encouraged to work in the school environment because of gender-related attitudes toward vocational preparation; economically, the relatively low salary of Jordanian teachers does not encourage men to work in teaching or counseling positions; socially, jobs in the Ministry of Education are not regarded as prestigious, particularly for men. As a result, males who graduate in psychology tend to look for jobs in administrative positions or to work in neighboring oil-rich countries to find better salaries. In addition, counselors generally prefer to work in secondary schools rather than preparatory or elementary schools because secondary schools are usually closer to the highly populated areas and work there carries more prestige.

In Jordan, the responsibilities of the school counselors cover a wide variety of activities (Al-Khofash & Hamdi, 1981). They perform the following activities: gathering information about the student to be used for counseling purposes, providing financial services, including identification of students with financial difficulties to provide them with assistance, advising students on problems of daily life, conducting case studies, identifying students with health problems or handicaps in order to provide them with appropriate services, identifying students with achievement problems to provide them with help, providing students who have school attendance problems with appropriate help, providing class guidance through classroom discussion of extracurricular topics, conducting group counseling for students with common problems, giving career and educational guidance and providing students with information regarding career and educational options, organizing parent–teacher meetings, establishing contact with students' homes and sending them brief notes regarding the school's news and educational suggestions, and conducting action-oriented research to identify factors related to common problems in schools and to suggest possible solutions.

With thousands of jobless doctors and engineers underlining the need for increased vocational guidance, more emphasis has been given to that counseling area since 1980. In that year, the Counseling Department at the Ministry of Education conducted in-service training programs for counselors in vocational guidance as well as many orientation programs to provide high school students and students planning to study abroad with information to help them with vocational and educational decisions (Abu-Ghazaleh, 1985).

Administering tests does not form part of the counseling services in Jordanian schools. First, although there are many tests of various types available in the Arabic language, only few of these tests have been standardized to Jordanian norms; second, few counselors have been trained to use standardized tests; third, the use of standardized tests is regarded as controversial in Jordan. Thus, the Department of Counseling trains and instructs counselors to use such nontest data as observation and cumulative records.

Administration of Counseling Services

The Ministry of Education's Counseling Department is housed within the Directorate of General Education. The head and the members of the counseling department work in several areas: recommending the appointment of counselors and counseling supervisors, conducting in-service training programs for counselors and supervisors, providing school districts with information and advice regarding educational practices, preparing schools and school districts for opening new counseling centers, conducting orientation programs to help students make vocational and educational decisions, and providing school counselors with relevant information (Department of Counseling, 1985).

Counseling and guidance supervisors are present in each school district: At this level, practitioners supervise counseling services in the schools, conduct educational research and provide counseling services to schools without counselors (Department of Counseling, 1985).

Training Facilities for Counselors

To be appointed, counselors must hold an MA in counseling or psychology, a diploma in guidance and counseling, a BA in counseling and mental health or a BA in psychology. Most counselors graduate from the University of Jordan where the majority of the faculty were trained in the United States. Behavioral, Rogerian, Cognitive and eclectic approaches are represented within the Department. Two kinds of BA-level programs are offered by the Department of Psychology at the University of Jordan (i.e., BA in Counseling and Mental Health and BA in Psychology). Obligatory 3-hour courses for the BA in Counseling and Mental Health are: physiological psychology, psychology of learning, experimental psychology, social psychology, psychology of personality, principles of psychological and educational measurement, methods of individual assessment, analytical statistics, principles of mental health, abnormal psychology, clinical psychology, problems and needs in childhood and adolescence, principles of psychological and educational counseling, modification of human behavior, counseling in the elementary school, special education, methods of teaching in special education, and a 9-hour practicum in counseling and mental health (Counseling Center, 1987).

Three-hour courses that are required for the BA in Psychology are psychology of learning, physiological psychology, experimental psychology, psychology of personality, social psychology, clinical psychology, sensation and perception, abnormal psychology, experimental psychology (2), principles of psychological and educational measurement, psychological readings in English language, analytical statistics, and cognitive psychology (Counseling Center, 1987).

The University of Jordan offers graduate programs in counseling and guidance at the diploma and MA levels. The obligatory 3-hour courses that are required at the diploma level are: problems and needs of childhood and adolescence, theories of counseling, behavior modification, principles and methods of counseling and guidance, group counseling, vocational and educational guidance, and field work in counseling (Counseling Center, 1987).

Obligatory courses for the MA include: personality theories, vocational growth theories, seminar in counseling and guidance techniques, research design and statistical methods, counseling theories, field work in counseling, seminar in MA thesis, and MA thesis. Students also take three elective courses (University of Jordan, 1983).

Further training for counselors is provided by the Ministry of Education. Short, job-oriented in-service training courses are held for newly recruited counselors, and refresher courses are conducted periodically.

Contributions

Those who work in the field of counseling at the University of Jordan or the Ministry of Education have made significant progress toward establishing a positive attitude to counseling in Jordan. They have drawn attention to the need for career guidance and have helped to introduce modern educational ideas and practices to Jordanian schools. In addition, several MA thesis and action-oriented research works have been devoted to counseling and guidance issues to be disseminated to the educational community at large.

Problems

Jordan, a poor country surrounded by oil-rich neighbors who offer salaries that are at least twice what can be earned in Jordan, finds its trained manpower tending to leave Jordan for the neighboring Gulf countries or Saudi-Arabia. This produces a shortage of qualified personnel in counseling as well as all other technical services. The shortage of appropriately qualified counselors (i.e., MA or Diploma in Counseling) thus has forced the Ministry of Education to appoint counselors with a BA in psychology. In the academic year 1984–1985 in the school district of Amman there were 2 counselors with MA Degrees in Counseling, 14 Diplomas in Counseling or Education, and 117 with BA Degrees (Amman School District, 1985). The problem occurs when insufficient training negatively influences counseling services as well as attitudes toward counseling. In order to solve the problem of insufficient counselor training, the Counseling Department at the Ministry of Education conducts continuous in-service training programs. In addition, the wide variety of school counseling activities is utilized to allow counselors to concentrate on services most appropriate to their training and to the nature of the school.

A second problem area in the Jordanian system can be seen in a lack of clear definition for the role of the counselor. Teachers, parents, school principals, and occasionally counselors themselves misunderstand the function of the counselor. This identity crisis over the role of the counselor of course is not unique to counseling in Jordan, for similar problems exist in the United States and have been the subject of study there (Cook, 1971; Sorenson, 1983). Attempts to solve this problem are starting with the emphasis on the school counselor's responsibility to define the counselor's roles and functions.

A third problem can be identified in the fact that the individual's freedom of choice is restricted in most of the Arab Middle Eastern countries (Bluhm, 1983; Moracco, 1979). The strength of family ties in Jordan, for example, requires individuals to give weight to their families' preference when they make educational, vocational, or marriage decisions. In these circumstances, the American model in career guidance programs that emphasizes, as Gibson and Mitchell (1981) state, the right and capability of the individual to make decisions and plans, cannot be applied. Counselors in Jordan, however, are trying to find ways around this problem by frequently working with the family to help an individual in the decision-making process.

SPECIAL EDUCATION IN JORDAN

Despite the increased interest in school counseling in Jordan, there has not been parallel attention given to special education. No special classes are held for students in Ministry schools who must be treated as special cases nor are specialized Ministry schools offered either for gifted students or for handicapped children. Because Jordanian schools do not differentiate between students according to their IQ scores, all students in the same class all over the Kingdom receive the same curriculum. Special education and rehabilitation programs, however, are provided to mentally retarded and physically handicapped hearing and visually impaired children in Jordan through 30 special centers. These centers serve students, aged 6–20 years, who comprise about 12% of all handicapped children (Elrousan & Yahya, 1984).

Jordan started its organized interest of the handicapped in the late 1930s. In 1939, a school for the blind was established in Jerusalem. After that time more voluntary, nonformal foundations were established to serve the handicapped with most of the foundations located in the West Bank of Jordan. Since the Israeli occupation of the West Bank in 1967, most of these centers and foundations have ceased to serve people on the East Bank of Jordan. The only place ready to receive the handicapped on the East Bank is a branch of the Holyland Foundation in Al-Salt.

Since 1967, several local and governmental efforts have been made on the East Bank and many centers have been established in Amman and throughout the Kingdom. A pioneer project for the gifted-talented students at the secondary school level was started in the city of Salt in the academic year 1984–1985 by a private foundation. Sixty male and 30 female students were selected to participate in the program from the upper 95th percentile of first-secondary students attending Salt schools on the basis of their mental aptitude, scholastic achievement, personality adjustment, creative abilities, and medical-physical fitness. Gifted-talented students are provided with an afterschool enrichment program in math, science, English language, and computer studies (Kaylani, 1985).

Several formal bodies offer and supervise various services for the handicapped in Jordan including teaching, vocational training, medical, and physiotherapy. The Ministry of Social Development offers the largest proportion of services. The Ministry of Health offers its services through medical and physiotherapy clinics. The Queen Alia Fund for Social Welfare provides funding for research studies. Much has been accomplished by this fund, which undertook a complete survey of the handicapped in Jordan in 1979. The Jordanian universities play significant roles by designing special training programs for personnel working in this field. The University of Jordan has its own school for the mentally handicapped, and a center for educating and training the physically paralyzed was established in 1983 at Yarmouk University.

Development and improvement of programs of special education in Jordan will require attention to problem areas and the following needs: more involvement in special education by mainstream schools, especially those controlled by the Ministry of Education; more training programs and in-service training for personnel working in the field of special education; constructing and cross-validating of reliable and appropriate measures for the purposes of identification and placement of the handicapped; more centers to provide a higher proportion of the handicapped with appropriate services; and more efforts to coordinate curriculum design and the practice of special education services in the various centers in Jordan.

FUTURE DEVELOPMENTS IN JORDANIAN SCHOOL PSYCHOLOGY

Based on the results of a survey of counseling services in 10 Middle Eastern countries, including Jordan, Day (1983) concluded that the profession of counseling has tremendous potential for growth and development in the Middle East.

The prospects for Jordan seem to be bright. First, the Jordanian Ministry of Education aims to appoint a counselor in each of its 3,000 schools. Although such an aim is too optimistic given Jordan's limited financial resources and the shortage of trained counselors at the present time, the goal is present. Second, the new BA program in counseling and mental health which has been implemented by the University of Jordan, may help in achieving the goal of increasing counseling services to more schools. Third, questions about the efficacy of school counseling and its accountability are being raised in Jordan. More emphasis is given to the evaluation process in counseling and the accountability and evaluation movement is expected to influence positively the quality of counseling programs in Jordan.

The needs identified by Saigh (in press) for development of school psychology in Lebanon are also relevant to the development of psychology in Jordan. Such needs include the establishment of legislation to regulate the practice of school psychology, the construction and validation of appropriate tools for human appraisal, and the development of training programs and in-service training for counselors and special education personnel. If such needs are met, perhaps most efficaciously through regional cooperation between Arab countries, the potential role of school psychology in the Jordanian educational system is indeed promising.

ACKNOWLEDGMENTS

We are grateful to Dr. Salma Jayyusi and Mr. David Lata, who provided us with very helpful suggestions and comments and helped us with editing.

REFERENCES

Abu-Ghazaleh, H. (1986). *Status and services of guidance and counseling at the Ministry of Education*. Paper presented at the Conference of Guidance and Counseling, Irbid, Jordan.

Al-Khofash, S., & Hamdi, N. (1981). *Psychological counseling*. Amman-Jordan: Institute of Educational Training.

Amman School District. (1985). *The annual report of counseling services in the academic year 1984–1985* (unpublished report). Amman-Jordan: Author.

Bluhm, H. P. (1983). The place of guidance in Egypt. *International Journal for the Advancement of Counseling, 6*, 31–37.

Cook, D. R. (1971). *Guidance for education in revolution*. Boston: Allyn & Bacon, Inc.

Counseling Center. (1987). *Student's guide*. Amman-Jordan: University of Jordan.

Day, R. C. (1983). Attitudes toward counseling in the middle east. *International Journal for the Advancement of Counseling, 6*, 143–152.

Department of Counseling. (1985). *The annual report of counseling services for the academic year 84–85* (unpublished report). Amman-Jordan: Ministry of Education.

Elrousan, F., & Yahya K. (1984). *Aspects and future plans for educating visually handicapped children in Jordan and the Middle East*. Paper presented at the International Conference of Educating Visually Handicapped, Paris.

Gibson, R. L., & Mitchell, M. H. (1981). *Introduction to guidance*. New York: Macmillan.

Kaylani, A. Z. (1985). *The pioneer program for the gifted-talented students at the secondary school level in the city of Salt*. Unpublished report.

Ministry of Education. (1982). *The statistical educational yearbook*. Amman-Jordan: Author.

Ministry of Education. (1984). *The Statistical educational yearbook*. Amman-Jordan: Author.

Moracco, J. C. (1978). Implementing self-concept in vocational choice in the Arab Middle East. *Journal of Vocational Behavior, 13*, 204–209.

Saigh, P. A. (in press). School psychology in Lebanon. *Journal of School Psychology*.

Sorenson, G. (1983). *Counselor's workbook: For a cognitive theory of counseling*. Los Angeles: University of California (mimeographed).

University of Jordan. (1983). *The University of Jordan catalogue* (Valid until 1985/1986). Department of Public and Cultural Affairs, Amman-Jordan: University of Jordan.

Chapter Twelve
School Psychology in Nigeria

B. N. Ezeilo
University of Nigeria, Nsukka

NIGERIAN EDUCATION

Nigeria is a West African country with a population of about 92.8 million. The population reflects approximately 270 different ethnolinguistic groups spread through the 21 states and the Federal Capital territory of Abuja (Arowolo & Daramola, 1986). There are about 38,211 primary schools with 359,701 teachers and 14,387,271 pupils. The ratio of primary teachers to pupils is 1:40. There are also 5,642 secondary grammar schools with 80,314 teachers and 3,059,088 pupils. The secondary teacher-pupil ratio is 1:38 (Federal Ministry of Education, 1986). Almost all the primary and secondary grammar schools are being managed by the government in terms of funding, and provision of teachers, materials, and equipment. Only a negligible percentage (about 0.04% of the primary schools, and 0.17% of the secondary schools) are privately owned.

The curriculum being currently operated is the 6:3:3:4 system of education that was introduced in 1983. This means that the child spends 6 years in primary school, and 3 years in junior secondary school if he or she passes the common entrance examination. The same curriculum is offered to all children until the end of the junior secondary education, that is the first 3 years of secondary education. The students are then divided into secondary grammar, technological, and vocational groups (Ukwuije, 1983), for another 3 years of secondary education called senior secondary education. During this period, the curriculum includes both academic and vocational subjects. At the end of the 3 years, the students may proceed to any of the tertiary institutions: the universities (for 4 years), the polytechnics (for 4 years), or the teacher's college (for 3 years). Alternatively, they may obtain jobs in industries or start their own private or corporate businesses.

Prior to the introduction of this 6:3:3:4 system, secondary education lasted for 5 years and the technical and commercial subjects, which form part of the present junior secondary curriculum, were de-emphasized. Education takes a high percentage of both the federal and state budgets, and adult literacy programs are being encouraged all over the country (Federal Ministry of Education, 1986). Primary school teachers usually complete a minimum of 2 years of post-secondary teacher-training programs in order to obtain the Teacher's Grade II Certificates. Three years of study in colleges of education or polytechnics are needed in order for teachers to obtain the Nigerian Certificate of Education (NCE) that is required for secondary school instruction.

SCHOOL PSYCHOLOGY

Training Facilities

In order to appreciate the position of school psychological services in Nigeria a brief history of psychology in Nigeria is given. Of the 26 Universities in Nigeria, 6 have departments of psychology. More specifically, the University of Ibadan, University of Nigeria, Nsukka, University of Ife, University of Jos, University of Lagos, and Ondo State University offer BSc degrees in psychology. In addition to this, Bayero University Kano offers psychology courses in its Department of Education. Four of the aforementioned universities offer graduate programs in industrial, social, developmental, and environmental psychology. Two universities are accredited by the Nigerian Association of Clinical Psychologists to train clinical psychologists at graduate levels. These institutions are the University of Nigeria Nsukka, which runs a masters as well as a doctorate program in its Department of Psychology, and the University of Benin, which has a subdepartment of clinical psychology in its Department of Mental Health of its School of Medicine. None of the aforementioned universities offers a specific program for training school psychologists. This is probably due to the fact that, to the author's knowledge, Nigeria has no trained professional school psychologist.

Many first degree holders in psychology are employed in schools first as teachers, who may in turn be assigned to counseling duties with reduced teaching loads. Some universities with faculties of education train guidance counselors and educational psychologists. Moreover, a number of colleges of education offer psychology courses.

There are three national associations that cater to the needs of Nigerian psychologists. The Nigerian Association of Clinical Psychologists (NACP) was established in 1979, to bring together clinical psychologists in Nigeria. The NACP is registered with the Federal Government of Nigeria. The Nigerian Psychological Association (NPA) was inaugurated in 1984 following a merger between the Nigerian Association of Psychologists (NAP) and the Nigerian Psychological Society (NPS). The NPS was established in 1970 and included graduates in education and counseling who had completed some psychology courses in the course of their training. The NAP, which came into being in 1981, consisted of professional psychologists (full members must have had at least a master's degree in psychology). As such the new NPA includes all members of the former NAP and professional psychologists from the former NPS. Full membership is restricted to individuals with a minimum of masters degree in psychology.

The third professional group is the Nigerian Association of Industrial and Organizational Psychologists which includes professionals in these fields. This was also inaugurated in 1984.

Scope of Services

From the foregoing one can see that psychology is a relatively young discipline in Nigeria. School psychology as a profession has not been well established. It is a field that needs to be explored. The need for school psychologists in Nigeria cannot be overemphasized. This observation has been made by a number of Nigerian psychologists (e.g., Eya, 1983; Uzoka et al., 1980), and educationists (e.g., Izundu, 1986; Nwokah, 1983; Shaikh & Martins, 1983; Ukwuije, 1983). These authors drew attention to the needs of the school child and the importance of providing psychological services in meeting these needs. In 1980, Uzoka et al. observed ''the UPE programme has brought to school pupils various psychological problems. The need for school psychological service has become more pressing than ever before'' (p. 12). Also Izundu (1986), in emphasizing the need for school psychologists in her ''model school personnel,'' noted that in a good school system it is not only the retarded child who needs help but also the gifted, the creative, and the geniuses, and that the presence of a psychologist becomes paramount in this case. Services closely related to school psychological services are being offered by guidance counselors. These services had been an integral part of the mandate of federal and some state secondary schools.

Psychological services for school-age children are provided at the University of Nigeria's Psychological Services Centre, the University of Ibadan's Psychology Clinic, and the University of Jos Psychology Clinic. The clientele of these facilities include primary and secondary school children as well as university students. Services include assessment, therapy, and research.

The only government-financed school psychological service seems to be the child guidance clinic started in Lagos in 1964 (Shaikh & Martins, 1983). Until 1972, it was operating as a grant-aided institution and was an arm of the Ministry of Education. Its attention was focused on assessment of handicapped children, remedial teaching of slow learners, and in isolated cases, secondary school counseling was provided. From 1973 to date its programs included ''school psychological services'' that are responsible for remedial programs in primary schools and counseling programs in secondary schools. The staff of this institution does not include professionally trained school psychologists. However, the child guidance clinic now known as Psychoeducational Service consists of the following units and provides the following services: Child Guidance Unit whose functions include diagnosis and placement of children as well as advising parents; School Psychological Unit for "remedial programs" in primary schools and counseling programs in secondary schools; and Special Education Unit that coordinates the teaching and administration in special education schools.

The nature of the problems handled at the child guidance clinic in Lagos include mental retardation, speech disorders, partial deafness, total deafness, visual impairment, physical handicaps, neurotic behaviors, psychotic behaviors, and specific learning disabilities. Cases of this sort are referred by school heads and parents, as well as hospital and public health departments. Although the problems handled at the child guidance clinic in Lagos occur in other parts of Nigeria, professional services as previously described are not available throughout the country. As such, children receive the attention of traditional healers, prayer house priests and prophets, general medical practitioners and special schools for the handicapped. Along these lines, the Guidance and Counseling Department of the University of Ibadan provides counseling services for school children. The services rendered in this regard include assessment and intervention. Unfortunately most of these services are delivered by practitioners with limited skills.

Special Problems

School psychology in Nigeria is handicapped by a lack of sufficiently trained personnel, and a lack of standardized tests. The need to develop and validate endemic tests is still relevant at this time (Ezeilo, 1978). The available literature reflects a paucity of research in the area of test development and validation. Work in this area in most cases is hampered by limited funds. This in turn may be related to lack of public awareness as to what school psychology can contribute to society. It is interesting to note however that the Nigerian Psychological Association and the Department of Psychology at the University of Nigeria Nsukka are presenting public enlightenment programs in an effort to rectify this situation. These programs include television and radio discussions, as well as newspaper articles of relevance to the psychological needs of children.

FUTURE DEVELOPMENTS

From the aforementioned, it is apparent that the practice of school psychology in Nigeria is markedly different than the practice of school psychology in the West. The point should not be missed however that the Nigerian government and

Nigerian psychologists are willing to advance the status of school psychology in the country. In so doing, these basic goals must be realized. Initially, there is need to establish graduate programs in school psychology. The government could facilitate the development of the profession by offering scholarships to students in this regard. It is also felt that effort should be directed to training of more special education teachers through a comparable increase in the number of special education training institutions. The development of endemically relevant and empirically validated diagnostic tests should be actively pursued. It is also felt that a number of existing occidentally developed tests may be suitable for use in Nigeria if they are empirically field tested. It is interesting to note that similar efforts have been highly successful in other developing countries (cf. Saigh, 1981; Saigh & Khuri, 1983).

As one might anticipate, the limited national budget may make it difficult to realize these goals at this time. It is hoped however, that puissant international organizations (e.g., UNESCO) as well as foreign agencies (e.g., Agency for International Development) will appreciate the need to provide more effective psychological services in the schools and that resources will be channelled in this direction.

REFERENCES

Arowolo, O. O., & Daramola, O. (1986). *Philosophy of population census in Nigeria*. Lagos: National Population Commission.

Eya, R. N. (1983, March). *Children in distress: Trends in modern care of the destitute in Anambra State*. Paper presented at the second annual conference of the Nigerian Association of Psychologists held at the University of Jos, Nigeria.

Ezeilo, B. N. (1978). Validating Panga Munthu Test and Porteus Maze Tests (wooden form) in Zambia. *International Journal of Psychology, 13*(4), 333–342.

Izundu, N. T. A. (1986, April). *Model school personnel for educational survival*. Paper presented at the third annual conference of the Nigerian Psychological Association, University of Nigeria Nsukka.

Nwokah, E. E. (1983, March). *A positive approach to the integration of communicatively-handicapped into society*. Paper presented at the second annual conference of the Nigerian Association of Psychologists, University of Jos, Nigeria.

Saigh, P. A. (1981). The validity of Lorge Thorndike nonverbal battery as a predictor of the academic achievement of international students. *Educational and Psychological Measurement, 41*, 1315–1318.

Saigh, P. A., & Khuri, A. (1983). The concurrent validity of mathematics anxiety rating scale for adolescents in relation to the academic achievement of Lebanese students. *Educational and Psychological Measurement, 43*, 633–637.

Shaikh, M. S., & Martins, J. O. (1983). The place of psychoeducational services in the universal primary education. In B. A. Babalola & I. S. Agiobu-Kemmer (Eds.), *The proceedings of the 12th annual conference of the Nigerian Psychological Society*, Port Harcourt, Nigeria.

Statistics Section—Federal Ministry of Education, Science and Technology, (1986). Unpublished document, Lagos Nigeria.

Ukwuije, R. P. I. (1983, March). *The new national education policy and continuous assessment.* Paper presented at the second annual conference of the Nigerian Association of Psychologists, University of Jos, Nigeria.

Uzoka, A. F., Eyo, I. E., Obi-Keguna, H. U. Okpara, E., Ibeh, G. A., Iwuh, I. I., & Ozioko, J. O. C. (1980, February). *Nigerian psychology and public policy.* Paper presented at the tenth annual conference of the Nigerian Psychological Society, University of Lagos, Nigeria.

Chapter Thirteen
School Psychology in South Africa

David Donald
University of Natal
Marg Csapo
University of British Columbia

INTRODUCTION

Education in South Africa is delivered through four essentially separate systems of education with a bureaucratically complex arrangement of departments of education falling within this framework.

Within the political policy of separate development a Department of National Education governs educational policy under the label of *general affairs*. Falling under this umbrella there are four distinct ministries of *own affairs*: The Department of Education and Culture (House of Assembly) for Whites; the Department of Education and Culture (House of Delegates) for Indians; the Department of Education and Culture (House of Representatives) for Coloreds (mixed race); and the Department of Education and Training for Black residents outside the national and independent homelands. Within the White ministry there are four historically independent provincial education departments: Cape, Natal, Orange Free State, and Transvaal (although these are nominally one). Apart from this, each of the six national homelands (Lebowa, Gazankulu, Kwazulu, Qwaqwa, KwaNdebele, and Kwangwane) and each of the four independent homelands (Transkei, Ciskei, Bophuthatswana, and Venda) have their own departments of education. Thus, South Africa's system of education consists of 18 different departments of education: 1 general, 11 for Blacks, 4 for Whites, 1 for Colored and 1 for Indians. The complexity and diversification does not stop there. Along the line of linguistic categories the system for White students is divided between the Afrikaners and the English, and among the Blacks it is divided among various tribes (e.g., Zulu, Tswana, Xhosa, etc.).

Comparison of the Four Systems of Education

Obvious differences are observable in comparing the four systems of education. More specifically:

1. Education for Black children is not compulsory. School attendance is compulsory for Whites and Colored students from age 7 to 16, and for Indian students from age 7 to 15 (Ormond, 1985).

2. Black students have to pay fees to attend school, whereas schooling is free for the other groups. They have to pay for texts, uniforms, stationary, and so on (De Lange, 1981a).

3. Educational per capita expenditure differs considerably among the four groups. For the 1982–1983 school year, the capita expenditure for a White student was U.S.$690, for an Indian student U.S.$430, for a Colored student U.S.$295 and for a Black student U.S.$56.50 (Ormond, 1985).

4. Differential representation at various levels of education is illustrated in Table 13.1 (Republic of South Africa, 1985). Black students are underrepresented in the secondary, tertiary, and special education categories. Colored students are underrepresented at the tertiary level, and Indian students to some extent in special education.

5. Access to education varies among the four groups. Whites, who comprise only 16% of the population, provide 75% of the pupils obtaining senior certificates and 82% of those who qualify for university entrance (Gordon, 1979). Comparatively few places exist for Blacks. About 50% of the Black students leave school before they reach the fourth year of education (Gordon, 1979). Opportunity for secondary technical education, commercial studies, or broader vocational choice is severely limited. In 1980 there were 10 residential and 1 nonresidential universities almost exclusively for White students, 1 for Colored, 1 for Asians, and 4 for black students. However, the White English universities have traditionally taken a stand against racism and, despite state policy, the number of Colored, Indian, and Black students enrolled in these universities has increased considerably in the past few years.

6. The differential capacity to retain students is best illustrated by Table 13.1, which shows the distribution of Black students according to the various levels of the school system. Additionally, Verwey, Carstens, and Du Plessis (1984) reported that although 55.7% of Black students are enrolled at lower primary level, this figure changes to 3.9% at the senior high school level. De Lange (1981a) reported that at the end of 1980 more than half (52.2%) of the school leavers were illiterate, and illustrated the low holding power of the schools by showing the percentage of children completing Grade 12 who entered school in 1963: Whites, 58.4%; Indians, 22.30%; Colored, 4.4%; and Blacks, 1.96%.

TABLE 13.1
1985 School Enrollment by Instructional Level and Race

Level of Instruction	*Racial Categories*							
	White		*Colored*		*Indian*		*Black*	
	N	%	*N*	%	*N*	%	*N*	%
Pre-primary	108,600	2.2	15,845	0.6	2,418	0.3	30,763	0.2
Primary	572,596	11.8	599,692	20.9	149,193	16.7	3,401,351	18.1
Secondary	433,485	8.9	198,109	6.9	85,342	9.5	822,277	4.4
Special education	42,748	0.9	11,224	0.4	2,376	0.3	4,331	0.0
Tertiary	196,188	4.0	22,896	0.8	22,005	2.5	64,614	0.3
Total	1,353,617	27.8	847,766	29.5	261,334	29.3	4,323,336	23.1
Total population	4,872,000		2,896,000		893,000		18,749,000	

Republic of South Africa: Educational Statistics, 1985.

7. Marked differences are found in pupil–teacher ratios. More specifically the following ratios are reported : schools for Whites, 18.2:1; for Indians, 23.6:1; for Colored students, 26.7:1; and for Blacks, 42.7:1 (Ormond, 1985). Moreover, primary classes for Black children with 60, 90, or 100 pupils exist (White, 1983; Csapo, 1987).

8. Preparation and qualification of teachers in each system of education differ. De Lange (1981a) considered senior certificate and professional qualification as the norm and showed that in the education system for White students, 3.36% of the teachers were underqualified; for Indian students, 19.70%; for Colored students, 66.14%; and for Black students, 85.0%. The shortage of qualified teachers and administrators is an alarming problem (Horrell, 1982).

9. The salary differential between teachers of White students and teachers of Black students is gradually disappearing. In 1974, a teacher in the education system for Black students received 38% of the salary of teachers of White students. By 1978, this percentage rose to 68% and by 1981 to 80% (De Lange, 1981a).

10. The different rate of population growth leads to underutilization of schools on the one hand and to overcrowding and denial of placement on the other. The declining rate of growth of the White population results in empty and half empty classrooms in the system of education for Whites, whereas schools for Blacks, many with double sessions, cannot accommodate the rapidly rising enrollment levels. Welsh (1978) estimated that, by the year 2000, with the present average annual growth rate of the Black population, Blacks will form 75.0% of the total population, the Whites will decline from 16.46% in 1980 to 13.24%, whereas the Colored and Indian populations will remain relatively constant at 8.99% and 2.83% respectively.

11. The language issue also affects students differentially. Secondary education for Black students is offered in English and Afrikaans, and because instruction is primarily in their native tongue in elementary schools, they are usually poorly prepared to continue their education in a second or third language. On the other hand, White, Colored, and Indian students begin and continue their education either in English or Afrikaans throughout their entire career.

SPECIAL EDUCATION SERVICES

The provision of special educational services is dispensed by several authorities within the various systems of education. Beside the four provincial departments of education, the Department of National Education has, until recently, also been involved with the education of White populations with special needs. The Department of Education and Culture (House of Delegates), the Department of Education and Culture (House of Representatives), and the Department of Education and Training have the responsibility for providing services for their own racial groups. The conspicuous lack of coordination of these services is further complicated by the involvement of provincial health authorities, the Department of Health, Welfare and Pensions, private welfare organizations, and the departments of education of the independent and national homelands.

In general, special education operates on the separatist model for Whites, Coloreds, and Indians. Special or adaptation classes and special practical high schools for mildly mentally handicapped students are well established in White education. The same system, although less well developed, operates for Colored and Indian students. For other handicapped students such as the blind, the deaf, cerebral palsied, epileptic, severely mentally handicapped, and the physically handicapped special residential or day schools are provided—again more liberally in White education but quite significantly in Colored and Indian education. Remedial, speech therapy, speech correction, and occupation therapy services are available through these special schools as well as for students in mainstream schools, again with a similar racial bias.

For black students, special education provision is extremely limited. Relatively few schools accommodate a proportion of severely mentally handicapped, blind, and deaf students but on the whole other special education services are so limited as to be nonexistant.

Table 13.2 illustrates enrollment figures in special education for 1985 (Republic of South Africa, 1985). At this time, there were 166 special schools for Whites, 40 for Coloreds, 15 for Indians, and 46 for Blacks.

SCHOOL PSYCHOLOGICAL SERVICES

School psychology in South Africa is characterized by a number of features that require initial elaboration.

First, given the highly complex sociopolitical and bureaucratic structure it is not possible to talk of one representative system. Strictly speaking, school psychological services differ not only across major ministerial dimensions but also across subdimensions (e.g., different departments within one ministry). To make any coherent sense of this complexity some simplification is necessary. Most rationally, and not necessarily following the bureaucratic dimensions, the total system is best understood as divided between services that are first-world oriented (those serving Whites, Coloreds, and Indians) and those that are third-world oriented (those serving Blacks).

Second, although school psychological services have existed in most departments for some time, in many cases this has been in little more than name. It is only in the past 2 decades that most real developments have taken place (Afri-

TABLE 13.2
1985 Enrollment in Special Education and Percentage in Relation to Total Population

	Racial Category							
	White		Colored		Indian		Black	
	N	%	*N*	%	*N*	%	*N*	%
Enrollment	42,748	0.9	11,224	0.4	2,376	0.3	4,331	0.0
Total population	4,872,000		2,896,000		893,000		18,749,000	

Republic of South Africa: Educational Statistics, 1985.

ca, 1977; Basson, 1977). In services to Coloreds, Indians, and Blacks the development, although still inadequate, has been proportionally most dramatic. Even for Whites, however, where services have existed in a more developed form for longer, real growth is comparatively recent. In one provincial education department, for instance, the number of school psychologists has grown from 3 to 43 (present ratio of students to psychologist, 3,000 : 1) in only 15 years.[1] This feature is important as dramatic changes in ratio radically affect the nature of services that are offered. The total situation, both first and third world, is therefore characterized more by a rapidly evolving pattern of service delivery than by any stable model.

Third, the possibility of professional registration in the category educational psychologist with the South African Medical and Dental Council only became effective in 1980. This has had two important effects. In the first place, the creation of the registration category, with accompanying criteria for training and certification, has stimulated dramatic growth in the number of university programs offering professional training for educational (school) psychologists (from 1 program in 1979 to 13 programs in 1987). In the second place, many school psychologists long employed by state departments either did not meet the criteria for registration or chose to become registered in an alternate category (e.g., counseling psychologist). The net result of these two effects has been a substantial growth of younger members of services with a background of professionally directed training mixing with, and at times conflicting with, older and usually more senior members of services with different views of service delivery. A tension between conservatism and radical reform of school psychology service is prevalent therefore and finds expression in anomalies, perhaps not unhealthy in the long run, at all levels of the system.

Fourth, within the overall context it is clear that South Africa is in the midst of political and social changes that are, and will have, profound effects on all aspects of its peoples' lives let alone on its institutional structures. School psychology is no exception. There are many in the country who are acutely aware

[1]Unless otherwise stated, figures quoted are from direct communication with officials concerned. In such cases published information is either outdated or nonexistant.

of the particular inadequacies and challenges that face the continued development of school psychology. What cannot be denied, is that there are vast areas of need and school psychologists are faced by a reality that is volatile, demanding and bewildering in its complexity.

With this background it will be appreciated that the following description of school psychological services in South Africa is relative. In the attempt to generalize, many variations and evolving patterns may be lost that in the future could prove to be significant. At this stage and given the overall complexity it is simply not possible to be more definitive.

Scope of Services

Within what have been termed the *first-world oriented services*, school psychological services follow a discernable general pattern. For each of the White, Colored, and Indian population groups there is a Ministry of Education and Culture. Within the Departments of Education concerned, school psychological services exist as subsections with their own hierarchical structures. All of these services, with some differences in nomenclature, have sections that deal with remedial services, with guidance and counseling, with the education of mentally handicapped students, and with specialized schools for other handicaps such as the blind, the deaf and the cerebral palsied. In some, medical and welfare services are included under the school psychological service and in others not. In all these services, but varying in extent, there are a number of clinics distributed in regions from which school psychologists, remedial teachers, speech therapists, and other associated professionals operate. In some services greater emphasis is put on itinerant school psychologists who, if they need, refer more problematic cases to the clinics whereas in other services the clinics have a more direct role.

The most dominant pattern of service delivery is the individual referral system. Schools, parents, medical, or other professionals refer students to the school psychological service for academic, behavioral, or emotional problems. School psychologists interview parents and teachers, assess the student on standardized tests or through observational or interview techniques and make recommendations that may involve, inter-alia; referral for more specialized assessment (e.g., medical or paramedical), referral for special education, parent or teacher counseling by the psychologist concerned, individual or family therapy by the psychologist concerned, or situational changes for the student. Because of the pressure of referrals, emphasis has traditionally fallen more on assessment and intervention by referral than on direct intervention. The evolving pattern of services is, however, rapidly changing this to give greater emphasis to direct therapeutic and counseling intervention by school psychologists.

A secondary pattern of service delivery that is evolving in some services with considerable rapidity and support is the consultative model. In these services, school psychologists are involved in time-allocated consultations on a regular basis with schools in their region, in consultations with teacher assistance teams, in inservice training particularly of specialized teachers, and in preventative and parent-directed programs. In high schools, as a widespread pattern, school psychologists regularly consult with counselors who act as the first agent in the referral system. High school counselors also handle vocational guidance under the direction of school psychologists.

Research and formal evaluation of curricular or other programs is only beginning to make itself felt as a legitimate activity for school psychologists.

In all services, mainstreaming has not become an issue. This, one suspects, is primarily because the cost of mainstreaming effectively would be prohibitive where the evolution of specialized education services on the separatist model has barely been established. Geographical factors might also play a part. Basically, however, there are more radical issues to be confronted in the society as a whole and what resources there are are too thinly spread to accommodate the demands of effective mainstreaming and the psychological and other professional support it needs.

As appears in the next section, differences—particularly in the ratio of students to school psychologists—do exist between the services for Whites and those for Coloreds and Indians. These differences have a clear effect on the delivery of services as previously outlined. However, the similarities are emphasized rather than the differences because, if anything, the gap is narrowing and the overall thrust and aim, although far short of adequate, is the same.

Tests and testing in all these services is highly controlled and reasonably sophisticated. A number of tests, mainly cognitive and scholastic, have been developed by a state agency, the Human Sciences Research Council, for local conditions. These include Junior and Senior Individual Intelligence Scales (Wechsler model) with norms established for different population groups. (Questionable although this may be at a fundamental level, it is practically useful in the present situation because of real social and educational differences.) A variety of group intelligence tests, aptitude tests, scholastic achievement tests, school readiness tests and local norms for various personality and vocational guidance inventories have also been established (Botha, 1984).

When one turns to school psychological services for Blacks in South Africa an entirely different picture emerges. As with all services, educational or otherwise, the shortfall is acute and desperate. For Blacks, school psychological services do exist in the Department of Education and Training as well as in the various Departments of Education of the national and independent homelands. In most cases, however, these services are minimal with student : psychologist ratios ranging from 28,000 : 1 to 35,000 : 1. Understandably the major need is for basic educational provision (classrooms, teacher numbers, and teacher upgrading) and resources are not readily directed to school psychological services. The principal function of existing school psychological services has been the application and control of group aptitude and scholastic achievement testing (norms for such tests having been established in the Black population), and the administration of a broad academic and vocational guidance programme in schools (Nieuwenhuis, Weideman, & de Klerk, 1984). Despite all this, some interesting and hopeful developments are taking place. First, progressively more Black school psychologists trained at, mainly, the open universities are filtering into the system. These psychologists, with a high level of professional training and a linguistic and cultural identity with their client populations are introducing some challenging innovations that cut across the first world model of service delivery (Brownell, de Jager, & Madlala, 1987). Second, in some services, notably the Department of Education and Training, necessity has given rise to a consultative model that optimizes the scarce resources of school psychologists. The evolution of a consultative model with the competency benefits that it generates for teachers would appear to have major potential in the present situation (Reynolds et al., 1984). Third, by default, a mainstreaming system exists in Black education because there are so few special education facilities. Ironically, without the traditional infrastructure of separatist special education, it is possible that mainstreaming could be maintained if consultative services could be sufficiently developed. Last, school psychological services are indeed slowly growing in numbers as well as level of training in Black education and much is being achieved in awareness, through pressure groups for improved services and through a search for more appropriate models of assessment (Gqubule, 1987) and intervention (Brownell et al., 1987; Mathabe, 1986). So much more would be possible, however, if resources were forthcoming.

Administration

All school psychological services in South Africa are state funded and fall under the different departments mentioned in the Introduction.

A typical service includes a head of school psychological and guidance services, a number of assistant or deputy heads in charge of the major subdivisions of the services (e.g., guidance and counseling; remedial services; special education, etc.) with school psychologists themselves divided into the ranks of senior school psychologist, school psychologist, and assistant school psychologist. Other professionals, such as remedial teachers, speech therapists, occupational therapists, social workers, and school counselors may be included in the service depending on its particular structure and the level of development of the service. Within this basic pattern considerable structural variation occurs across departments in the number and nomenclature of subdivisions and personnel as well as in regional organization.

In the case of White education, services have been formally established since the mid 1940s (Basson, 1977), and in Indian, Colored, and Black education since the 1960s (Africa, 1977). At present the respective ratios of school psychologists to students is:

Whites	: 2,750 : 1 (average over 4 provinces)
Indians	: 8,800 : 1
Coloreds	: 9,000 : 1
Blacks	: 28 – 35,000 : 1 (depending on the department concerned)

In White education, and to a lesser extent in Indian and Colored education, a number of special schools for severely mentally handicapped, cerebral palsied, blind, deaf, epileptic, and physically disabled exist as well as various reform schools and schools of industries. In most of these, a much higher ratio exists that approaches 80 : 1.

School psychologists in White services have in the majority, a masters (6 years) degree in psychology and, by regulation, must be trained and experienced teachers. Some have a BEd. (4-year) degree only and very few have doctorates. In Indian and Colored services, many recent appointments hold similar qualifications although a lower standard has prevailed in the past. In Black education, the minimum requirements is that a school psychologist should hold a bachelors (3-year) degree in psychology and be a qualified and senior teacher (often ex-principal; Nieuwenhuis et al., 1984). In general, school psychologists are not required to register with the South African Medical and Dental Council if they are in the employ of a state education department. In the past at least, this has meant that the appointment of school psychologists has favored educational experience and seniority rather than psychological and professional training. With the recent upsurge of training programs for school psychologists, however, this trend is changing and more, in all services, are going through a masters level professional training with the additional year's internship requirement. These school psychologists are eligible for registration and most, in fact, seek it despite not being obliged to do so. Educational psychologists in private practice must be registered, however. Outside the universities, not many of these exist although there are a significant number of registered clinical and counseling psychologists, who, through private practice, offer an alternative to the states' provision of school psychological services. Because they attract a fee paying population, however, this alternate service tends to favour the already privileged middle classes.

Training Facilities

As mentioned, professional training in school psychology has experienced a major upsurge in South Africa in the past decade. Basson (1977), bewailed the total lack of professional training programs at that stage and the widespread use of school psychological services as career ladders for general promotion rather than for a specialized professional service. As illustrated in Table 13.3, today there

TABLE 13.3
Master's Level Professional Training Programs in Educational Psychology

University	*Ave. Intake as at 1986*[a]	*Race Group*[b]
U. of Bloemfontein	5*	White
U. of Cape Town	4	open
U. of Fort Hare	4*	Black
U. of Natal (Pietermaritzburg)	6	open
U. of Natal (Durban)	6	open
U. of Port Elizabeth	4	White
U. of Pretoria	15	White
U. of South Africa	6	open
U. of Stellenbosch	6	White
U. of Western Cape	3*	open
U. of Witwatersrand	8	open
U. of Zululand	4*	Black
Rand Afrikaans U.	6	White

[a]In those cases marked with an asterisk courses have only recently been approved and intake is an estimation.

[b]Strictly speaking all universities are 'open' at postgraduate level. What is indicated is the admission tendency to date in each case.

are 13 professional training programmes in universities across the country meeting the requirements for professional registration.

The minimum requirements for training as laid down by the Professional Board for Psychology of the S.A. Medical and Dental Council are as follows:

> *Admission requirements*: Four years of psychology (i.e., B. Hons or B. Ed. degree) plus a 1-year teaching qualification. Most universities require teaching or other relevant experience as an additional requirement and select candidates by interview and past record.
>
> *Curricular requirements*: The masters program involves 1 year of taught course work with a supervised practicum requirement of 15 hours per week. In addition, there is a research dissertation requirement and then a 12-month supervised internship in an approved setting(s). Criteria are laid down covering the general curriculum content and applied skills that must be included in the program. Broadly, these include relevant professional, ethical, and theoretical issues and content as well as diagnostic, intervention, and consultative skills. Systematic exposure to local specialized institutions and interprofessional consultation is also included. Taking the practicum and internship requirements together, over 2 years, trainees spend 70% of their time in supervised case- and field work experience.

Although all training programs are obliged to meet these requirements (courses being formally submitted for approval to the Professional Board and subsequently regularly inspected), considerable variation in the detail and focus of curricula exists. The University of Natal (PMB) for example, which runs the most long established program, has a strong clinical and consultative bias. Other programs are more counseling oriented, whereas yet others are more educationally oriented. Most programs are eclectic in their philosophical orientation with behavioral, psychoanalytic, Rogerian, community, systems, or other approaches being accommodated according to staff competence and current program development.

Contribution

Because professional educational psychology, particularly in a university context, is relatively recent in origin contributions in this particular field on more than a limited, local level have been relatively few. (In psychology, more generally, the contribution of a number of South Africans has been significant. This, however, is not the place to review these.) Recently, however, some significant work focusing on the particular problems of South Africa has started to emerge, interalia, Basson (in press); Brownell et al. (1987); Dawes and Donald (1987); Fouché, Hammond, and Hammond (1987); and Skuy (in press).

It is to be hoped that this trend will grow in momentum particularly as South Africa is faced with many challenging and urgent research issues in the field of school psychology.

Special Problems

South Africa is so beset with problems that it is difficult to specify those that are *special*. However, problems that can be regarded as unique or particularly pressing in the context of South African school psychology are the following:

1. *The inequality of services*. This is the most glaring problem and has been well defined within this chapter. The need, however, cannot simply be seen in terms of improving school psychological services for Coloreds, Indians, and particularly Blacks—numbers of school psychologists, level of training, and ancillarly service infrastructure—but must also be seen in terms of improved basic education as this is *fundamental* and influences all else (Donald 1984).

2. *The administrative inefficiency of the present departmental structure*. The present plethora of education departments causes overlap, wastage of scarce resources, regional confusion, administrative blocking and feeds into, as it is fed by, a political policy that is increasingly and radically untenable both morally and practically.

3. *The lack of appropriate assessment tools and models of intervention*. Especially in the Black community, there is a need to develop appropriate tests and assessment techniques. This does not mean a simple collection of norms on es-

tablished or face-lifted tests. In many cases, it requires a conceptual restructuring in terms of social and cultural norms, expectations, and realities. Beyond this but also related, is the question of appropriate models of intervention. Given the extent of the need in the Black community as well as social and cultural factors not to mention the stresses and pressures created by political upheaval, it is clear that first-world oriented models of intervention are not necessarily the most appropriate. On-going and radical research into alternative approaches and their effectiveness is badly needed.

Some of these problems were addressed in the recommendations of the de Lange Commission for School Psychology (1981b). Basically, through its recommendation of a Co-operative Education Service Centre (CESG) incorporating a Section for Education and Guidance (SEG) in each educational service area, it recognized the need to rationalize professional service delivery under one central authority and to distribute it regionally rather than racially. Even though this addresses the problems mentioned previously under 1 and 2 it does not really address the central issue in 3 as the model proposed has been clearly conceptualized as a first-world school psychological service. Apart from this, the recommendations move too far beyond present state policy and with little action since 1981 it is unlikely that anything like the recommendations will be enacted.

In conclusion, South Africa has major problems to face in the development of its school psychological services. In some significant areas there have been developments that are encouraging but the three major remaining areas of need are: (a) Political change—without which development is unlikely to move beyond its present inefficient and cumbersome pattern; (b) Resources, both financial and professional—without which the fabric and infrastructure cannot be built; and (c) Research—without which the appropriate goals and directions cannot be defined. These are areas in which the international community, if it is concerned, can help.

REFERENCES

Africa, H. (1977). School psychology among the blacks in the Republic of South Africa. In C. D. Catterall (Ed.), *Psychology in the schools in international perspective* (Vol. 2, pp. 145–154). Colombus: Calvin D. Catterall.

Basson, C. J. (1977). School psychological services in white schools in the Republic of South Africa. In C. D. Caterall (Ed.), *Psychology in the schools in international perspective* (Vol. 2, pp. 155–166). Colombus: Calvin D. Catterall.

Basson, C. J. (in Press). A preliminary overview of potential sources of work related stress for the educational psychologist in the Republic of South Africa. *Educational Psychology in Practice*.

Botha, L. (1984). *The catalogue for scholastic achievement and diagnostic tests, aptitude and proficiency tests*. Pretoria: Human Sciences Research Council.

Brownell, A. J., de Jager, A. C., & Madlala, C. F. (1987). Applying first-world psychological models and techniques in a third-world context. *School Psychology International*, *8*, 34–47.

Csapo, M. (1987). *Perspectives in education and special education in southern Africa*. Vancouver: Centre for Human Development and Research.

Dawes, A. R., & Donald, D. R. (1987). Orientations to child management: A comparison of teacher-counsellors and high school principals with regard to child versus institutional advocacy. *South African Journal of Psychology, 17*(4), 131–136.

De Lange, J. (1981a). *Provision of education in the RSA*. Pretoria : Human Sciences Research Council.

De Lange, J. (1981b). *Investigation into education. Education for children with special education needs*. Pretoria : Human Sciences Research Council.

Donald, D. (1984). Key issues in the development of applied educational psychology in the contemporary South African context. *South African Journal of Psychology, 14*(2), 29–33.

Fouché, G. W., Hammond, E. J., & Hammond, J. C. (1987). *The child witness*. Pietermaritzburg: University of Natal Press.

Gordon, L. (Ed.). (1979). *Survey of race relations in South Africa, 1978*. Johannesburg : South African Institute of Race Relations.

Gqubule, M. (1987). *Mental retardation : A case study of a ten year old moderately retarded African girl from a low socio-economic and sub-cultural background*. Unpublished masters dissertation, University of Natal.

Horrell, M. (Ed.). (1982). *Survey of race relations in South Africa, 1981* Johannesburg: South African Institute of Race Relations.

Mathabe, N. R. (1986). *Guidance in a modernizing context: an analyis of the guidance needs and expectations of students in the high schools of Bophuthatswana*. Unpublished doctoral dissertation, Rhodes University.

Nieuwenhuis, F., Weideman, B., & de Klerk, J. (1984). *Skoolvoorligting-stelsels in die Republiek van Suid- Afrika*. Pretoria: Raad vir Geesteswetenskaplike Navorsing.

Ormond, R. (1985). *The apartheid handbook*. Bungay: Penguin Press Books.

Republic of South Africa. (1985). *Educational statistics*. Pretoria: Government Printer.

Reynolds, C. R., Gutkin, T. B., Elliott, S. N., & Witt, J. C. (1984). *School psychology. Essentials of theory and practice*. New York: Wiley.

Skuy, M. (in press). A comparison of the guidance received and desired by black and white pupils in South Africa. *International Journal for the Advancement of Counselling*.

Verwey, C., Carstens, P., & Du Plessis, A. (1984). Research Institute for Educational planning. *Education and Manpower Production (Blacks)* (No. 5). Bloemfontein: University of Orange Free State.

Welsh, D. (1978). The nature of racial conflict in South Africa. *Social Dynamics, 4*(1), 36.

White, D. (1983). *Teachers for Africa*. Inaugural address. Johannesburg: University of Witwatersrand.

Chapter Fourteen
School Psychology in India

M. K. Raina
National Council of Educational Research and Training

INDIAN EDUCATION

Among the many tasks that India faced immediately after the attainment of independence in 1947, reconstruction and expansion of her system of education was one of the most stupendous. The newly independent country assumed responsibility for an educational system that had become very outdated after years of colonial rule. The Indian government had to quickly reconstruct a modern and viable system of national education. This required the creation of, among other qualities, universal free elementary education, programs to reduce adult illiteracy, a rational language policy including the adoption of Indian languages as the media of instruction, restructuring secondary and higher education by introducing and modernizing vocational education and a diversified curriculum, raising educational standards at all levels, and improving methods of teaching and examinations, improving its research facilities, and improving special education services and resources for the retarded (Kamat, 1980).

Today, India's educational system is one of the biggest in the world. Education is broadly perceived as a seamless continuum of lifelong learning, essential for human resource development at every age level. It is strongly committed to improving the status and character of people, developing the intellectual, social, and emotional characteristics of its people, and enabling them to meet their basic needs of daily life (Sixth Five Year Plan, 1980–1985).

India is a vast country with 31 states and union territories. Its population in 1980 stood at 559 million, having recorded a growth rate of 83% since the 1951 census. In 1978, the child population in the 6- to 10-year age group was 84,016,000, of which 78% live in rural areas. Children ages 11 to 13 number 4,733,000, of which 74% live in rural areas. About 82% of children between

6 and 10 are enrolled in school. That percentage drops to 37 for those ages 11 to 13.

Primary responsibilities for education rest on the individual. Thus, one finds few uniform educational patterns within the country. Differences exist in the age of school entrance, the number of years required at the elementary and secondary stages, the curriculum, and other important aspects of education.

The Fourth All-India Educational Survey (1980) recorded that the number of recognized educational institutions in the country on September 30, 1978 was 634,144 out of which 88% were located in rural areas, 90% provided education at the primary stage, 23% at the middle stage, 7% at the secondary stage, and 2% at the higher secondary stage. Of the 556,873 institutions in rural areas, 91%, 21%, 5%, and 1% provided education at primary, middle, secondary, and higher secondary stages, respectively.

Among the primary schools, 39% were supported by the state government, 55% were under local bodies, 4% were private aided, and 2% were private unaided. Of the primary schools, 94% were government or local body schools. In most of the states, the majority of the schools supported by the state or local government were run as government schools or as local body schools. Of the 112,404 middle schools, 45,306 (40%) were government schools, 38% local body schools, 17% private aided and 5% private unaided schools. As in the case of primary schools, the majority 78% of the middle schools were either run by the government or by the local bodies. Of the 47,104 secondary and higher secondary schools, 14,338 (30%) were government, 9% local body, 57% private aided, and 4% private unaided schools. Of the secondary and higher secondary institutions, nearly 61% were managed by the private sector.

The total enrollment attending at the school stage in the recognized institutions was 95,137,549 of which 37% were girls and 70% living in rural areas.

In 1978, there were 2,940,337 teachers in educational institutions. Of these 44% were in primary school, 28% in middle school, 19% in secondary, and 10% in higher secondary schools.

About 26% of the teachers are women at all levels. About 87% are formally trained as teachers. Differences in the preparation of primary and secondary teachers are not apparent.

The pupil–teacher ratio at the national level is 41:1 at the primary stage, 25:1 at the middle stage, and 18:1 at the secondary and higher secondary stage.

During the period from 1950-1951 to 1975-1976 the total number of educational institutions rose from a little less than 250,000 to over 625,000 (i.e., by 2.5 times), whereas student enrollment increased from a little below 25 million to over 100 million. The number of teachers correspondingly increased fourfold, from 0.7 million to 3 million. The total outlay on education increased from about 1.2% of the national income to a little over 3%. Literacy rates increased 17% in 1951, to 29% in 1971, to an estimated 33% or 34% now.

PSYCHOLOGY IN INDIA

The foundations of scientific psychology were laid in India in 1915 with the establishment of the Department of Psychology at Calcutta University, the first of its kind in the country. Subsequently, departments of psychology were started at the universities of Mysore and Aligarh in 1924 and 1932, respectively. In 1946, Patna University started departments of experimental and applied psychology. Since its independence, scientific psychology in India has grown rapidly with a steady rise in the numbers of universities providing psychology courses in teaching and research, and is regularly offered in professional institutions of agriculture, nursing, engineering, medicine, management, and education (Raina, 1984; Ramalingaswami, 1978).

PROFESSIONAL ASPECTS OF PSYCHOLOGY IN INDIA

Psychology is accepted and recognized as an independent and useful field of study, research, and training.

> Psychology occupies a unique place among the social sciences, in the sense that it is both an academic discipline as well as a profession. As far as the professional side is concerned, the university courses have proved inadequate. Most of the courses run by the departments of psychology, whether in the colleges or in the universities, are academically oriented so that graduates in psychology have sought and have been mainly absorbed in teaching and research positions, or have taken up various positions in the government or private concern where training and knowledge of psychology is not of any particular relevance. . . . Unfortunately, our postgraduate programs also lack an adequately professional base. As a result not only has psychology failed to develop as a profession in India, but many psychology graduates are employed in professions other than the academic where the knowledge in psychological skills acquired can be put to practical use. The subject has thus, by and large, continued to be an academic discipline. (Rath, 1979, p. 71)

The stunted growth of the professional aspects of psychology has been due, in part, to its being tagged to philosophy. According to Rath (1979):

> This has not only stunted its growth but has inevitably given it a largely non-practical and theoretical orientation which is but a natural consequence of its association with a purely theoretical and academic subject like philosophy. In places where the subject has emerged out of the departments of education, it has managed to get a certain amount of professional bias largely in areas of mental testing, guidance and counseling. (p. 71)

SCHOOL PSYCHOLOGY

School psychology, also called *educational psychology*, does have an important place in India (Paliwal, 1977). The first survey of psychology in India (Mitra,

1972) found educational psychology to be developing quickly and was expected to catch up with other areas. It recorded a tenfold increase in 20 years and was surpassed only by developmental psychology and personality. The teaching of educational psychology began in colleges of education from their beginning. However, as an applied branch of psychology, it never attained much status in faculties of education, or departments of psychology (Buch, 1972). Ramalingaswami's (1978) survey indicates that educational psychology was taught at the MA level as an optional course in 30 universities, in guidance and counseling in 17 universities, in techniques of vocational psychology in 15 universities, in educational and vocational guidance in 8 universities, and in test construction and measurement in 4 universities. However, educational psychology forms an especially important ingredient in the education of teachers. It is recognized that "the expansion of formal education will require increasing numbers of teachers in classrooms; and if the quality of education is to be maintained or improved, adequate steps will have to be taken to train teachers effectively, and to that end, to create a fairly developed and up-to-date science of educational psychology" (Buch, 1972, p. 82). The latest survey of teacher education in India (Singh, 1983) indicates that educational psychology is offered as a compulsory course in all the universities in India as a complete paper or combined with such courses as health education, educational measurement, educational evaluation, and statistics.

Psychology not only is being taught in universities and professional institutions but recently has been introduced in schools. The need for introducing psychology has been addressed by the National Council of Educational Research and Training in its document *The Curriculum for the Ten-Year School: A Framework* (1975):

> The students in the classes IX and X are usually in the age range of 14 to 16 years. These two years however, are crucial from the point of view of development of personality. While from the onset of puberty there are problems of adjustment which the young child has to cope with, it is at this stage that these become acute and additional preparation for a transition from the life of a school student to that of a productive person has to be undertaken. It is therefore, necessary to give the child some psychological insight into his problem and the knowledge that may help him to understand his behaviour as well as that of others around him. (p. 12)

The main objective of teaching psychology in schools, as indicated in the *Framework* is "to help the adolescents to cultivate an insight into their problems of growth, development, social relations, personality and adjustment to life and work." Psychology is offered as one of the elective subjects for the Senior School Certificate Examination of the Central Board of Secondary Education.

Despite appreciating the crucial role that psychology plays in education, the field of school psychology as commonly understood (cf. Kratochwill, 1981) unfortunately is one of the most neglected and relatively inactive areas in contemporary Indian psychology. "Though our school system is patterned after the British system, the position of a school psychologist and the vocational psychologist so well known in England have become almost unknown in Indian set-up'' (Pasricha, 1976, p. 39). This is not absolutely correct because in India we have school psychology characterized by a more omnibus professional that combines the roles of guidance counselor, career masters, district psychologists, special educators, and psychometrists. Guidance, in fact, was introduced in Calcutta University's Department of Applied Psychology in 1938 with a view to conduct research in the field of educational–vocational guidance.

The appointment of the Secondary Education Commission in 1952 (Report of the Secondary Education Commission, 1954) influenced considerably the development of the guidance movement in India. The commission recommended diversification of courses and emphasized the need for educational and vocational guidance. Guidance was described by the committee to cover the entire range of student problems and to be available at all levels of schooling. The importance of guidance services currently is greatly emphasized in view of the introduction of vocational preparation within school.

In addition to supporting guidance services, the Secondary Education Commission also recommended special services for various categories of special and disabled children. Opportunites for integrated education, vocational training, and economic rehabilitation have been created in order to help integrate the disabled and the nondisabled and to place the disabled children in ordinary schools with the help of special teachers, aides, and resources in order to more effectively meet the varying needs of different types of handicapped children.

Services for these types of children are discussed in following sections.

Administration

Following recommendations by the Secondary Education Commission that guidance bureaus be established at state levels with coordination provided at the national level, the Central Bureau of Educational and Vocational Guidance was established in 1954 by India's Ministry of Education along with an offer to help state governments should they decide to establish guidance bureaus for themselves. P. H. Mehta's (1983) recent survey of the status of guidance services in the country indicated that 19 states or union territories have a bureau providing educational and vocational guidance services, whereas 10 lack a state level guidance agency. The bureaus are providing testing and career choice services and disseminating information regarding courses and vocations available to students with different interests and aptitudes. The objectives of the bureaus as stated by Odgers (1962) are:

1. to create a guidance consciousness and understanding on the part of headmasters and other educational leaders in the state in order to create a readiness for the initiation of guidance services in the secondary schools;

2. to train guidance personnel for the secondary schools in the state;

3. to provide supervisory and consultative services to the guidance units in secondary schools;

4. to set up an information service in the state bureau and to supply useful educational and occupational information to the guidance units in secondary schools, preparing such materials and in some instances securing them from other sources for distribution;

5. to construct and standardize, or adapt and restandardize psychological tests for use by the bureaus and by school guidance units having trained counselors;

6. to prepare and publish guidance aids and tools, including bulletins and newsletters for use by school guidance units, headmasters, and teachers;

7. to provide counseling and guidance services at the State Bureau, to provide services not available in the schools, to serve as laboratory for trainees, or to serve as a demonstration unit and to provide continuing experience for state bureau staff members; and

8. to conduct research necessary for the preparation of materials, the evaluation of guidance programs, or the development of improved techniques such as the prediction of success in the different streams of the multipurpose schools.

Three of the 19 state-level guidance agencies have an independent guidance existence, with the head reporting to the director of education or some other senior official in the Directorate of Education. Few of the state-level agencies appear to be a part of the Office of the Directorate. They are generally extremely small units.

Most agencies have no more than one professionally qualified staff member. Apparently only 6 of the 19 heads of these state-level agencies have a diploma in guidance, whereas 13 are not professionally qualified.

Guidance Services in Schools

P. H. Mehta (1983) reported that approximately 10,500 schools have a guidance service. Of these, less than 2% have a full-time counselor, whereas 12% have a guidance program conducted by a part-time counselor (i.e., by a teacher counselor or visiting counselor). The remaining guidance programs are conducted by a careers teacher (i.e., educational and occupational information service without testing or counseling). The program is often quite limited and is conducted haphazardly even in those schools that reported guidance programs conducted by a full-time or part-time counselor.

Mehta concluded that, although an increase occurred between 1963 and 1981 in the total number of schools offering some kind of guidance services, the increase is not very significant in light of the increased number of schools during this period. The pace of expansion of school guidance services needs to be increased considerably. The quality and availability of school counselors also is far from satisfactory.

Training Facilities

The National Council of Educational Research and Training (NCERT) and some other institutions and departments of education are offering diploma or refresher programs for the training of school psychologists. University departments generally offer graduate courses in psychometrics and vocational psychology as part of their MA courses (Status of Psychology in Indian Universities, 1982). NCERT has offered a postgraduate diploma in educational and vocational guidance since 1958. The objective of the course as stated by the council is to train counselors for guidance bureaus in various states, and for schools and training colleges to teach guidance and counseling to prospective school teachers and counselors. Admission requirements for the course include a master's degree in psychology or education in the second division. The course is 9 months and full time in duration and consists of theoretical and supervised practice. The theoretical courses include: principles and procedures of guidance, counseling, psychology of adjustment, theory of vocational development, occupational information in guidance, measurement and evaluation in guidance, and basic statistics for guidance. The supervised practice includes testing, group guidance, counseling, occupational information and vocational development, and a practicum in self-understanding. A few state Bureaus of Educational and Vocational Guidance and the St. Xaviers Institute of Education, Bombay also offers courses in educational and vocational guidance.

More than 150 institutions in India currently provide services for the mentally retarded for diagnosis, treatment, education and training, rehabilitation, sheltered employment, and care and management. In addition, the National Institute of Mental Health and Neurosciences, Bangalore, organizes teaching courses in psychology, mental hygiene, and psychiatry for graduate students; conducts research in the field of psychiatry, neurology, and neurosurgery; and organizes postgraduate courses of teaching for nurses in the field of psychiatry (D. S. Mehta, 1983).

The four National Institutes for the Handicapped (i.e., one each for the visually handicapped, deaf, orthopedically handicapped, and mentally handicapped) organized training programs for teachers. The National Institute of Public Cooperation and Child Development, New Delhi, was established as an apex organization in the field of public cooperation and child development. It reviews and revises training curricula and teaching methods for various training courses, particularly in the field of child development. Its plans include establishing extension demonstration units like child guidance clinics, child-care centers, and nutrition demonstration units to strengthen its training programs and to develop innovative models.

Contributions

Psychology in India continues to be largely an academic discipline and it has not developed much as a profession. Some organizations (e.g., the National Council of Educational Research and Training, National Institute of Public Cooperation and Child Development and the four National Institutes for the Handicapped) have made significant efforts to train school psychologists. Many other organizations have directed their efforts to meet the special education needs of children. Many institutions, particularly NCERT, have taken a lead in facilitating test administration, training, and the development of good test libraries. Psychology as well as school psychology are interacting more with other social sciences and taking steps to further advance psychology as a discipline and as a profession. For example, the second survey of psychology in India (Pareek, 1980) found a tendency to seriously question and challenge the validity of impressions and the ready-made solutions offered for problems in clinical, social, and educational psychology. One finds immense diversity of interests shown through research in the wide variety of problems on which work has been reported (Pareek, 1980). Many restricted and specialized areas have emerged in the field of counseling and therapy. Indigenous approaches, especially that of Yoga, have received scientific scrutiny uncovering the scientific principles underlying the phenomenon. Yoga seems to be beneficial in providing relief for disturbed conditions, and in enhancing human happiness (Murthy, 1980). Psychology is expected to offer conceptual and intervention insights and to be socially relevant. Indian psychologists have made considerable and valuable contributions in different areas as noted in two major surveys of psychology in India (Mitra, 1972; Pareek, 1980; Raina, 1984). However, much remains to be done in the specific area of school psychology and psychological services.

Problems

In many countries, psychology is a distinct and defined specialty for the practice of psychology. However, many and diverse topics are pertinent to the practice of psychology in the schools. Indeed, school psychology cuts across and impinges on other important psychological fields including clinical, counseling, developmental, learning, and educational psychology (Kratochwill, 1981). Unfortunately, this is not true for India and many other developing countries. Teacher-training programs place special emphasis on educational psychology without realizing that teachers seemingly make little use of this knowledge in their professional work. Most of the knowledge of psychology that is imparted to them seemingly remains on a verbal level and is soon forgotten. Teachers develop few skills and attitudes that enable them to function in their professional settings as psychologists as well as teachers. Unfortunately, the need for school psychologists is not clear. The teaching of educational psychology is generally believed to be sufficient to enable teachers to understand and to solve problems associated with learning and mental health. This notion needs to be changed and a strong case made for a distinct and specialized field of school psychology that also could involve the types of practices found in other countries.

In India and many other developing countries, "counseling has not yet developed as a profession; therefore, the counselors and educators often do not appreciate the importance of the counselor's position in a school set-up" (Pasricha, 1976, p. 283). Despite the fact that there are professional school psychologists and guidance personnel in almost all states, persons of high caliber generally have not been attracted to these areas as a profession because of lack of job prospects and remuneration (Rath, 1979).

The status of tests and measurements is another problem that has hindered the development of school psychology in India. "The subject is replete with instances of what is characterized as 'psychometric borrowings,' and it is not surprising that many tests and tools adopted from the West are meaningless and irrevelant to our cultural context. This phenomenon has been ridiculed as a plain case of adoptology" (Rath, 1979). Many tests of questionable value have flooded the market. Concerned by this, the Indian Psychological Association has appointed a Test Commission to screen tests and provide certificates of merit (Status of Psychology in Indian Universities, 1982). Researchers and test-users have not been fully aware of problems in using tests on pre-literate and unsophisticated populations, of forging new items to suit the Indian population, and of the need to develop new testing techniques and strategies that are culturally more appropriate. Psychometricians with strong backgrounds in measurement, cognitive, and behavioral psychology are needed to develop tests and tools suitable to our culture.

Research in psychology, particularly in school psychology, has remained "handicapped because the investigators were not sufficiently innovative in developing techniques suited to the study of problems peculiar to this country" (Pasricha, 1976, p. 321). After surveying research in the area, Pasricha pointed out that, although research is basic to the development of guidance and counseling, it remains unorganized in India.

The programs currently organized are not only limited in scope but remain largely uncoordinated. At times one finds duplication of efforts and also neglect of a broad spectrum of programs that are urgent. The programs do not prepare professionals who would fulfill the roles of the school psychologists as proposed by the Thayer Conference (Cutts, 1955).

FUTURE DEVELOPMENTS

A recent government of India document (Report of the Working Group on Education and Culture, 1980) envisages education in terms of the formal system of teaching—learning aimed at certain minimum standards of achievement as well as the preparation of individuals to enable them to discover their talents, sharpen their abilities, realize their potentials, and contribute their best to the nation's development. Given these progressive attitudes toward education by the Indian government, and the growing awareness among psychologists about the need to provide psychological services in India, Indian school psychologists are in a strong position to advance their professional status as well as the mental health in India. The current governmental concern about vocational education should enhance the professional role of school psychologists. However, various efforts must occur to organize the profession. This requires sustained efforts to convince educational administrators and planners about the need for such a service so that broad-based and coordinated programs can be established. Persons interested in school psychology should work to establish their own professional society in order to facilitate the communication of professional information and to coordinate activities with interested agencies and organizations. Some well thought out suggestions have been made by the UGC Panel of Psychology (Rath, 1979) relating to professional objectives of psychology, reorientation of research, tests, and measurement.

Teacher education programs that attend to the teacher training in special education also are needed. Such programs must be broad based in recognition of the wide scope of special education. For an effective role, and a high level of competence, professional psychologists including school psychologists cannot escape the responsibility of building linkages with allied sciences. The building of these linkages is possible when agencies attain a level of maturity so as not to be thwarted by the initial threat and feeling of insecurity in the absence of a clear identity (Pareek, 1980).

In countries like India that have much diversity, complexity, disparity, and disability, school psychological services have a bright future. Indeed, what was said only a few years ago still has much merit (Bardon, 1976):

> The years ahead are full of promise for improved service to children and to schools. It is believed that there is much to be gained by continuing analysis of the specialty of school psychology, which perhaps more than any other specialty in psychology mirrors the times and serves as an indicator of what may be ahead for all of professional psychology. (p. 790)

REFERENCES

Bardon, J. I. (1976). The state of the art (and science) of school psychology. *American Psychologist, 31*, 785–791.

Buch, M. B. (1972). Educational psychology. In S. K. Mitra (Ed.), *A survey of research in psychology*, (pp. 80–125). Bombay: Popular Prakashan.

Cutts, N. (Ed.). (1955). *School psychologist at mid-century*. Washington, DC: American Psychological Association.

Educational systems in the states and union territories in India. (1982). New Delhi: National Council of Educational Research and Training.

Fourth all-India educational survey (1980). New Delhi: National Council of Educational Research and Training.

Kamat, A. R. (1980). Educational policy in India: Critical issues. *Sociological Bulletin, 29,* 137–206.

Kratochwill, T. R. (Ed.). (1981). *Advances in school psychology.* Hillsdale, NJ: Lawrence Erlbaum Associates.

Mehta, D. S. (1983). *Handbook of disabled in India.* New Delhi: Allied Publishers.

Mehta, P. H. (1983). Guidance services in India towards the end of 1981: Report of a status survey. *Indian Educational Review, 18,* 1–16.

Mitra, S. K. (1972). *A survey of research in psychology.* Bombay: Popular Prakashan.

Murthy, H. N. (1980). Counselling and therapy. In U. Pareek (Ed.), *A survey of research in psychology,* (pp. 333–371). Bombay: Popular Prakashan.

Odgers, J. C. (1962). *State bureaus of educational and vocational guidance: A survey report.* New Delhi: National Council of Educational Research and Training.

Paliwal, T. R. (1977). Psychology in the schools in India. In D. Catterall (Ed.), *Psychology in the schools in international perspective* (pp. 168–182). Columbus, OH: International School Psychology.

Pareek, U. (Ed.). (1980). *A survey of research in psychology.* Bombay: Popular Prakashan.

Pasricha, P. (1976). *Guidance and counselling in Indian education.* New Delhi: National Council of Educational Research and Training.

Raina, M. K. (1984). Psychology in India. In R. J. Corsini (Ed.), *Encyclopedia of psychology* (pp. 133–135). New York: Wiley.

Ramalingaswami, P. (1978). Psychology in India: A challenge and an opportunity. *Indian Educational Review, 13,* 22–42.

Rath, R. (1979). *Reorientation of teaching and research in psychology in the Indian universities.* New Delhi: University Grants Commission.

Report of the secondary education commission (1952–53). (1954). Delhi: Ministry of Education and Culture.

Report of the working group on education and culture (1980–85). (1980). New Delhi: Ministry of Education and Culture.

Singh, L. C. (1983). *Third national survey of secondary teacher education in India.* New Delhi: National Council of Educational Research and Training.

Sixth five year plan. (1980–1985). New Delhi: Planning Commission.

Status of psychology in Indian universities. (1982). New Delhi: University Grants Commission.

The curriculum for the ten-year school: A framework. (1975). New Delhi: National Council of Educational Research and Training.

Chapter Fifteen
School Psychology in the People's Republic of China

Joseph C. LaVoie
University of Nebraska at Omaha

To understand education and psychology in the People's Republic of China, one must have some information about the history of this country. The People's Republic of China came into being on October 1, 1949. Prior to 1949, Chinese educational philosophy contained a strong Confucian element along with some influence from Dewey. Yee (1973) noted that before 1949, psychology in China had a distinctly western influence, and the ideas of Dewey were subscribed to by a large number of psychologists. Dewey's concepts of an active learning process, the relatedness rather than the separateness of stimulus and response, and the view of mind as descriptive of problem solving (McDonald, 1964) were some of the ideas that Chinese students, who were educated in the United States during the period, came into contact with. The Confucian emphasis on morality and the virtues of kindness, uprightness, decorum, wisdom, and faithfulness provided basic precepts on which education was based. Perhaps the most important contribution of Confucius was his thinking about the effects of postnatal influences on mental development. Over 2,500 years ago, he proposed a relationship between nature and nurture. According to Liu (1982), Confucius suggested that people are alike because of nature, whereas their differences are the result of practice. This Confucian idea was developed further by scholars who followed him. In their refinement of Confucian thought, they recognized the contribution of innate factors to mental development, but they also emphasized that experience, in the form of education, contributed more to mental development than innate factors (Liu, 1982).

The most notable Dewey influence was his delineation of pupil aims, teacher aims, and the means to be used to acquire the teacher aims (McDonald, 1964). Equally important was the proposition that pupil interest and discipline were connected, and the view that the pupil was an active learner (i.e., the child is motivated to solve his or her own problems). Thus, intellectual problem solving by the child was seen as preparation for life. This assumption by Dewey fit with the Confucian principles, which probably accounts for their coexistence in Chinese educational philosophy.

For a number of years after its inception, the People's Republic of China was dependent on the Soviet Union for economic and military aid. The Soviet model of centralized authority was used in planning (Europa Yearbook, 1986). The Russian influence infused into the educational system as well, and the Russian system of education became the model for China. The goal of Chinese education, like that of the Russians, seems geared toward what Bronfenbrenner (1970) labeled "collective upbringing." Thus, you find a highly structured preschool/kindergarten, with emphasis on regimentation and skill acquisition. This format continues throughout the school years as the student remains with his or her classmates and teachers come to the students' classroom to teach the lesson, rather than the converse as occurs in the junior and senior high schools in the United States. Children in China, like their Russian counterparts, start primary school at age 7, and continue on through middle school (junior and senior high school). Also like the Russians, teachers are viewed as friends, and the emphasis in the two systems is on character education. Both societies have "Young Pioneers," a communist youth organization intimately tied to the school. The use of student monitors in the classroom, and the implementation of social criticism from one's peers, as a control process, are similar in both countries.

Although an ideological split between the two countries occurred in 1960, the vestiges of the Russian model of education are still present from preschool programs through the university curriculum. Mao intended to develop a distinctive form of Chinese socialism (Europa Yearbook, 1986), but this distinctiveness failed to materialize. Similarly, Deng Xiaping's economic reforms have been blocked from influencing the political ideology of the country. Western-style democratic change, labeled *bourgeois liberalization*, has been quickly stifled. Note that the recent demands for democratic change came from certain elements in higher education. Although the number of western-trained educators in the People's Republic of China is increasing, their ability to infuse a western style of education may be blocked.

The history of psychology in the People's Republic of China follows a similar trend to that of education. Zhang Houcan (1985) noted that from 1849–1949 psychology in China was largely a translation of western psychology. After the establishment of the People's Republic in 1949, Pavlovian conditioning was adopted as the psychological model and Russian textbooks were used. Marxism, Leninism, and Mao's teachings were assimilated into the model to create a Chinese system of psychology. But psychology was totally abandoned during the Cultural Revolution because it was considered a "pseudoscience," and contrary to Marxist–Leninist thought. Psychology reappeared after the Cultural Revolution (1966–1976) and the field is rapidly expanding today. Psychology departments can be found in the major universities, and psychology faculty are located in departments of education in normal universities. Both educational and developmental psychologists can be found among the faculty in these departments of education, but as yet there is not a defined field of school psychology.

THE EDUCATIONAL SYSTEM

Article 44 of the revised constitution of the People's Republic of China states: "Citizens of the PRC have the right and obligation to receive education. The state promotes the all-around development—moral, intellectual, physical—of young people and children" (McCowen & McLean, 1984, p. 123). The 1985 statistics (Europa Yearbook, 1986) show that 14.8 million children received some type of preschool/kindergarten (i.e., 3- to 6-year-olds) education, 133.7 million children were enrolled in a primary school, and 47.06 million attended some type of middle school (similar to the junior and senior high school in the United States). These students were instructed by a corps of about 10 million teachers, resulting in student–teacher ratios of 27:1 in preschool, 25:1 in primary school, and 16.4:1 in the middle school.

The goal of education is to foster intellectual, esthetic, moral, and social development in the child. For the Chinese, society and self are inextricably bound. Humans are infinitely malleable; therefore, the philosophy guiding education is that of direct positive influence. Imitation and modeling are important teaching methods. The role of the teacher is to eliminate ignorance and to provide a nurturing climate. Excellence in education is measured in terms of the speed with which children learn. Children are taught to understand and accept correct social roles, and to behave appropriately from a Marxist–Leninist perspective. Behaving appropriately is a function of acquiring the culturally specified feelings or affective development, and this acquisition is the product of moral education (Lee, 1987). Note the emphasis on moral education, and the similarity to the Russian model of education that was discussed earlier. The objective of moral education is obedience and proper behavior. A primary goal of education then, is to mold the child into a useful individual—one who contributes to the culture.

These goals of education are transformed into curriculum. At the preschool/kindergarten level the child receives instruction in hygiene, sports, ethics (moral education), language, general knowledge (understanding of people and environment that helps to develop attention span, memory, imagination, and problem solving), arithmetic, music, and art (State Education Commission, 1986b). At the primary level, the curriculum consists of Chinese, mathematics, foreign language (usually English), ethics/moral education, social science, natural science, fine arts, and physical education. Chinese lessons require up to 40% of the total class periods, with an additional 25% taken up with mathematics (State Education Commission, 1986c). The same general type of curriculum is offered for middle-school students. Political education, based on Marxist–Leninist philosophy, is required so that all middle-school students acquire a socialist consciousness and culture (State Education Commission, 1986d). Not all primary-school graduates attend a secondary school. In 1985, about 70% of primary students were admitted into junior middle school, and 46% of these graduates were admitted to senior middle school (State Education Commission, 1986d).

According to the State Education Commission of the People's Republic of China (1986a), 96% of the school-age children (7 years of age or older) were attending school in 1985. A primary education is compulsory in one third of the counties in the People's Republic, and a compulsory ninth-grade education is projected for 1990. The Ministry of Education is responsible for pedagogy at the national level. The ministry delegates some of this authority to bureaus of education at the provincial (state) level, and these in turn delegate some responsibility to bureaus of education at the county and city–town levels. Standardized textbooks are produced by the Ministry of Education, and there is an attempt to standardize education as much as possible. However, schools and teachers are encouraged to use supplementary materials. The Ministry of Education also has an Institute for Research in Educational Sciences that conducts research in the areas of educational and developmental psychology (Liu, 1982).

Scope of Services

In the United States, there is an interface between school psychology and special education. Although there may be some disagreement about the role and functions of school psychologists, for most practitioners the role consists of assessment, diagnosis-prescription, consultation, and problem solving (Reynolds, Gutkin, Elliott, & Witt, 1984). There is no defined area of school psychology in the People's Republic of China, although school psychologists from Hong Kong have provided some services and training for psychologists in South China.

Assessment/Diagnosis-Prescription

Educational psychology is a recognized field and some educational psychologists are involved indirectly with assessment/diagnosis-prescription in the form of curriculum development and entrance examinations. Other types of assessment are largely absent. Zhang (1985) reported that psychologists are becoming aware of the importance of psychological testing for the detection of learning disabilities. Several western tests, such as the WISC–R, WAIS, Stanford–Binet, Bender–Gestalt, Draw-a-Man, California Psychological Inventory, MMPI, and the Embedded Figures Test have been translated into Chinese (Liu, 1982; Zhang, 1985). But the cultural bias in these tests is recognized, so assessment instruments for ages 0–6 years are now being developed to provide early detection of learning disabilities (Zhang, 1985). One such instrument is the Peabody Picture Vocabulary Test that has been revised by Gong and Gua (1984). Their re-standardization of the test was done with 3½- to 8-year-olds, and it resulted in appropriate scales for MA, IQ, and percentiles. This assessment device has now been used in screening more than 5,000 young children for learning disabilities. Adaptive behavior-rating scales or similar types of instruments have not been used. The need for these types of instruments is not recognized, although such information may be useful in designing training programs for developmentally delayed children.

School psychology roles are partly assumed by medical doctors in pediatrics clinics. These clinics, located in hospitals, serve children from birth to 4 years. The children are brought to the clinics by their parents on a regular basis for health checks. If some type of developmental problem is detected during the regular health screening, the pediatrician may elect to use a test such as the Denver Developmental Screening Test. Most often, the problem is detected initially by the parent who notices that the child is different in some way. The parent then takes the child to the doctor because he or she thinks that the doctor can prescribe treatment (usually medicine) that will correct the child's condition. Among the tenets in the belief system of the Chinese is a very strong faith in the healing power of medicine (Clayre, 1985).

This belief in the power of medication to correct an existing condition is exemplified in the case of a family in which both parents were college teachers. When their second child was about 1 year of age, they noticed that he was displaying some very strange behaviors, such as rocking, pulling his hair, hitting his head against the wall, and that he was mute. They took this child to several pediatric clinics to seek a remedy for this peculiar behavior pattern. Over the next 4 years they spent 1,000 Chinese dollars (U.S. $270) seeking a cure, but none could be found. During my stay at this university, I was asked to visit the child who was now 5 years old. After observing the child for a brief time, it became evident that he was autistic. Unfortunately, there was no available facility to place the child in, so I arranged outpatient care for him at a local psychiatric clinic. The clinic staff did not recognize the autism, although after I explained it, they were able to find some written descriptions. The chief psychiatrist at the clinic placed the child on a tranquilizer-type drug to reduce his hyperactive and self-destructive behavior. The medication made the child more manageable for his parents, and over time they were able to toilet train him, but his maternal grandfather thought that the child was too lethargic, so the parents stopped administering the drug, and the child was taken to a small village where the grandfather lived. In this setting, there were no available services, so the child will continue in his infantile state.

Modification of IQ. There is much interest among Chinese researchers in improving existing mental abilities, specifically intelligence and memory. One such attempt has been reported by Wu (1985), who proposed that increasing the efficiency of brain activity through mental exercise should increase IQ scores in children. To test this hypothesis, Wu had students in Grades 7 and 12 complete a problem solution, within 10 minutes, each morning for a period of 64 school days. Another group of the 7th-grade students were used as a control. Wu reported that posttests revealed an increase of five IQ points for the 7th-grade students and six IQ points for the 12th-grade students who were exposed to the daily problem-solving experience. These results, Wu argued, demonstrate that children's IQ can be improved through training.

Consultation and Problem Solving

The absence of psychological assessment and applied psychologists in the schools makes the detection of learning disabilities difficult, although in the more severe cases parents and teachers are aware that the child is different in some way.

Visual/Hearing Impaired. Children who are physically impaired (blind or deaf) are more easily detected, and therefore more educational opportunities are available for them because they are a salient subpopulation. For example, Armfield (1985) published a study in which he compared normal versus hearing-impaired Chinese students using the Raven Matrices Test. He found that the hearing-impaired scored consistently lower than similar aged groups of normal hearing children.

Most of the 330 special education schools, with a total enrollment of 39,684 students (State Education Commission, 1986e) and a student–teacher ratio of 6:6:1, serve the visual/hearing impaired. The curriculum for these special education students is the same as that for normal students, with some additions. Schools for the blind stress music to increase the student's appreciation for life (State Education Commission, 1986e). Schools for the deaf stress vocal training to develop the child's ability to speak and lip-read, as well as sports and exercise to develop and coordinate physical strength (State Education Commission, 1986e). Children enter these schools at 8 years of age and receive the typical 5-year primary curriculum over a period of 8 years (Armfield & Lu, 1983). Vocational and technical skill training is provided to prepare the student for a useful role in society. For example, at schools for the deaf, boys recieve training in woodworking and girls learn how to sew. Following graduation, students enter regular factories or factories for the blind and deaf.

Mentally Retarded. Certain groups of children, particularly those with some type of learning disability, are receiving little or no special training, and those who receive some special education are not being trained according to their assessed needs. Children with mild, moderate, and severe learning disabilities are often found in the same classroom with normally functioning children, with little or no attempt at individualized instruction. To illustrate this situation, I met a 12-year-old girl who was placed with her fifth-grade class even though she could not read or write. She would spend the entire day in school sitting at a desk staring at the other children. My assessment found her to be moderately mentally retarded. This girl is now attending a newly opened special education class in a school operated by volunteers.

Only four schools for the mentally retarded plus 160 classes associated with primary schools were available in 1985 (State Education Commission, 1986e). The curriculum at these schools consists of the usual primary school classes. According to Armfield and Lu (1983), students are expected to achieve at about 50% of the level expected for the normal student. Lower functioning children are given more training in vocational and self-help skills, with less emphasis placed on academic skills (Armfield & Lu, 1983). Music, sports, and games are provided to help students develop attention (State Education Commission, 1986e). In several cities, various types of organizations have organized classes for the mentally retarded. These schools are run by volunteers. One such school in Guangzhou (South China) is supported by a women's group. Special education teachers and school psychologists from Hong Kong have been providing some teacher training and student assessment at this school. At the present time there is one school in the entire nation for training special education teachers (Piao, 1981; State Education Commission, 1986e).

Gifted Children. There is some attempt to provide special services for gifted children, if higher status middle schools that provide more academically challenging programs are considered. Examinations are used to identify these children at the sixth and eighth grades, so that they can attend special "key" middle schools, at least one of which is located in each province. These key middle schools will have the more academically capable students who therefore are more likely to obtain higher scores on entrance examinations for the prestigious universities. Liu (1982) reported that 15 districts have special programs for extremely gifted children who are labeled *super-normal.*

Administration

The absence of a recognized field of school psychology prevents any organized attempt to provide psychological services for children. Education is controlled nationally, although lower units of government also have some authority, and all units of government contribute to the cost of supporting education. Any psychological services that might be available would have to be obtained from psychologists at universities or medical clinics at hospitals. Thus, the available psychological services have no connection with the schools whose students they might serve. Parents who seek medical/psychological services for their children have to pay a fee.

Administration and supervision of programs for the visual and hearing impaired, as well as those who are mentally retarded, are carried out by a Special

Education Bureau in the Ministry of Education at the national level. This bureau is responsible for finances, teaching materials, and supervision of the programs. Volunteer schools for the mentally retarded are financed and supervised by citizen committees.

Training Facilities

Departments of psychology are located in major universities, such as Beijing University, Beijing Normal University, Hangzhou University, and East-China Normal University at Shanghai. There is at least one normal (teacher-training) university in each province or city, and these universities have either a department of psychology or a psychology faculty in the department of education. The theoretical orientation followed in most departments is the Russian model, so students receive training in Pavlovian conditioning and the Luria–Vygotsky model.

According to LaVoie's (1987) report on undergraduate education in psychology, theories receive major attention, but neural and biochemical bases of memory and learning, and some aspects of perception are discussed. Liu (1982) contended that the goal of psychology is to integrate theory with practice. At normal universities, students are instructed in child development and a course in educational psychology is offered. No training is given in tests and measurement or assessment. Therefore, those students with training in psychology who might be available to work as applied psychologists in the school have no training in those areas that are so critical to their functioning. Students in an educational psychology course might receive some experience in observing kindergarten children on the playground and in class, and they may serve as an assistant teacher in a primary classroom. The typical undergraduate program is 4 years, and an additional 3 years is required for a master's degree. Graduate training in psychology does not seem to differ greatly from the undergraduate curriculum. A few doctoral programs in psychology are being opened. The training in these programs seems to be quite individualized, but again the training models the undergraduate program.

A need for training in applied psychology is recognized (Zhang, 1985), but as yet no programs have been developed. There is one normal university that trains special education teachers for the fields of visual/hearing impaired, and mental retardation (Piao, 1981). A type of psychoeducational clinic has been opened in a few universities. One such clinic can be found at South China Normal University in Guangzhou. Children with various types of suspected learning problems can be referred to the clinic. Assessment and diagnosis is done by psychologists at the clinic, and medical personnel are available for consultation. Some type of remedial program, such as mental exercises, may be developed for the child. Because these clinics are just starting, their role and mission are not well defined.

Contributions

Given the absence of any recognized school psychologists, as we know them, what types of support services are available to schools and families? Some of these services have already been identified, but they will be mentioned again in this section. Three types of services can be used. Pediatric clinics at hospitals provide services to the families and school for the young child through kindergarten. A few psychoeducational clinics at universities are able to diagnose certain types of learning disabilities and to prescribe some type of remedial program for these children. Perhaps the major service agent is the classroom teacher. Although they have no training in applied psychology, teachers in most schools function in a clinical practitioner role. When teachers observe that a child is experiencing some learning difficulty, they assign special exercises to motivate the student to achieve at the level of his or her classmates. Parent conferences are commonly held, and teachers often visit the families of problem students to determine what familial or environmental influences might be interfering with the student's mastery of the required educational materials. Students experiencing learning problems are frequently kept after school to complete extra assignments and to receive remedial help from the teacher (Armfield & Lu, 1983).

Special Problems

It is evident from this review that the major problem with school psychology in the People's Republic of China is that this discipline does not exist. Therefore, applied psychologists are not available to school systems. This void in psychological services is filled in part by pediatricians and other medical personnel, including nurses at pediatric clinics. A few educational psychologists at newly opened psychoeducational clinics at normal universities provide some services, but the most likely practitioners are teachers who are not trained for the role.

The psychology profession in the People's Republic is aware of the urgent need for applied psychologists in the schools, but there is a tremendous need for psychologists in every specialty area. Few clinical psychologists are available in psychiatric clinics to serve the mental health needs of the country whose population is in excess of one billion people. Psychology faculties at universities lack well-trained academic psychologists. Much of the current problem can be traced to the 10-year Cultural Revolution during which time psychology was banned from the university curriculum because it was contrary to Marxist–Leninist thought (LaVoie, 1987). For this 10-year period, psychology was not taught on university campuses and all research projects were terminated. The impact of this drastic action is beyond comprehension.

The educational system in the People's Republic faces other problems as well. Although several western assessment measures, such as the various tests alluded to previously, have been translated into Chinese, the cultural bias and inappropriateness of these measures for Chinese children are recognized. But only limited resources are now being allocated to developing appropriate measures. Much of the available test development effort has been channeled toward improving the admission examination procedure, because the Chinese use examinations to determine admission to certain middle schools and to universities.

A third problem is the lack of qualified psychology faculty at universities to develop a training program in school psychology. To my knowledge, there are no trained school psychologists to serve as trainers for other psychologists. There are several school psychologists in Hong Kong who could serve as adjunct faculty at selected universities to train school psychologists, but no attempts have been made to initiate such a cooperative training program.

FUTURE TRENDS

In all likelihood, school psychology or a form of applied psychology will emerge in the educational system of the People's Republic of China. The need for this discipline is recognized, and some progress is being made. The introduction of psychoeducational clinics at some normal universities, and the consultation services of school psychologists from Hong Kong are likely catalysts for a major change. At the present time, the People's Republic is undertaking a massive overhaul of its educational system. What results from this effort will set the direction for educational modernization for the foreseeable future. What role, if any, psychological services play in the education system of the future will be determined by the policy that is now undergoing a review. The need for psychological services in the schools is recognized by leaders in the field of psychology, but educational policy is made by political, not educational, authorities.

ACKNOWLEDGMENTS

I would like to acknowledge the contribution of Professor Aaron Armfield in providing me with various draft papers and other reports of his work while at South China Normal University. The sponsorship of my alternative work assignment at South China Normal University by the International Studies Program at the University of Nebraska at Omaha is appreciated. Finally, I want to express my heartfelt gratitude to my colleagues and friends at South China Normal University for helping me to see and understand China through "Chinese eyes."

REFERENCES

Armfield, A. (1985). A comparison of high ability and low ability pupil scores on Raven's Standard Progressive Matrices at the primary school attached to South China Normal University and the

Guangzhou School for the Deaf/Mute, Guangzhou, People's Republic of China. *School Psychology International, 6*, 24–29.

Armfield, A., & Lu, T. Z. (1983). *Education for all children: A challenge for China*. Unpublished paper, University of Nebraska at Omaha.

Bronfenbrenner, U. (1970). *Two worlds of childhood: U.S. and U.S.S.R.* New York: Russell Sage Foundation.

Clayre, A. (1985). *The heart of the dragon*. Boston: Houghton Mifflin.

Gong, Z., & Gua, D. (1984). An intelligence screening test for preschool and primary school children—Picture Vocabulary Test. *Acta Psychologica Sinica, 16*, 393–401.

Europa Yearbook (Vol. 1). (1986). London: Europa Publications.

LaVoie, J. C. (1987). Undergraduate education in psychology in the People's Republic of China. *APA Monitor, 18*, 38.

Lee, L. C. (1987, April). *China's integrated approach to child care and socialization*. Paper presented at the biennial meeting of the Society for Research in Child Development, Baltimore, MD.

Liu, F. (1982). Developmental psychology in China. *International Journal of Behavioral Development, 5*, 391–411.

McCowen, R. C., & McLean, M. (1984). *International handbook of education systems* (Vol. 3). New York: Wiley.

McDonald, F. J. (1964). The influence of learning theories on education. *The sixty-third yearbook of the National Society for the Study of Education*. Chicago: University of Chicago Press.

Piao, Y. X. (1981). Special children and their mental development. *Acta Psychologica Sinica, 4*, 394–400.

Reynolds, C. R., Gutkin, T. B., Elliott, S. N., & Witt, J. C. (1984). *School psychology: Essentials of theory*. New York: Wiley.

State Education Commission of People's Republic of China (1986a). *Recent achievements in China's education system*. Beijing: Author.

State Education Commission of the People's Republic of China. (1986b). *Preschool education in China*. Beijing: Author.

State Education Commission of the People's Republic of China. (1986c). *China's primary school education*. Beijing: Author.

State Education Commission of the People's Republic of China. (1986d). *Secondary school education in China*. Beijing: Author.

State Education Commission of the People's Republic of China. (1986e). *Education for the handicapped in China*. Beijing: Author.

Wu, T. (1985). A second experiment on the method of raising the level of children's intelligence. *Acta Psychologica Sinica, 17*, 38–45.

Yee, A. H. (1973). Psychology in China bows to the cultural revolution. *APA Monitor, 4*, 1.

Zhang, H. C. (1985). *Psychology in China: Then and now*. Unpublished manuscript, Beijing Normal University.

Chapter Sixteen
School Psychology in Hong Kong

Grace Y. M. Yung, Winnie C. Y. Lau, David C. Kwok
Education Department of Hong Kong

Cho-yee To
School of Education, The Chinese University of Hong Kong

EDUCATION IN HONG KONG

Hong Kong has a land mass of 1,068 square kilometers (412 square miles) and is one of the most densely populated places in the world. In 1985, the population was estimated at 5,466,900. It was also estimated that 98% of the population were of Chinese origin. Demographic data also revealed that 25% of the population were students reflecting an enrollment of 1,369,741 pupils in different categories of registered schools. The total expenditure for education in the fiscal year 1985–1986 amounted to HK$7,806 million (HK$910.8 million in capital expenditure and HK$6895.18 million in recurrent expenditure) or U.S.$1000.84 million. This expenditure in effect amounted to 17% of the government's budget (Knight, 1986).

In 1985, there were 737 primary schools and 424 secondary schools in Hong Kong (Statistics Section, Education Department, Hong Kong Government, 1986). These schools may be classified into three types according to their source of support (i.e., government schools, aided school[a] and private schools). The majority of schools in Hong Kong are aided schools. Primary education was made free in all government and aided schools in September 1971 (Knight, 1986). The provision of 9 years of free and compulsory education was introduced in September 1978. Children start primary school at the age of 6 and remain in school until the age of 15 or until they complete junior secondary (high) school.

In the primary schools, a broad-based curriculum offering a balance of academic and cultural subjects is presented. Entry to primary schools is arranged by the Primary One Admission System (i.e., a centralized scheme allocating children to places in schools within their districts and taking into account parental

[a]aided schools: schools managed by sponsoring bodies (e.g., missionary schools, fraternal associations, charity organizations) but with full funding from the government.

preference). Primary school graduates receive junior secondary (high) school billets through the Secondary School Places Allocation System. This system places students in junior secondary (high) schools on the basis of students' internal performance, scaled by a centrally administered Academic Aptitude Test, as well as parental preference.

At the secondary level, four types of schools are apparent. More specifically, students may enroll in Anglo-Chinese grammar schools, Chinese middle schools, technical schools or prevocational schools. The Anglo-Chinese grammar schools and Chinese middle schools differ mainly in the medium of instruction. Both offer a 5-year secondary program that consists of a broad range of academic and cultural subjects culminating in candidacy for the Hong Kong Certificate of Education Examination (HKCEE). Students with satisfactory HKCEE grades may enroll in a 2-year course of study. Graduates of this program may sit for the Hong Kong Advanced Level Examination (HKALE) and students with satisfactory HKALE grades may enroll in the University of Hong Kong or tertiary courses. A number of Anglo-Chinese and Chinese middle schools offer a 1-year course of study leading to candidacy for the Hong Kong Higher Level Examination that is used to screen applicants to the Chinese University of Hong Kong. Secondary technical schools also provide preparation for the HKCEE. Qualified candidates may continue their studies at technical institutes, the Hong Kong Polytechnic or the City Polytechnic of Hong Kong.

General teacher-education programs are provided by three colleges of education under the supervision of the Education Department of Hong Kong. These colleges offer 2-year or 3-year full-time teacher-training programs for students with satisfactory HKALE or HKCEE results. These programs are designed to prepare students for teaching careers in primary or junior secondary (high) schools. Teacher-training colleges also offer a 2-year part-time in-service program for special education teachers. Postgraduate professional programs leading to the certificate or diploma of education are offered by the University of Hong Kong as well as the Chinese University of Hong Kong for university graduates who wish to pursue a secondary teaching career. Technical teacher training is provided by the Hong Kong Technical Teachers College.

With respect to special education, a flexible range of provisions are in effect. More specifically, on-site remedial support services are provided on a withdrawal basis during school hours. A peripatetic teaching service is available within the regular schools for exceptional students. Moreover, off-site support services for exceptional children are provided at Resource Teaching Centres and Adjustment Units.

SCHOOL PSYCHOLOGY

Scope of Services

Psychological services are administered by the Department of Education through the Psychological Services Unit. The unit currently provides services for a wide range of students. More specifically, services are provided on a regular basis at two special education centers. Services in this context involve assessment, intervention, and staff training. Educational psychologists also serve on preschool stimulation programs for the mildly retarded. Viewed along these lines, educational psychologists provide recommendations on program development and instructional procedures. They also conduct psychoeducational testing.

Psychological services are also provided by practitioners who serve on the staff of Adjustment Units. Efforts are also directed toward the early indentification and treatment of elementary school students with intellectual or behavioral problems. Teachers assess elementary school children against criteria that are set by the Educational Department. Educational psychologists subsequently provide more formal assessments in those instances involving considerable variation from developmental norms and remediation is provided as needed.

Direct intervention services are available for older students at special education centers. These centers operate on a cost-free open referral system that is heavily utilized. Services involving assessment and intervention are regularly provided. Back-up services are also provided by special education centers to front-line workers (e.g., student guidance officers, guidance teachers, and school social workers) who work within the educational system. Counseling services are provided by student guidance officers (i.e., primary school teachers who have completed a 6-month preservice student guidance training program). These officers strive to organize prevention programs, manage children with mild learning or behavioral problems, provide parental guidance, and refer more severe cases to appropriate mental health agencies.

Viewed from a different perspective, the educational psychologists who serve on the staff of the Psychological Services Unit have been actively engaged in a number of applied research projects. For example, the WISC–R was translated for use with Cantonese-speaking Chinese children in 1978 and further adapted to minimize cultural bias. The instrument was subsequently validated as based on the performance of 1,100 Cantonese-speaking children between the ages of 5 and 15 and endemic norms were established. Investigations subsequently established the factor component and construct validity of the scale (Lee, Priester, & Yung, 1986). In a similar vein, the administration instructions of the Raven's Progressive Matrices and Bender Gestalt Test were translated and the instruments were normed on local samples. Research is currently being directed toward the development and validation of endemic measures for diagnosing specific learning disabilities.

The Psychological Services Unit is also engaged in a number of training activities. Students from the Educational Psychology Program at the University of Hong Kong, social work students from the Chinese University of Hong Kong and the University of Hong Kong as well as students from post-secondary institutions regularly receive supervised field training from the staff of the Psychological Services Unit. Lectures, workshops, and formal seminars are also provided for Colleges of Education, parents, guidance counselors, and social workers.

Administration

The cost of operating the Psychological Services Unit is borne by the government and services are delivered without charge. In a similar vein, the services of the special education centers and adjustment units are funded by the government. The Psychological Services Unit is directed by a principal educational psychologist who in turn is assisted by two senior educational psychologists. At the moment, the Psychological Services Unit employs 18 educational psychologists, 11 educational counselors and 9 psychologist assistants. All personnel are native Chinese who are fluent in Chinese and English.

Psychologists are free to practice their training once they receive a master's degree from a recognized institution. Although there is no legislation to regulate the practice of psychology in Hong Kong, the Hong Kong Psychological Society advises on the adequacy of professional entry level qualifications and strives to insure ethical conduct within the field.

Training Facilities

Approximately half of the educational psychologists in Hong Kong were trained at Universities in the United Kingdom, namely, University College London, the University of Manchester, and the University of Strathclyde. The rest were trained at the University of Hong Kong. In general, the curricula for these programs reflect a combination of courses in the areas of assessment, intervention, special education, instructional methods, consultation, child development, and research methods. A substantial portion of each program is devoted to providing supervised field experiences in divergent educational and clinical settings.

Contributions

One of the roles that the Government has entrusted to the profession involves serving as a child advocate. This involves acting for children in matters relating to their basic welfare and well-being. As the most readily available service to school children, it is possible to claim that the Psychological Services Unit has worked toward the promotion and maintenance of social adjustment of school children by insuring that their needs are met.

As part of the Education Department, the Psychological Services Unit is in a unique position to effect changes in the system of education and has influenced official policy as to the designated role of the profession. Using feedback from the field, the Psychological Services Unit has established additional mental health services such as the Secondary School Guidance Program and the Schools Support Scheme. These additional avenues of support have been instrumental in improving the scope and quality of pastoral care.

PROBLEMS AND FUTURE TRENDS

The rapid urbanization of new towns has created population centers in areas that were scarcely populated in the past. Crowded living environments, departures from traditional mores, and a higher percentage of working parents are presenting added demands on the schools. With this in mind it is not surprising to note that there is a prodigious demand for school psychology services and additional lines will have to be created within the Psychological Services Unit. It is also apparent that additional psychological tests will have to be developed in as much as foreign tests generally include culturally biased items and inadequate norms. As such, it is anticipated that more time, energy and funds will have to be devoted to test development in the future.

REFERENCES

Knight, B. (Ed.). (1986). *Hong Kong 1986—A review of 1985*. Hong Kong: Hong Kong Government Publications.

Lee, L. M., Priester, H. J., & Yung, Y. M. (1986). Factor Analysis of the Hong Kong Wechsler Intelligence Scale for Children (HK-WISC). *Educational Research Journal, 1*, 58–62.

Statistics Section, Education Department, Hong Kong Government. (1987). *Enrollment Summary September 1986*. Hong Kong: Hong Kong Government Publications.

Chapter Seventeen
School Psychology in Japan

Fujiro Shinagawa
Senzokugakuen University
Professor emeritus of Tokyo Gakugei University

Masahiro Kodama, Akira Manita
The Research Division of Consultation and School Psychology
School Education Center, The University of Tsukuba

There are no school psychologists in Japan as frequently observed in other countries (Kicklighter, 1976; Meacham, 1983; Saigh, 1984; Whittaker, 1982). There are neither psychologists employed by the school system nor any school psychological practitioners employed outside the schools.

Although there is not a vocation of school psychology, some school psychological services are provided. Many psychologists working outside the schools offer assistance in resolving psychological problems exhibited by school children. However, they have little impact on the Japanese school system. Knowledge of the status of Japanese school psychology requires an understanding of the conditions governing its educational system including its administrative characteristics.

Japanese schools usually require their teachers to engage in various kinds of activities for school children in addition to teaching (e.g., guidance, counseling, homeroom activity, clerical work). All staff members except clerical personnel are employed as instructional staff and hold teaching licenses. Other specialists including psychologists are not legally allowed to provide educational or psychological services as they lack the authority under Japan's educational codes. Thus, Japanese laws do not allow school psychologists as traditionally conceived in other countries to work in Japanese schools.

GENERAL FEATURES OF JAPANESE SCHOOL EDUCATION

After the war, drastic changes occurred in the Japanese educational system. In 1947, a new education system was inaugurated, promulgated by two important pieces of legislation: the Fundamental Law of Education and the School Education Law. A "multitrack" system that diversified education broadly into vocational and higher educational courses in the pre-war years was changed into a "single-track" system. A 6:3:3 system was created in which children are provided opportunities for a 6-year elementary education; 3 years lower secondary education (junior high school), and 3 years upper secondary education (high school). The first years are compulsory; all children ages 6 through 14 have equal educational opportunity according to the law.

Since the enactment of the Board of Education Law in 1948, every local government has its own board of education. Most elementary and lower secondary schools are administered by municipal boards of education in cities, towns, and villages. According to education statistics in 1983, fewer than 1% of elementary schools and 5% of lower secondary schools were privately administered (Statistical Abstract of Education, 1984). Almost 100% of Japan's children are enrolled at the elementary or secondary levels.

As of 1983, 94% of graduates of compulsory courses (i.e., Grades 1–9) were admitted into upper secondary schools. Those who wish to advance to this upper level must pass the entrance examination. Two types of school courses are offered: the general and the specialized. General courses provide students with general education needed to satisfy advancement into higher education (e.g., a college preparatory program). Specialized courses focus mainly on vocational education for those students who aspire toward a particular vocational area as their future occupation.

As of 1983, 70% of students were registered in general courses. Most of those schools offering the general courses (71%) are administered by prefectural boards of education. The others are privately (29%) and nationally (<1%) controlled by the central government.

Japan has been called a "degreeocratic society" (Galtung, 1971), an educational career-centered society. The Japanese society has a strong emphasis on providing programs for students who aspire to receive a higher education or to enter into prestigious universities. According to 1983 education statistics, more than 30% of high school graduates were registered at universities (male 27%, female 11%) and junior colleges (male 11%, female 22%). Most institutions of higher education in Japan are established and maintained privately; 72% of universities and 84% of junior colleges are privately administered. The enrollment rate of students at private institutions reaches 75% and more.

Prefectural governments are obliged to organize special education institutions for physically and mentally handicapped children who cannot be educated at ordinary elementary and secondary schools. The number of pupils enrolled at those schools was about 94,000 in 1982.

The Ministry of Education takes a role as a guiding and advisory agency for the administration of education. According to the guideline of the Ministry of Education, the curricular mode in ordinary education should employ a lecturing style. The students are grouped by age and their other developmental similarities. Because of their homogeneity, children either fail to move to the next grade or to drop out of the school during the compulsory courses. Class size and the numbers of teachers are arranged according to the kinds of schools. More than 70% of the elementary schools have 31 or fewer students per class, whereas there are 41-50 students per class in more than half of the secondary schools.

Japanese teachers are responsible for various school activities in addition to their teaching duties. Teachers at the elementary level teach all subjects and spend much of their school time managing both instructional and clerical duties for their students. Teachers at the secondary school level teach in their major field, and assume responsibility of their home class and administrative duties in the school (e.g., the advisor for the traffic safety training program may be expected to devise the school program to coordinate it with those in the community).

PSYCHOLOGICAL PROBLEMS OF SCHOOL CHILDREN

Japanese children display various behavioral problems. School refusal (i.e., school phobia), drop out, attempted suicide, home violence, school violence, and delinquency are some of the more frequent examples. The Ministry of Education reported in 1981 the rate of long-term absences among those refusing to attend school to be .2% in elementary schools and .6% in lower secondary schools.

Although the incidence of *home violence*, a term used to refer to children who display violence toward their parents, is unclear, the number of cases is thought to be considerable and is most frequently observed among youngsters in lower secondary schools. It often coexists with refusal to attend school or delinquency.

The Ministry of Education reported in 1982 the number of cases of school violence requiring police protection and commitment to be 1,803. In addition to these severe cases, the Ministry reported incidents of 10,000 or more offenders and about 5,000 victims, most of whom were teachers. School violence is a new phenomenon in Japan and draws much social attention. In 1982, 599 cases of child suicide were reported (White Papers of Japan, 1983). A tendency exists for suicide to occur at lower age levels, even in elementary school age.

Increases in juvenile delinquency also are noted. Increases were noted in juvenile offenses that are both minor (e.g., pilfering and theft of bicycles or school items), as well as major (violent crimes, speed gangs, and school violence). Also, the age for determining juvenile delinquency was lowered. Nearly 80% of these offenders are less than 17 years old. Common characteristics among juvenile delinquents are their psychological instability, discontentment with school life, alienation, hopelessness, and lack of self-control.

The Japanese culture highly respects education and excessively values academic development. This has resulted in severe and competitive entrance exams for the better schools. The competitive circumstances facilitate inadequate and inappropriate interpersonal relationships among pupils and between them and teachers. There is often a lack of mutual understanding and communication. These conditions tend to promote delinquency, inability to keep up with classroom studies, and mental illness. This unduly high emphasis on academic achievement causes fundamental problems in Japanese education.

SCHOOL PSYCHOLOGICAL ACTIVITIES

As previously indicated, Japan does not have school psychologists who exclusively provide psychological services in schools. Such services are provided by teachers, educational supervisors, psychologists, and other specialists and are provided in various institutions. We compared the roles of school psychologists in England and the United States (Meacham, 1983; Williams, 1971) and found functions common to Japan (Table 1) that can be classified into four categories as follows: school, department of education supervisor, psychoeducational clinic, and clinic or hospital.[1]

There are four independent roles of school psychology: (a) having direct contact with children; (b) educating or training of school staff; (c) planning, managing, and system designing; and (d) investigating and research. Thus, Japanese school psychology covers eight areas: psychological testing; interviews with pupils, teachers, and parents; therapeutic guidance and referral; case conferences; lectures for staff and parents; educational planning; investigating; and research. Not covered are areas of managing, screening, diagnosing, and evaluating.

Training Program

Most Japanese universities and colleges at undergraduate and graduate levels provide a number of psychological courses in which students are educated to be psychologists. However, none of the universities provides a school psychology course. Described here are the training programs in school psychology; they are directed mainly toward teachers.

Teachers in Japan have an obligation to provide various kinds of counseling for children. Some teachers who are called *guidance teachers* or *teacher counselors* are specially trained to consult with and counsel pupils as a part of a school's activities. These guidance teachers or teacher counselors also are engaged in counseling in community-based counseling provided through the psychoeducational centers found in each region. In addition, some of them serve in administrative leadership roles, formulating guidance, and consulting principles to be enacted

[1]School, department of educational supervisor and most of psychoeducational centers are controlled by local board of education. Most of psychoeducational clinics are attached to institutes and universities. In clinic or hospital (e.g., Child Guidance Clinic) controlled by the Ministry of Welfare and Home of Delinquency controlled by the Ministry of Justice are included.

TABLE 17.1
School Psychologist's Role Provided by Institutions

	INSTITUTION			
Psychologist's Role	*School*	*Dept. of Educational Supervisor*	*Psycho-educational clinic or center*	*Clinic or Hospital*
1. Psychological testing				
group	0		0	0
individual	0		0	0
2. Interview with pupils	0		0	0
3. Interview with teachers & parents	0	0	0	0
4. Therapeutic guidance & referral	0		0	0
5. Case conference	0		0	0
6. Lecture for staff		0	0	
7. Lecture for parents	0	0	0	0
8. Managing, supervising, system-designing				
9. Screening, diagnosis evaluation				
10. Educational planning	0	0		
11. Investigating, research	0	0	0	

Note: Circles mean the functional roles provided by institutions.

through educational supervisors who work in the Educational Committee of the local governments. Thus, teachers who are assigned as guidance teachers play a significant role in school psychology both inside and outside school.

Training programs for them can be classified into four sections: *Section 1*: study meetings within schools, and research and study meetings voluntarily organized outside of schools (e.g., National Organization of Psychoeducational Consultation); *Section 2*: study meetings organized by the educational committee of local governments; *Section 3*: short-term study programs in which teachers are sent to study school psychology from 2 months to 1 year at a university or a research institute; and *Section 4*: long-term study programs in which teachers chosen by each local government are enrolled into a graduate department of psychology in a national university of education for a 2-year master's education. They receive their normal salaries during the study period.

The training and educational programs for school psychologists in various institutions in Japan are briefly outlined here.

Among Japan's national universities, five or six (Fujiwara, 1984) provide graduate departments of education. They include clinic courses on school psychology in which students are trained in educational consultation in order to help participants manage school psychological problems when they return as teachers.

Several other departments in the university such as educational psychology, clinical psychology, education, and sociology also offer training and educational programs. These programs aim at educating specialists in each respective field and thus are not necessarily concerned with issues most central to school psychologists and educational consultants. These specialists extend their assistance to teachers when required.

In addition to those training and educational programs previously mentioned are some private training institutions concerned with school psychology. They promote the development of practical skills and technologies on psychological diagnosis, counseling, treatment, and social welfare.

History and Administration

The history of school psychology (Shinagawa, 1964) is briefly described here.

In 1917, the first psychoeducational clinic in Japan, The Institute of Child Culture, was established by a psychologist, Dr. R. Kubo, in Tokyo. After that, many centers or clinics were established: Otsuka Child Guidance Clinic at Tokyo (1919), the Osaka City Vocational Guidance Clinic (1920), the Tokyo City Child Guidance Clinic (1921), the Tokyo Kojimachi-ku Psychoeducational Clinic (1925). The Psychoeducational Clinic (1936) attached to Tokyo Bunrika University was the first institute at a national university in Japan. (The name of the university later was changed to the Tokyo University of Education and then renamed the University of Tsukuba). The current name of the clinic is The Research Division of Consultation and School Psychology, School Education Center, The University of Tsukaba. Child Guidance Clinics were established in 1948 in almost all prefectures and controlled by the Ministry of Welfare. Juvenile Retention and Classification Home and Family Court were established in 1948 in every prefecture, and controlled by the Ministry of Justice. Psychoeducational centers appeared in 1952 sponsored by Tokyo Kita-ku Education Association. The Psychoeducational Clinic attached to the Tanaka Institute for Educational Research began in 1953. The Board of Education of the Tokyo Municipal Government established in 1958 its Psychoeducational Clinic attached to the Tokyo Municipal Institute of Educational Research. This center serves as a major resource to many other psychoeducational centers located in each district (Ku) in the metropolitan area. This clinic is the only one in which psychologists are employed as regular staff members. In other centers, staff members are teachers and psychologists committed to their work on a part-time basis. Since 1958, a number of institutes have been established to conduct research and extend psychological services. Many universities and colleges have counseling centers and some have psychoeducational clinics. These university staffs offer consultation or counseling services. All public institutions such as psychoeducational centers or clinics controlled by the Board of Education provide free services to their clients. In private clinics, clients must pay for services according to the type of diagnosis or therapy.

FUTURE PROSPECTS

School psychology in Japan has not yet become an important part of its institutionalized education program. We have indicated that Japan has a particular educational administration that inhibits the development of school psychology. Some psychological services are offered but not enough to satisfy the need for professional school psychologists. Due to the lack of school psychologists, no one is responsible for planning mental health programs in the school or for advising school administrators and teachers on the curriculum and mental hygiene issues.

In view of the need to promote sound mental and psychological development among school children, school psychology hopefully will be incorporated into school system practices in the near future. The Japanese government plans to initiate a series of educational reforms. Seizing upon this opportunity, we have highly recommended that the government should institutionalize school psychology.

REFERENCES

K. Fujiwara (Ed.). (1984). *A study of psychoeducational consultation*. Tokyo, Japan: Kaneko-Shobou.

Galtung, J. (1971). Social structure, education structure and life long education: the case of Japan. In *Review of national policies for education: Japan*. Paris: OCED.

Kicklighter, R. H. (1976). School psychology in the U.S.: A quantitative survey. *Journal of School Psychology, 14*, 151–156.

Meacham, M. L. (1983). The development of school psychology in the state of Washington: a personal perspective. *Journal of School Psychology, 21*, 1–7.

Saigh, P. A. (1984). School psychology in Lebanon. *Journal of School Psychology, 22*(3), 233–238.

F. Shinagawa (Ed.). (1964). *School psychological consultation*. Tokyo, Japan: Nihon-Bunka-Kagaku-sha.

Statistical Abstract of Education, Science and Culture: 1983 edition. (1984). Tokyo, Japan: Research and Statistics Division Minister's Secretariat, Ministry of Education, Science and Culture.

White Papers Of Japan 1981-1982: Annual abstract of official reports and statistics of the Japanese Government. (1983). Tokyo, Japan: The Japan Institute of International Affairs (1984).

Whittaker, M. (1982). School psychology in three european countries. *Association of Educational Psychologists Journal, 5*, 63–64.

Williams, P. (1971). The educational psychologist in England and Wales. *Journal of School Psychology, 9*, 157–166.

Chapter Eighteen

School Psychological Services Down Under: An Australian Perspective

Martin H. Ritchie
The University of Toledo

School psychological services in Australia represent a blend of British and American influences as well as the unique influence of an emerging Australian culture. Colonized by Great Britain one century after the American colonies, Australia retains the pioneering spirit of a growing nation. Australia is the sixth largest country in the world, about the size of the continental United States, with a population of only 16 million (Australian Bureau of Statistics, 1986). Over 70% of the people live in modern metropolitan areas along the coasts. The remaining people are scattered in small settlements and large cattle or sheep farms in the interior regions of the continent known as the outback. Living conditions in the outback are difficult. Families must be self-sufficient, as the nearest neighbors may be hundreds of kilometers down a dirt track. Traveling to schools is impractical for many children, who must either board in city schools or learn by correspondence and "school-of-the-air." The stark contrast between urban and outback regions presents a real challenge to the provision of school psychological services.

THE AUSTRALIAN EDUCATION SYSTEM

The Australian education system was modeled on the British system and includes both public (state) and private schools. Three quarters of all students attend public schools. The government bears 94% of the cost of education, the state governments providing 60% and the Commonwealth (federal) government 40%. Both public and private schools receive government funding (Australian Bureau of Statistics, 1986).

School attendance is compulsory between the ages of 6 and 15 years. Most public school systems consist of preschool, 7 years of primary, and 5 years of secondary schooling. Years 11 and 12 have traditionally been for those wishing to pursue tertiary studies. About half of all students remain for year 11 and a third complete year 12. Australia has numerous colleges of advanced education, universities, and technical and further education centers. There is no tuition fee for tertiary institutions, although there are quotas on enrollments making entry highly competitive.

Guidance and special education services are generally available from preschool to year 12 and are administered by the education departments of each of the six states and two territories. These education departments have authority over budget, curriculum, and personnel for the entire state or territory. Approximately 1% of Australia's 3 million students attend special schools (Australian Bureau of Statistics, 1986).

SCHOOL PSYCHOLOGY

Role of the School Psychologist

School psychologists in Australia are usually called *guidance officers*. Their role combines elements of the British educational psychologist, the American school psychologist, and school counselor. Their duties vary depending on their location and whether they serve primary or secondary schools, or both. Typically these duties include diagnostic assessments; special education placements and referrals; consultation with parents, teachers, and other professionals; educational and vocational guidance; counseling; and to a lesser extent, program development, evaluation, and research (Jenkins, 1976). The majority of school psychologists are city-based and serve one or two schools, are responsible for fewer than 1,000 students, and have the support of remedial teachers, speech therapists, special education consultants, and clinical psychologists. School psychologists in the country areas may be responsible for 20 schools and 3,000 or more students spread over an area the size of New Mexico and have little in the way of specialist support services.

Historical Development

School psychology in Australia evolved from clinical psychology, vocational guidance, and psychometrics. In 1928, the Vocational Guidance Bureau was established in the New South Wales Department of Education to provide information to students on jobs and university entry requirements. In 1934, the same department set up child guidance clinics to provide diagnostic testing for children not coping in schools (O'Neil, 1983). The Australian Council of Education Research (ACER) was founded in Melbourne at about the same time and provided a variety of education and psychological services including the standardization and distribution of tests. The ACER today serves a function similar to that of the Educational Testing Service in the United States (Connell, 1980). Vocational guidance bureaus and child guidance clinics were opened throughout Australia in the 1930s and 1940s and were administered by psychologists most of whom were trained in the United States or the United Kingdom (O'Neil, 1982).

Many teachers were engaged in the army psychological testing service during World War II. After the war, some gained employment as school psychologists in the state education departments (Parry, 1984). In 1945, the Australian Branch of the British Psychological Society (later the Australian Psychological Society) was formed and began to oversee the training of psychologists (O'Neil, 1983). Today, school psychologists are employed in every Australian state and territory.

Training

The training of school psychologists in Australia is shared by the universities and the state education departments. Each state has at least one college or university offering a degree recognized by that state's education department as prerequisite to employment as a school psychologist. The actual degree may be in educational psychology, counseling psychology, school psychology, or school counseling and may be offered at the diploma (bachelor's plus one year) or master's level. Degree programs are found in both education and psychology departments and typically include units in educational psychology, developmental psychology, research, psychoeducational assessment, behavior therapy, consultation, counseling, and vocational guidance. Many programs require units in special education (Keats, 1976a).

Teachers who meet the requirements for school psychologists in their state apply directly to their state education department. Those selected undergo inservice training and supervised internship, which usually lasts 1 year with full pay. Provisions are sometimes made for them to continue their university studies during their in-service training year. Selection of school psychology is highly competitive and most successful candidates have several years' teaching experience and at least one degree beyond their teacher certification (Davies, 1983).

Special Problems

Three problematic issues facing school psychologists in Australia are service delivery, professional recognition, and the policy of normalization in the schools. School psychologists in many parts of the world are faced with the problem of choosing the most appropriate model of service delivery. In Australia, school psychologists have operated primarily from a direct-service model. This involves providing service to individual students as they are referred. It is a remedial model in which intervention occurs only when a problem is detected or suspected (Meyers, 1973). This model is functional in urban areas, where caseloads are manageable and support services are plentiful, but it is impractical in the outback or country areas, where some school psychologists are able to see an individual child only two or three times a year and are unable to refer the child to support services. This has necessitated new approaches to provision of services that emphasize more efficient methods of early detection and referral as well as indirect intervention based on consultation with parents and teachers. Although school psychologists trained in urban settings find the initial challenge of providing services in the outback daunting, those with experience in the country areas are offering valuable insights into service delivery strategies that are applicable to all settings, including the cities. Some examples are in-service training for teachers, parent education, and self-enhancement programs for children (Burnett, 1983).

School psychologists in Australia are moving toward professional recognition. This movement has been somewhat hampered by the confusion surrounding their identity as either educators or psychologists. Although similar to the problems of role experienced by American school psychologists, the situation in Australia is unique because part of their professional training remains within the parameters of state education departments. Because of this, many school psychologists view themselves, and are viewed, first as educators and second as psychologists (Keats, 1976b). This serves to enhance their referent power in working with teachers but at the expense of expert and legitimate power as defined by Martin (1978).

Some school psychologists are registered as psychologists by state registration boards. Registration usually requires a master's degree plus supervised internship and is not mandatory in all states and territories in order to practice as school psychologists (Taylor, 1982). Although there are moves to upgrade training standards and to make registration mandatory, state registration boards are reluctant to raise standards so high that state education departments are unable to recruit school psychologists eligible for registration from the ranks of their teachers.

School psychologists have been among the first to face the challenges of normalization, or mainstreaming in schools. Traditionally, school psychologists in Australia have served as the gatekeepers to special education (Nixon, 1976). Their recommendations, based on their assessments and diagnoses, have been influential in determining which children received which services. Under the current policy of deinstitutionalization, school psychologists are once again being asked to take major responsibilities for determining which children can benefit from less restrictive placements. Not only the children but the teachers as well have encountered problems of adjustment. Many teachers in regular schools feel unprepared to meet the educational and social needs of newly integrated students. Many special education teachers are having to redefine their expectations when faced with a new class composition. Implementing the policies of normalization and deinstitutionalization has highlighted the need for school psychologists to provide consultation and in-service training to teachers from both the regular and the special schools.

Australia's Contributions to School Psychology

Australia is making significant contributions to school psychology in the areas of indirect services, training, and research. The extreme isolation of the outback has given rise to innovative strategies for furnishing educational and psychological services. Because transportation to schools is impractical, primary schooling takes place in the home with parents acting as surrogate teachers with the assistance of the correspondence school and school-of-the-air. Daily lessons and materials are sent to the parents by the correspondence school. Parents, some with limited educational backgrounds, must be able to understand the lessons and follow directions sufficiently to guide their children through the curriculum. This kind of curriculum planning requires special attention to detailed instructions, sequential development of materials, and the use of simple language. School psychologists are learning from this example to prepare their psychological reports and recommendations in such a way as to be clearly understood and implemented by parents in the absence of other support services.

Daily lessons are supplemented by two-way radio interactions with the school-of-the-air. This enables teachers to interact with students and to provide support to the parents. School psychologists are making use of the two-way radio in providing parent consultation and counseling services. As more remote, country areas are linked by Australia's satellite network, the provision of psychological services over vast distances will take on new dimensions.

Formal cooperation between universities and education departments has helped reduce the gap between theory and practice in the training of school psychologists. During their practicum or internship students are teamed with school psychologists who supervise them in the performance of the same duties they will have to perform in the schools (Davies, 1983). Students are teamed with several psychologists during their internship, enabling them to experience a variety of situations and problems. This arrangement reduces the initial shock experienced by some psychologists during their first year by exposing them to real situations while they have the support of supervisors from both the university and the education department. This arrangement also encourages university instructors to keep abreast of current needs in the field and reflect these needs in their teaching and research.

Australia is making significant contributions to school psychology through research. Early research efforts concentrated on the renorming of existing psychometric instruments. A strong psychometric movement has evolved from these efforts, resulting in the development of instruments such as the Barrett-Lennard

Relationship Inventory (Barrett-Lennard, 1962), the Sheppard School Entry Screening Test (Sheppard, 1972), and the Learning Preference Scale (Owens & Straton, 1980), to mention a few.

It would be difficult to present a representative sample of all the areas of research being conducted by Australian school psychologists. A cursory review of recent professional journals reveals a variety of research reporting on self-concept and achievement (Hattie & Hansford, 1982), social skills training (Kafer, 1982), consultation (Ritchie, 1983), matching students to school environment (Cotterell, 1982; Fraser & Fisher, 1982; Marjoribanks, 1980), and emerging roles of the school psychologists (Maggs & White, 1982).

FUTURE TRENDS

School psychology in Australia is still emerging as a profession. In the next decade changes are likely to occur in four areas of professionalization; training standards, specialization, registration, and the establishment of a professional association.

The ratio of school psychologists to students is improving in Australia. This relieves pressure on universities to turn out large numbers of school psychologists quickly, thus allowing universities to improve training standards and to increase the length of training. The Australian Psychological Society (APS) is currently upgrading its standards for APS-approved programs, a trend that is likely to continue in the near future. As training standards improve, it is likely that more programs will offer school psychologists the opportunity to specialize in specific areas such as psychometrics, counseling, vocational guidance, and working with specific learning disabilities. In the future, school districts may be able to employ several school psychologists with complementary areas of specialization, thus improving their psychological services.

Legal recognition through licensure or registration is a valued attribute of a profession (Ritchie, 1979). With improved training standards more school psychologists will be eligible for registration. It is likely that registration will eventually become mandatory for school psychologists in Australia. In a similar vein, recognized professions are usually governed by an autonomous or semiautonomous professional association (Ritchie, 1979). Today there is no such association for school psychologists in Australia. Most school psychologists belong to local teachers' unions and many are members of the Australian Psychological Society. Some states have recently formed guidance officer's associations and there is a current movement to form a national association (Parry, 1984).

School psychologists are well established in Australia. Just as Australian culture is still evolving, so is the role of Australian school psychologists. They have always been among the first to turn educational innovations into educational practices and are likely to continue to do so.

ACKNOWLEDGMENT

Reprinted by permission of the *Journal of School Psychology*, *23*, 13–18, as published in 1985.

REFERENCES

Australian Bureau of Statistics. (1986). *Year Book Australia 1986.* Canberra: Author.

Barrett-Lennard, G. T. (1962). Dimensions of therapist responses as causal factors in therapeutic change. *Psychological Monographs*, *76*(2, Whole No. 562).

Burnett, P. C. (1983). A self-concept enhancement program for children in the regular classroom. *Elementary School Guidance and Counseling*, *18*, 101–108.

Connell, W. F. (1980). *The Australian Council of Educational Research, 1930–1980.* Hawthorn, Victoria: ACER.

Cotterell, J. L. (1982). Matching teaching to learners: A review of a decade of research. *Psychology in the Schools*, *19*, 106–112.

Davies, G. J. (1983). *The training of guidance officers in Australia.* Brisbane: Queensland Department of Education.

Fraser, B. J., & Fisher, D. L. (1982). Effects of classroom psychosocial environment on student learning. *British Journal of Educational Psychology*, *52*, 374–377.

Hattie, J. A., & Hansford, B. C. (1982). Self measures and achievement: Comparing a traditional review of the literature with a meta analysis. *The Australian Journal of Education*, *26*, 71–75.

Jenkins, N. R. (1976). The role and functions of school counsellors. *Australian Psychologist*, *11*, 53–59.

Kafer, N. F. (1982). Interpersonal strategies of unpopular children—Some implications for social skills training. *Psychology in the Schools*, *19*, 255–259.

Keats, D. M. (1976a). Professional courses for the training of educational psychologists in education. *Australian Psychologist*, *11*, 83–93.

Keats, D. M. (1976b). Psychologists in education. *Australian Psychologist*, *11*, 33–42.

Maggs, A., & White, R. (1982). The educational psychologist: Facing a new era. *Psychology in the Schools*, *19*, 129–134.

Marjoribanks, K. (1980). Person-school environment correlates of children's affective characteristics. *Journal of Educational Psychology*, *16*, 49–55.

Martin, R. (1978). Expert and referent power: A framework for understanding and maximizing consultation effectiveness. *Journal of School Psychology*, *16*, 49–55.

Meyers, J. (1973). A consultation model for psychological services. *Journal of School Psychology*, *11*, 5–15.

Nixon, M. (1976). Educational psychology: An optimistic view. *Australian Psychologist*, *11*, 65–71.

O'Neil, W. M. (1982). *The beginnings of modern psychology.* Sydney: Sydney University Press.

O'Neil, W. M. (1983). One hundred years of psychology in Australia. *Bulletin of the Australian Psychological Society*, *5*, 8–20.

Owens, L., & Straton, R. G. (1980). The development of a cooperative, competitive, and individualised learning preference scale for students. *British Journal of Educational Psychology*, *50*, 147–161.

Parry, S. F. (1984). *An overview of the organization and scope of education department guidance services in Australia.* Unpublished master's thesis, University of Queensland, St. Lucia, Australia.

Ritchie, M. H. (1979). The professional status of counseling. *Dissertation Abstracts International*, *40*, 681–A.

Ritchie, M. H. (1983). Brief behavioural consultation: A case example. *School Psychology International*, *4*, 237–244.

Sheppard, M. J. (1972). *A teacher's school entry screening test.* Sydney: Robert Burton.

Taylor, K. (1982). The registration of psychologists in Australia: An updated summary. *Bulletin of the Australian Psychological Society*, *4*, 20.

Chapter Nineteen
Psychological Service in New Zealand

D. F. Brown
Department of Education, Wellington, New Zealand

This chapter was written during a period of significant change. The New Zealand Government has embarked upon a reorganization of the public sector that includes a major review of its educational and psychological services. Concurrent with this reconsideration of the administration of education and the delivery of psychological services within education has been the first complete reappraisal of special education services since the 1940s, titled the *draft Review of Special Education* (1987).

INTRODUCTION

New Zealand is a country approximately the size of the Great Britain. Situated in the South Pacific Ocean, it consists of two main islands and some smaller ones enjoying a temperate climate and a long history of political stability. It has a population a little over 3 million with approximately 564,000 students of compulsory school age. Approximately 684,000 students attend primary and secondary schools. About 168,000 students are in full- or part-time tertiary education including trades training (Department of Education, 1986). The population is of predominantly European extraction whose forebears migrated to New Zealand during the 19th century. About 10% of the population is of Polynesian origin. The Maori population migrated to New Zealand 800 to 1,000 years ago and are presently enjoying a resurgence of cultural interest and identity. Pacific Island migrants came to New Zealand largely in the last 30 years. These new immigrants are making an increasingly vital impact on the multicultural nature of the population.

The Department of Education is at the center of the administrative pattern of the education service. Education is compulsory from 6 to 15 years. The vast majority of children begin school at 5 years and a high proportion continue for 1 to 3 years beyond their 15th birthday. Education in New Zealand is artificially divided into four sectors. Early childhood, primary (elementary), secondary, and tertiary. These sectors are administered by a variety of boards and councils that have some degree of autonomy but are regulated by the central department. Most governing bodies are democratically elected and employ professional staff or have them seconded to them by the Department of Education.

The Department of Education, under the control of the Minister of Education, is charged with the administration of the Education Act of 1964 and its admendments, and regulations made under the act. This is the core legislation for education in New Zealand. The act is enabling in the Westminster model of government and sets the legal basis for the administration and practice of education across the country.

The department has very wide functions that extend over all levels of education from the kindergartens through the universities and over private as well as public institutions. It shares its administrative responsibilities with other statutory bodies including the university authorities, controlling authorities, and with many voluntary agencies. In addition to administering the provisions under which grants are made to other authorities, the department:

- inspects schools and teachers;
- recruits and regulates the training of teachers;
- issues syllabuses and controls many examinations;
- prepares codes of practice for buildings:
- authorizes school conveyance systems and provides and maintains a school bus fleet of its own;
- awards bursaries and boarding allowances;
- publishes the Education Gazette, and a range of textbooks and brochures for schools;
- directly controls the Correspondence School, the National Film Library, a psychological service, some special schools, and a curriculum advisory service;
- conducts in-service training courses;
- provides services for schools in the Pacific Islands and engages in international co-operation in education within the framework of UNESCO and other agencies; and
- advises the government on policy matters.

The psychological service consists of 165 established positions. Psychologists work fom 41 centers ranging in size from 2- to 11-person teams. Each team is self-sufficient administratively. Centers are established in all cities and major towns but some centers have a significant rural hinterland that requires a considerable amount of travel. Each year, the Department of Education awards 13 studentships to well-qualified teachers (see later comments on training) for a 3-year study program. These are available on full teaching salaries and can be taken up at one of the two universities offering postgraduate training.

Approximately 90% of all students in primary and secondary schools (elementary through high school) attend state (public) schools. About 8% attend private schools that are integrated into the state system and supported by state funding, whereas another 3% attend totally private schools.

Although the gap between the lowest and highest income groups in New Zealand appears to be widening, New Zealand has never had a significant differentiation among family incomes. Government policies and the general egalitarian nature of society in New Zealand have tended to produce checks and balances in income distribution that have ensured that few families fall below generally accepted poverty lines. The mean income in New Zealand dollars in 1986 was $27,196 (U.S. $17,700) (Dept. of Statistics, 1986).

SCOPE OF SERVICES AND CONTRIBUTION TO EDUCATION

The Role of the Psychological Service

The psychological service of the Department of Education has moved from a fundamental concern with diagnosis and programming for individual children to a comprehensive special education consultative role. Psychologists now work for a wide range of schools and agencies, and they place a particular emphasis on their work with parents. They are closely involved with teacher support and inservice training. In recent years, the role of the service has expanded to include a systems analysis of education functions and a coordinating, supervisory role with a growing itinerant delivery of special education resources. The most rapidly expanding program in this area is a guidance unit model for behaviorally disordered and slow-learning students.

The Guidance Unit Model

This model is likely to undergo further adaptation over the next year or two. Basically, the unit is based on a well documented empirical model (Thomas & Glynn, 1976). It replaces the special class approach that separates students from the peer group for special education. In place of these special classes, small teams of support staff work in an itinerant model where the child is retained in its regular classroom and the support teacher assists the regular class teacher with behavior change programs in the academic or social-learning areas. The teams consist of a psychologist, itinerant specialist teacher, the principal of the regular school, and the regular classroom teacher. Psychologists act as team leaders on a consultative basis and work in very close interrelationship with the teams. The model is a problem-solving, data-based, educational approach to the needs of students and their teachers.

When Beaglehole wrote *Mental Health in New Zealand* (Beaglehole, 1950), he noted the capacity of psychologists to meet the majority of so-called mental health needs in the community. Beaglehole saw the delivery of this assistance cast in the child guidance model espoused in Britain and the United States during the 1930s. This was, indeed, the model of delivery that the Department of Education psychological service adopted, and the gradual expansion of the service into the 1960s saw this model proliferated.

Their early work, based on this child guidance model, saw them, no less than their British counterparts, "continuing to make forays (into the schools) from isolated clinics" as Booth, Potts, and Swann (1983, p. 39) put it. The purpose of these visits was often to classify students and to recommend placement in special education programs. This reactive approach is not difficult to understand given the medical model on which it is based. It is worth noting, however, that it was one element of an emerging pattern of work. At the same time, psychologists were attempting to link family with school where they could, and to do so from a position of independence from the school system itself. The child guidance approach was not one that would effectively meet the needs of schools. However, it did serve to establish the psychological service in a community setting from which it could exercise a degree of independence that could not have been achieved otherwise. I discuss this aspect of the psychologist's role later.

Psychologists and School Program Development

As psychologists developed a better understanding of the very real contribution they could make to educational programs within the school, they began to increasingly center their work on school program development. Two influences were at work to encourage this approach. The first of these was undoubtedly the pragmatism of many psychologists who, as trained and experienced teachers, saw an obvious need to be intimately involved with the staff of the schools they served. These psychologists recognized the implicit need to ensure that teachers identified with the psychologist's perspective of a child's need if change was to be effected. This led to a determination to work in schools, within their systems rather than outside them, hoping to have their advice acted upon by others (e.g., Brown & Hallinan, 1972).

The second influence has been the opportunity to apply the principles of learning to classroom settings. Stemming largely from the United States, the literature on this major development encouraged many psychologists to apply behavior analysis to children in the classroom setting and even to schools themselves. A strong local application of research practice began to emerge in New Zealand (e.g., Glynn, 1986, 1987). This approach sealed what was now to be an inevitable trend toward a closely interactive association between psychologists and schools.

Functions of Psychologists

A particular feature of the work of psychologists has been their capacity to deal with children across settings. They are not confined to schools, indeed they are established in centers in the community in order to ensure their independence. In this way, psychologists have been able to carry out two important functions. The first of these is their ability to receive referrals from any source. Twenty percent of referrals come from parents. Even though referrals come from parents and others, psychologists may manage them through the school if it is appropriate to do so. Thus, a systems approach remains a viable option yet the confidentiality of parent and client data is upheld.

Because psychologists can work outside the school setting and outside school hours, their work is not restricted by either of these parameters as it might be if they were seen exclusively as "school psychologists." Although this model is common in some other countries (the author has worked in a somewhat similar organization in the United Kingdom) there is an added advantage in New Zealand that the education system is a national one with no boundaries set by local education authorities. This rather happy state of affairs allows the psychologist, or at least the psychological service, to stay with a child as it moves through the educational system from early childhood to high school or across the country from one school to another 1,000 or more miles away.

The second function that is of particular importance is that the psychologist can act as an advocate for the child. The Department of Education accepts the notion that, although psychologists are officers of the department, they also fill this important advocacy role. As a consequence, psychologists can take an independent position with school authorities and even with the department itself where a psychologist feels compelled in the best interests of the child to do so.

The Advocacy Role. This advocacy role is, to some extent, a requirement of a psychologist working within the constraints of the ethnics of the profession. Since 1984, psychology has been a registered profession in New Zealand with its own disciplinary procedures. The Act of Parliament that established the registration procedures is itself a constraint against actions that would not be in the best interests of a client. However, for the period since the psychological service has been in existence the Department of Education has accepted that the complexity and sensistive nature of the psychologist's work requires this particular recognition and has willingly given it.

The Changing Role

The changing role of psychologists in education has seen emphasis placed on new developments as they have, in turn, become necessary. The move to consultation rather than psychometric examination; teacher support rather than indirect, written advice; home–school liaison rather than some kind of distant, expert commentary to parent or schools, have shifted the psychologist further away from a clinical, often medical model to a more apparent educational approach. The growing confidence among psychologists that there is an educational validity about their role has been noticeable since the 1970s in particular. Many psychologists are making a more confident assertion of the utility of their role. Where a problem has clear educational characteristics they are now less willing to accept the medical model that so often sets hierarchical structures, and that relies more upon epidemiological data and the establishment of pathology (e.g., Thomson 1987).

Related Services

The orientation of the psychological service was originally toward the primary (elementary) sector of education. Consequently, psychologists have a long history of providing an assessment and advisory role to primary schools, including the intermediate schools that provide a 2-year educational program for 11- and 12-year-old students. At present, the psychological service provides three related services.

The earlier and more traditional model of diagnosis and advice is offered across all sectors of education and to a wide range of other referral agencies, including parents. Department of Education data indicate that psychometric testing has reduced markedly in the last decade. Between 1978 and 1985, the numbers of children tested for intelligence were reduced in those psychological service centers where statistics were available from 68% to 28%.

There is also a clinical role that places psychologists in a one-to-one relationship with clients, offering a service that is community wide but that concentrates on children or the adults who work most closely with children—most usually their parents.

A consultative, co-worker relationship spreads across all four sectors of the education service offered as well as to a wide range of other agencies involved with children, including parents. In this role, psychologists share skills in assessment and program development, and may coordinate or take a direct role with those working closely with children. This role often involves leadership in in-service training, program development, and program delivery. However, these services provide an educative function and lead to the objective of self-sufficiency of the co-worker.

There can be no doubt that this last activity is now the predominant one. Psychologists are developing increasingly effective means of working in this consultative model.

Two Important Aspects

A special word must be said about two aspects of the work of psychologists that are becoming increasingly important in any discussion of the role of psychological services in schools. The first of these is assessment, the second is teacher support.

Assessment. In the New Zealand education setting, assessment has now come to be seen as a systematic process of collecting data for the purpose of assisting in educational decision making about students. It is concerned less with placing a child in one of several diagnostic categories, predicting performance, or making statements about presumed causes of a disability or handicap than it is with establishing educational programming. Its chief function is to determine learning needs in specific terms within the context of a careful evaluation of the environment, available teaching strategies, and the curriculum itself.

In order to be effective, assessment must include recognition and understanding of the cultural, language, and value systems of the students and it must take cognizance of the effects of sexism in limiting learning opportunities.

Demands for psychologists to assist in schools will range from the need for minor modifications in the regular classroom program to the need for specialized resources in a special unit. The personnel involved in assessment, therefore, will vary in different cases from the class teacher or tutor and the senior staff of the educational facility through a limited range of specialist involvement to a multidisciplinary group. As the person who has the most contact with the student in the educational setting and who is most likely to have to implement any remedial strategies, the classroom teacher is a key person in assessment. Parents may be included in assessment as is their right.

In educational settings it is necessary for the model of assessment to be educational. Assessment, therefore, must be based on the actual service provided by the educational facility: the teaching of a curriculum in its broadest sense. By adopting this model, the psychologist accepts the implications for the kinds of records kept and for the kinds of reports that are provided for parents and others. The model discourages the use of tests that do not relate to the teaching needs of the students, including those from ethnic minorities.

The psychologist plays an essential role in ensuring that this particular model of assessment is developed. It is fundamentally an educational rather than a medical model and it is an absolute requirement that it will have education and social validity based on well-founded educational practices. It requires a focus not only on the student but on the learning environment. It is a continuous process because the conditions in the student's environment are constantly changing.

No such process of assessment can be carried out without a form of leadership that demonstrates a clear conceptual understanding of this model. The psychological service is, in this sense, making a major contribution to a significant and wide ranging conceptual shift. The shift moves from a search for pathological conditions toward the identification of factors that are preventing a child from learning.

Teacher Support. Teacher support becomes a significant element of the work of psychologists if the model of assessment just noted and the consultative, co-worker relationship is to be fostered. In the absence of sufficient psychologists to ensure that all children with special educational needs can be dealt with individually, and even presuming that this were a desirable approach, psychologists will remain a scarce resource in our school systems. Therefore, it is essential that psychologists are able to work with school teams to make the teachers and managers of the school proficient in strategies that will permit the schools to become self-reliant if not self-sufficient. Among a number of models that have been advanced to meet this objective in New Zealand, the Staff Sharing Programme (Gill, 1986) is coming to be more widely adopted. This program involves psychologists in the development of teacher self-reliance across a wide range of problem-solving strategies aimed at identifying and dealing with social and academic maladaptive behaviors.

Early Intervention

A further significant development of the work of psychologists has been in early intervention. This work was established in three centers in New Zealand in the mid 1970s. One was developed at a large psychopaedic hospital by psychologists and health professionals working with intellectually handicapped children. Another was specific to one university center, whereas the third, first named "Dawnstart" (Straton, 1985) was established in 2 large cities by the Department of Education psychological service. These programs have now been extended to 12 cities. Psychologists play a central role in that they act as leaders of an educational team and as co-workers with professionals from health and voluntary agencies.

A major purpose of these early intervention programs is to assist the child who is at risk of developmental disability to attain optimum development and functioning. Educational psychologists have the capacity to add to these programs important insights to a child's early cognitive development. They also can make a major contribution to the educational perspective not always found in early intervention work. This approach extends the concept of early intervention beyond its purely physical development role. It ensures that from the beginning psychologists can make their unique contribution with long-term educational objectives being set.

Because the family unit is the most crucial source of learning and support to the child, psychologists focus their early intervention programs not just on the child but on the family environment as well. Parents are recognized as an integral part of the team. This cooperative model of parent professional cooperation establishes a positive relationship with the family and ensures the parental right of close involvement in assessment, program planning, and decision making from an early stage.

Although early intervention programs concentrate in the age group 0 to 3 years, the department places a great deal of importance on the transition phase into early childhood facilities and into school. The department has established the position of adviser on handicapped children with the intention of making an education input to early intervention programs and ensuring the continuity of programming throughout the early years and into school. These advisers work from the psychological service, enabling the team of psychologist and specialist teacher to make a significant educational input. The principles of parental involvement, a problem-solving approach, and interdisciplinary cooperation are essential for successful outcomes.

Training Facilities

Training is presently undertaken at Auckland University in the North Island and the University of Otago in the South Island. Comparisons of training programs with those in other countries are difficult to make. The author has personally visited a number of training sites in Australia, the United States, and the United Kingdom without being able to draw any major conclusion about comparability because of the diversity of training programs. At present, however, it is necessary for a candidate for training in New Zealand to have completed a successful teacher training (3 years at a teachers college and 2 years of classroom teaching) and to hold a first degree in educational psychology (3 years at a university). Successful applicants then will be given a further training program (3 years of postgraduate study and practicum that includes 1 full year of supervised internship). If one follows a recent analysis of training programs in the United States (Brown & Minke, 1986) it appears reasonable to suggest that the New Zealand training programs are the equivalent of the upper level of training programs available in the United States, both in content and in depth of study.

Special Problems

In many ways, New Zealand's psychological service has made a unique contribution to educational developments. In his analysis of the work of the service, *The New Zealand Educational Psychologist: A Comparative Analysis*, Bardon (1980) remarked on the capacity of the New Zealand psychological service to respond quickly to policy changes. In fact, psychologists are part of the policy feedback loop in the Department of Education and are contributors to policy formation as much as they are agents of policy. Thus, as their professional development has determined a move away from normative and usually, for New Zealand, understandardized tests to an ecological assessment approach for example, the psychological service has been in the van of change.

However, one particular problem facing the psychological service at present is some degree of uncertainty over its organizational structures. The service has been established as an integral part of the Department of Education. At present, the New Zealand Government is reviewing all its operations and is attempting to separate out regulatory and service delivery functions from policy-making activities. One possible scenario for the future may see the psychological service detached from the Department of Education to become some kind of free-standing servicing agency, available on a contract basis to the schools and educational institutions of New Zealand.

Such a move would be taken in the name of greater efficiency and effectiveness. Its effect might be to move psychologists from the collegial network of fellow teachers and educators and to convert them to outside consultants and advisors called upon to identify, if they could, with the educational world. Whether psychologists in such a setting could hold the same commitment to an educational model that places them as members of an integrated education service remains to be seen.

FUTURE TRENDS

The role of the psychologist in the school system comes under closer scrutiny as the system itself begins to examine its educational programs and procedures for exceptional children. Glaser (1977) suggested that as educators have come to understand individual differences they have dealt with them by exclusion. This has led to the gatekeeping role referred to by Ysseldyke, Reynolds, and Weinberg (1984) and to the deliberate establishment of a separate stream of special education.

In New Zealand, no less than in most other industrial countries, the viability of a parallel system of education, with special education running alongside its regular counterpart, has been called into question. In the Department of Education *draft Review of Special Education* (1987) produced for public discussion two central points emerge.

The first of these is the notion that, rather than continue to mainstream students who are handicapped, we should mainstream special education itself. All of it! This would mean that special education would become a support service. Special classes and units would be continued for students who needed such specialist resources. But they would be fully integrated into the organizational structure of regular education. That this could be achieved in New Zealand may be a matter for debate, but it would be easier in this country than in many others simply because mainstreaming has always been the "only option" for many of the more isolated rural communities.

The *draft Review of Special Education* places upon psychologists in education an enormous responsibility. This is to act as facilitators of change in the development of quite radical rearrangements of administrative and teaching practices. As noted in an address to the New Zealand Psychological Society (Brown, 1986) it will be a moot point if psychologists all wish to take up this task, but somebody must. In a sense, it is an attempt to break the shackle of labeling, misplacement, and often unproductive educational endeavor. Glass (1983) referred to this problem when he said, "It is my premise that most people who are labelled as 'handicapped' in our schools are diagnosed so arbitrarily because of nonspecific symptoms that most questions of treatment are, perforce, irrelevant!"

In order to develop a more rational approach in special education, psychologists will be asked to extend the work many of them have already begun. The trend toward a more genuinely consultative exchange between psychologists, teachers, and parents will become more predominant as the intentions of the review begin to be translated into educational practice. Psychologists will contribute the practical skills and up-to-date knowledge of how to go about such complex tasks as mainstreaming. They will be expected to reflect the lessons of the literature (e.g., Biklen, 1985; Bishop, 1986), and to operationalize them in the New Zealand setting.

An equally significant contribution will come from their conceptual understanding of what such a total mainstreaming approach will mean for the educational system as much as for individual teachers, parents, or schools. At the time of writing, psychologists are taking a major part in public discussions following the distribution of the *draft Review of Special Education* to every school, special interest group, advocacy group, and voluntary agency throughout the country.

This quite massive consultative effort will set the scene for special education as a support service in New Zealand for many years to come. It will have major implications for regular education. Ultimately, it may lead to the merging of the parallel streams of education into one main stream. Psychologists are seen as the lynch pin in this change. Their special knowledge and particular skills will be a critical element in the successful reorganization of the educational provisions for students with special needs in New Zealand.

REFERENCES

Bardon, J. I. (1980). *The New Zealand educational psychologist: A comparative analysis*. Wellington, New Zealand: New Zealand Council for Educational Research.

Beaglehole, E. (1950). *Mental health in New Zealand*. Wellington, New Zealand: New Zealand University Press.

Biklen, D. P. (1985). Mainstreaming: From compliance to quality. *Journal of Visual Impairment & Blindness, 80*(1), 58-61.

Bishop, V. E. (1986). Identifying the components of success in mainstreaming. *Journal of Visual Impairment & Blindness, 80*(9), 939–946.

Booth, T., Potts, P., & Swann, W. (1983). *An alternative system: A special imagination* (2nd ed.). Milton Keynes: The Open University Press.

Brown, D. F. (1986, August). *The contribution of psychology to special education—Recent developments in New Zealand.* Paper presented to the annual conference of the New Zealand Pychological Society, Dunedin, New Zealand.

Brown, D. F. (1987). *Early intervention programmes—The Department of Education perspective.* In Mitchell & Brown (Eds.), *Future directions for early intervention* (pp. 6–8). Auckland, New Zealand: Downs Association.

Brown, D. F., & Hallinan, P. (1972). *An experimental approach to psychological services in schools.* Wellington, New Zealand: Department of Education.

Brown, D. T., & Minke, K. M. (1986). School psychology graduate training: A comprehensive analysis. *American Psychologist, 41*(12), 1328-1338.

Department of Education. (1986). *Education statistics of New Zealand.* Wellington, New Zealand: Author.

Department of Education. (1987). *draft review of special education.* Wellington, New Zealand: Author.

Department of Statistics. (1986). *Household expenditure and income survey.* Wellington, New Zealand: Author.

Gill, D. (1986). *A staff sharing scheme: A school based management system for working with difficult children.* Auckland, New Zealand: Department of Education.

Glaser, R. (1977). *Adaptive education: Individual diversity and learning.* New York: Holt Rinehart & Winston.

Glass, G. V. (1983). Effectiveness of special education. *Policy Studies Review, 2* (Special No. 1), 65–78.

Glynn, E. L. (1986). *Antecedent control of behaviour in educational contexts.* In K. Wheldall, Merrett, & T. Glynn (Eds.), *Behaviour analysis in educational psychology* (pp. 215–229). Kent, England: Croom Helm.

Glynn, E. L. (1987). Effective learning contexts for exceptional children. In D. R. Mitchell & N. N. Singh (Eds.), *Exceptional Children in New Zealand* (pp. 158–167). Palmerston North: Dunmore Press.

Straton, E. A. (1985). *Early intervention services.* In N. N. Singh & K. M. Wilton (Eds.), *Mental retardation in New Zealand: Provisions, services, and research* (pp. 120–135). Christchurch: Whitcoulls.

Thomas, J. D., Glynn, E. L. (1976). *Mangere guidance unit: Evaluation of behavioural programmes.* Research Report, University of Auckland, Auckland, New Zealand.

Thomson, C. (1987). *Report on child assessment units: Report to the health education welfare committee.* Wellington, New Zealand: Department of Education.

Ysseldyke, J. E., Reynolds, M. C., & Weinberg, R. A. (1984). *School psychology: A blueprint for training and practice.* Minneapolis, MN: National School Psychology Inservice Training Network.

Chapter Twenty
School Psychology in Canada: Views on its Status

Florent Dumont
McGill University

PRESUPPOSITIONS OF THE ANALYSIS

The effort to assess the condition of school psychology in Canada is complicated by a number of problems that need to be acknowledged at the very outset. The first and most formidable has proven to be the issue of determining which psychological services fall within the purview of this profession (e.g., Bardon, 1986; Monroe, 1979; Weininger, 1971; White & Harris, 1961). The fact that so many practitioners who provide psychological services in schools across the country are not in agreement about what they should be doing is at least *prima facie* evidence that there is little consensus in practice, if not in theory, as to what constitutes the profession of school psychology, and the academic disciplines which underpin it.

Another problem is that there has been, in various provinces of Canada, a proliferation of disciplinary specialties in psychology. Professionals trained in these disciplines have gone forth to carve out a market for their services. They have not been respectful in all cases of traditional territorial markers. When they have found employment in a school system, they have been brought face to face not only with a clientele that they can serve, and very often serve well, but with other psychological specialists, some of whom may be resentful of encroachments in what they perceive to be their own domain. It is not uncommon to find in an urban school district in Canada not only accredited school psychologists, but also clinical psychologists, psychoeducators, psychiatric nurses, guidance counselors, counseling psychologists, psychometricians, and other psychology-based professionals. Very often one or more of these specialists is not in evidence. When, however, several are, the potential for ferment and excitement where they come face to face at work is easy to imagine.

As the reader may be aware, Canada is a culturally diverse society with a relatively small population distributed over a vast land mass. Moreover, matters bearing on formal education fall under 10 separate provincial jurisdictions. The unstandardized manner (across, and sometimes within, provincial jurisdictions) in which school systems have consequently been organized makes it exceedingly difficult, if not impossible, to present a national perspective on the organization of school psychology. This chapter consequently reflects a subjective cull of certain of the more salient and interesting developmental aspects of the profession in various parts of Canada.

STRUCTURAL VARIABLES IN THE EDUCATIONAL SYSTEM

Cultural Mosaic

In language, culture, socioeconomic patterns, and distinctive national lifestyles, provinces and territories differ dramatically from one another. Canada is constituted in part by a large number of Amerindian nations and Inuit peoples, each with its distinctive language and culture. To respect and indeed foster these cultures is national policy. In addition to the large number of Caucasians of French, English, Irish, and Scottish extraction who long ago established their respective language and culture in various parts of the land, later immigrants from Europe, the Middle East, the Caribbean islands, and the Far East have continued to add to Canada's numbers—and to the complexity and random pattern of its cultural mosaic. These historical movements have not been without their influence on the various regional school systems and the configuration of psychological services that they provide to their constituents.

The heterogeneity of Canadian society is prized by its citizens. A price, of course, has to be paid for this in terms of specialization of services that correspond to the characteristics of the different populations being served. The Special Needs Researcher of the Northwest Territories (NWT), for example, reported that the "following linguistic groups are provided for in schools across the NWT: Inuvialuktun (Inuktitut), Loucheux, Innuinaqtun, North Slavey, South Slavey, Dogrib, Chipewyan, Cree, English and French" (Arsenault, personal communication, 1987). If the development of adequate school systems in such a vast and sparsely inhabited yet culturally diverse territory has been difficult, providing specialized psychological services is proving to be a challenge of epic proportions. All the provinces of Canada face comparable if less acute needs. The governments of, say, the prairie provinces must be sensitive not only to their Amerindian and Métis populations, but to large communities of Hutterites, Doukhobors, and Mennonites. And in addition to a vigorous and cohesive Ukrainian population whose sense of language and community is well defined, there are more recent streams of immigrants (e.g., Polish and, lately, Vietnamese) that have yet to find a well-defined place in the larger community.

Some Commonalities

In all this diversity there are nevertheless some commonalities cutting across jurisdictions governing the services that are provided to school children. For example, in response to a questionnaire that the author directed, in the winter of 1987, to the ministries of education of all the provinces, it was unanimously reported that children with special educational needs are mainstreamed, if it is at all possible. They revealed a philosophical and applied concern for the normalization of the school environment for those with handicaps as well as those who function "normally." The principle of "least restrictive alternative mode" is accepted and operative. If, for example, a child has an IQ that is in the range extending below 70 or so, or has a sensory handicap that severely compromises participation in the normal classroom, separate classrooms are provided. But even in these cases partial integration, say, for 40 minutes per day, is often attempted. "Separate but equal" is not an acceptable environmental formula for children with exceptional needs, unless it is a professionally demonstrated desideratum.

Professional Diversity

Psychological services are provided to students and to school personnel by a broad array of specialists. Foremost among them in most provinces are school psychologists, that is, those who are professionally engaged in the various branches of applied educational psychology in school settings. In addition to school psychologists are vocational guidance specialists, social workers, guidance counselors, counseling psychologists, psychometricians, student affairs "animateurs," psychoeducators, special education teachers, reading consultants, psychiatric nurses, and, indeed, until quite recently, criminologists.

In several jurisdictions, school psychologists are simply all provincially accredited psychologists who have been employed by a school board. In some settings they are employed to help teachers better understand cognitive processes in such disciplines as mathematics or reading, to conduct in-service workshops in techniques to increase text comprehension and recall, to counsel in the area of inferential processes or proportional thinking, and to help teachers in other domains of teaching and learning. In other settings they deal directly with pupils who have problems of a socioaffective nature, conduct workshops on identifying children with depressive symptomatology, and develop programs to combat increasing levels of vandalism and interpersonal violence. Still others are employed to work as psychometricians: to test and assess pupils in view of making placement decisions, to detect rather than solve problems, to refer rather than perform therapy.

Although all of these competencies and functions fall within the purview of school psychology and are frequently written into a single job description, these responsibilities usually are not reserved by law to this psychological specialty. Confusion arises because clear exclusionary criteria do not exist for determining which professions are responsible for providing each of the various services. Even within the same school district individuals working in different psychology-based professions can be called on to perform overlapping if not identical tasks. Differences also exist between provinces. Counselors are mandated to do intelligence and personality assessment within certain jurisdictions, whereas elsewhere such work is restricted to clinical psychologists or school psychologists with a psychometric specialization.

The Tax Base

The funding of education and the ancillary psychological support services are largely provided by the provincial governments. Only in what concerns the Territories and the indigenous peoples of the country is such funding assured by the federal government. This prevents serious discrepancies in quality of services from arising between regions of the same jurisdiction as a function of the tax base that is constituted by their relative wealth or poverty. Although the public funding formulas for the education of children vary considerably from province to province, the discrepancies in the outlay of monies per capita of the provincial population (Table 20.1) do not seem directly related to those formulas. For example, municipal sources of educational funds were considerably higher in 1983–1984 in Ontario (29%), Manitoba (25%), and Alberta (22%) than in Québec (2%), New Brunswick (0%), Prince Edward Island (0%), and Newfoundland (2%) (Table 20.2). In Canada, regional disparities in wealth are compensated for by federal transfer payments to the less affluent provinces. This redistribution of national income allows more funds to flow into the school system of such provinces than otherwise would.

Determining the relative quality of the school services provided to children in the various provinces and territories of the country is complicated by consideration of such variables as licensure and accreditation standards for teachers and other school professionals, salary structures for school employees, levels of unemployment (and other social pathogens), and population densities. That task is clearly beyond the scope of this chapter.

SCHOOL PSYCHOLOGY

What Are School Psychologists Hired to Do?

"School psychology was born in the prison of a test, and although the cell has been enlarged somewhat, it is still a prison." This sentiment, expressed some

TABLE 20.1
Total Expenditures on Education in Relation to Selected Socioeconomic Indicators, Canada and Provinces, 1983.

	Expenditures Related to Indicators		
Province	*Personal Income*	*Population*	*Labor Force*
	%	dollars per capita	
Canada	9.1	1,227	2,508
Newfoundland	13.5	1,240	3,336
Prince Edward Island	9.6	961	2,184
Nova Scotia	10.5	1,135	2,650
New Brunswick	10.9	1,094	2,672
Québec	10.5	1,318	2,796
Ontario	7.9	1,168	2,257
Manitoba	9.3	1,170	2,413
Saskatchewan	9.6	1,213	2,561
Alberta	9.0	1,324	2,488
British Columbia	7.6	1,088	2,211

Note: Adapted from *Education in Canada: A statistical review*. Statistics Canada (December, 1986), pp. 242–243.

years ago by Sarason (1977, p. 27), may or may not be true, depending on (a) one's attitudes toward testing, and (b) the character of the school system where one is practicing this profession. It would seem unfair however to blame school psychologists for having imposed a narrow and suffocating role on themselves without consideration of the pressures that the school and the general public have applied to that same end. Scientific advances always arise from a predisposing social and political context (Dumont & Lecomte, 1985; Mannheim, 1936). The genuine need for quantification as well as the lure of a technology-textured learning environment long ago pushed Canada and other parts of the Western world in a psychometric direction. School psychologists as well as other science-based professionals have been swept along in that tide.

The job descriptions for psychologists that are published by various ministries of education in Canada always include assessment and diagnosis, but they also include such clinical responsibilities as direct intervention with emotionally troubled, conduct-disordered children, as well as consultative work among teachers developing individualized or group treatment programs for children with cognitive or behavioral deficits. Their responsibilities, at least on paper, can seem overwhelming. They may include personal psychotherapeutic counseling of students, modification of inappropriate teacher behaviors relative to particular pupils, development of preventive programs in areas of socioaffective disorder, consulting with parents, community agencies, and those professionals who collaborate with them within the school district, adapting remedial programs for application to particular elementary school classrooms, and developing programs to improve

TABLE 20.2
Expenditures on Education, Percentage Distribution, by Direct Source of Funds, Canada and Provinces, 1983–1984.

		Direct Source of Funds by Government Level		
Province	*Total*	*Federal*	*Provincial*	*Municipal*
	$'000s	Total (with other sources) = 100.0%		
Canada	30,532,402	9.0	68.0	15.4
Newfoundland	714,521	7.1	85.3	2.4
Prince Edward Island	119,482	10.9	83.1	nil
Nova Scotia	977,503	9.8	73.3	8.8
New Brunswick	774,471	8.8	86.1	nil
Québec	8,578,138	6.1	85.3	2.2
Ontario	10,304,286	7.9	53.9	28.9
Manitoba	1,226,310	13.7	53.5	24.8
Saskatchewan	1,205,245	14.1	54.1	25.2
Alberta	3,107,356	7.9	63.7	21.9
British Columbia	3,069,623	10.3	76.9	5.3
The Territories	455,467	63.9	27.9	1.3

Note: Adapted from *Education in Canada: A statistical review.* Statistics Canada (December, 1986), pp. 240–241.

the psychoemotional climate of the school (e.g., Ministère de l'Education du Nouveau-Brunswick, 1982, pp. 2–6).

The actual work of school psychologists may not encompass all these areas because of pressing caseloads. School psychologists often feel forced to ceaselessly test, appraise, diagnose, and recommend placement—particularly when there is not an adequate number of psychometricians or guidance counselors available who are qualified to help them in this aspect of their work.

An official conceptualization of the psychological services provided in a school milieu, published by the Ministère de l'Education du Québec (1986), is of interest. Although there are few substantive differences between the services offered in Quebec and those offered in other provinces, differences exist in their configuration and breadth. This official guide groups 41 discrete psychological services into those that (a) are specifically provided by psychologists, and (b) are although psychological in character, of a generality that allows them to be performed by specialists in different disciplines.

The activities detailed in this document cannot all be identified in a chapter of this length. Among those activities provided only by psychologists are, for example, distinct group activities that require a specificity and level of training possessed only by this professional group. A representative example is the sexual education workshop; it is of interest to note that it is characterized by (a) the added participation of health and social welfare personnel, and (b) an emphasis on the emotional and relational aspects of healthful sexual development. Those psychological services that are not conducted by a specific category of specialist include preventive interventions directed at potential school leavers, sensitivity sessions dealing with the social integration of handicapped persons, violence in the school, drug abuse, and the social integration of ethnically diverse pupils.

This schema addresses the controversial question that ministries of education as well as accrediting bodies continue to wrestle with (viz., which psychological services must be delivered by an accredited psychologist?). This question is a troublesome one for the prosperous as well as the poorer provinces. The cost of employing adequate numbers of staff with doctorates to deal with the variety of psychological problems that require attention in the school is regarded as prohibitive. It simply cannot be done. And as the research programs of our advanced degree students become increasingly specialized, the funding ministries are aware that the schools cannot be expected to provide the professional mirror-images of these basic science specialties. Moreover, because the ratios of psychologist to students that prevail in the various school districts of the country range from 1:2000 to 1:13,747, it is understandable that ministries of education as well as universities are looking at ways to design training programs that will more closely correspond both in breadth and degree level to the needs of the provinces' school systems.

What Training Is Required?

The educational requirements for accreditation as school psychologist in the provinces and territories of Canada are so diverse that one can make few meaningfully general statements about them; on the other hand, one cannot adequately describe them in a chapter of this length. The diversity of those requirements is comparable to that which one might find, for example, in any five countries of Europe chosen at random. Defining training requirements in Canada is further complicated by the fact that certain provinces have assigned school psychology tasks almost entirely to other professions, each of which has its unique training requirements.

Although provinces generally do not insist specifically on accreditation as a school psychologist for those they intend to hire in a school psychology position, they do insist that such recruits be certified as *psychologist* by an authorized provincial body. This enables school districts to match their needs with candidates that have particular configurations of courses, practica, internships, and job experiences. This is particularly adaptive as within the specialized psychology labeled *educational*, one must further specialize in developmental psychology, tests and measurements, instructional design, special education, or cognitive science (among others). The internship preferred by school boards is one in an educational setting that presents learning experiences that correspond closely to the challenges of the position being recruited for. As the academic component of educational psychology programs in some universities provides only a general foundation in the discipline, more intense and narrow specialization for the psychologist who is school bound is provided in individualized internships.

As the widely divergent demands that school boards make of school psychologists (and other professionals providing them with psychological services) require varying levels of education, applicants with degrees inferior to the doctorate are often hired by them. For example, certain school districts seeking a psychologist for a position that does not require doctoral level research competencies might hire a psychologist with a terminal master's degree if the job applicant had the needed clinical and consulting skills.

Finally, in some provinces, psychology-based tasks are performed by professionals trained not as school psychologists but as school counselors, clinical psychologists, or psychometrists. All may be registered as psychologists. The highly permeable professional boundaries that separate them invite conflicts as to who has the right to practice in one domain or another. One can always hope that all of these professionals are so heavily burdened that presumed encroachments onto each other's domains will not be resented, but welcomed with relief.

Difficulties Facing the Practitioner

Certain problems that face educational psychologists arise from the very nature of the settings in which they work. For example, work in regions such as the Northwest Territories that are climatically harsh, isolated, and sparsely settled or have unusual demographic features present challenges for which most school psychologists are ill prepared. There are other problems attributable to the very nature of a profession still in the process of defining itself on a continental scale. One can characterize the former category of problems as microstructural, and not easily generalizable to the country as a whole; the latter category as macrostructural, and dealing with systems and social structures that are nationwide. The latter is most useful to focus on in this chapter.

The education ministry of one of the more populous provinces traced many difficulties to a lack of clarity in the laws that govern the delivery of psychological services to schools. In response to inquiries made by the author, an officer of that ministry (personal communication, 1987) reported that "hiring practices for boards are in confusion" and that "interference by the outside licensing agency with school procedures is becoming an issue." Other complications, reported by this respondent, that flow from this sociolegal matrix are: (a) widespread controversy concerning the university degree level that should be required for professional practice, (b) "lack of networking [and] professional development activities mainly [deriving from] confusion re jurisdiction," and (c) the great disparities that prevail in defining the roles of those who provide psychological services to school boards. Although most provincial ministries may not be readily prepared to concede that they labor within disabling legal structures, the theoretical issues that are raised therein are widely debated, outside of Canada (American Psychological Association, 1987) as well as within.

Vague role definitions for *school psychologist* take a heavy toll. Teachers cannot be expected to make fine distinctions among the tasks that different kinds of psychologists should undertake, especially when administrators and other school board personnel are themselves uncertain of the constraints that the professional specialization of their support staff creates. When teachers have detected a problem that can be characterized as *psychological*, they initially tend to expect the school psychologist to be professionally equipped to treat it. This view is naive, often leads to disillusionment among teachers and a consequent deterioration in the latter's professional relations with psychologists, and promotes a sense of inadequacy and diminished self-esteem among those asked to provide psychological expertise.

School psychologists frequently feel a teacher distrust of their services that derives from at least two sources. Teachers often receive advice and in-service training from psychologists who have never been teachers themselves. The suspicion is widespread among teachers that psychologists and other professionals do not know what the teachers are up against. Teachers frequently judge professional contributions by school psychologists as unrealistic and patronizing. Many school psychologists feel they must counteract such preconceptions before beginning a consultation. In the words of one school psychologist who had worked years in the prairie provinces, "With every teacher who was new to me, I began the consultation by recounting an incident from my own teaching experience."

Second, individual psychologists have been expected (often unfairly) to provide schools and other institutions with a breadth of psychological services in which no single professional could possibly acquire expertise. This difficulty has a twofold root. School systems in many parts of Canada, when recruiting for school psychologists, commonly advertise simply for certified psychologists. There are several reasons for this. In some cases they want to cast their net over as large a pool of prospective employees as possible because they know from experience that professionals, particularly those with doctoral-level training, have not been interested in coming to their region in significant numbers. One department of special services tried to provide psychological services to several sparsely populated regions within its jurisdiction. The plan fell through because there was an insufficient number of qualified applicants. Although this view comes from a region with a number of geographic and demographic peculiarities, it is common in all the vast regions of the country that are remote from the large population centers. Also, school psychology is not considered a distinct psychological specialization such that certain school psychology services are normally provided only by accredited school psychologists.

Those who qualify in every sense as school psychologists construe their professional roles in ways that frequently are not fully consistent with the roles imposed on them by their employers. Moreover, among school psychologists, there is a great deal of diversity in the kinds of postgraduate professional programs in which they have been trained. One Canadian educational psychology department offers academic programs of cognitive science, developmental psychology, tests and measurement, educational technology, computer applications in education, special education, adult education, instructional design, and others. Future school psychologists usually specialize in one of these areas; the more advanced the degree, the greater the level of specialization. However, their school-based internships cannot adequately focus on more than a narrow segment of the total spectrum of specialties. Needless to say, they may not be truly qualified to be hired for professional work in more than one, at most two areas.

Tensions between as well as within different professions are widely reported in Canada. The former occur among school psychologists when tasks are imposed on them that can more properly be addressed by other professions. For example, children diagnosed as school phobic frequently are referred by school psychologists to a community mental health clinic. Some have been known to be referred back to the school for treatment by the school psychologist. Finely nuanced directives from the governmental ministries controlling referrals for various categories of problems still need to be developed in some provinces in order to prevent these difficulties.

The problem of overlapping mandates can be partially addressed by the strategy of restricting services that can be described by the use of the words "psychological," "psychologist," or "psychology" to those who are "duly registered psychologists." One province has issued a ministerial directive bearing on the psychological testing and assessment of pupils that requires this. However, this policy is complicated by the fact that innumerable psychoeducators, speech pathologists, school couselors, and psychometricians, among others, are certified psychologists in that province. The knottier question is how one distinguishes psychological from educational assessments except, in many instances, in the most arbitrary way.

Heavy testing, diagnostic, and referral burdens are placed on school psychologists. Indeed, in response to the question, "what are generally considered the most important contributions that school psychologists make within and outside the school context?" one province reported only one task in 1987: "intellectual assessment." Similarly, in parts of the country where the school psychologist is mandated to provide a broad spectrum of psychological services, the more isolated, less adequately staffed school districts require so much direct assessment that time for indirect, consultative work with teachers and other school personnel does not exist. To further complicate this issue, some provinces have authorized other school-based professionals to provide services, principally of a clinical nature, which school psychologists might otherwise have been able (and preferred) to deliver themselves.

CONCLUSIONS

"There are . . . many (most would argue too many) *opinions about*, or accounts of *perceptions of*, the role and function of the school psychologist" (Ysseldyke, 1986, p. 27). Opinions exist, of course, in the absence of certitude, and it is this that makes it difficult to assess what is happening in the profession of school psychology in Canada. One cannot be quite sure that those who work in this profession are making fine distinctions between what they think their clientele expect school psychologists to do, what they personally would prefer to be doing themselves, what the profession "officially" indicates that its practitioners should be doing, and what they think they actually are doing.

An analysis of this field is complicated by the fact that it is hardly less true today in Canada than it was a generation ago in the United States that "the role of the school psychologist varies in scope and character with the philosophy that prevails in specific schools" (Gottsegen, 1960, p. 2). Perceptual bias and doctrinal distortions are present in every source of information, whether it is a ministry of education or the parent of a school-phobic child being helped by a school psychologist. Cross validating even the most significant classes of perceptions available to us would be an enormous research task that one could easily suspect would only lead to the conclusion that there is no consensus on major issues.

Forecasting the future of any profession is always a temerarious enterprise. It is all the more so when, given the diversity and fluidity that characterizes the field, we are not quite certain where we are in the present. Janzen (1987), speaking of the evolution of school psychology in Canada, indicated that many of the growing pains of this profession that may only be remembered in the United States as history are the daily fare of Canadian school psychologists: role confusion, identity diffusion with related disciplines, the struggle for "recognition and academic respect" in psychology departments. For the profession there still remain major tasks: standardization of training and accreditation norms, development of school psychology organizations, journals, and the cultivation of formal and informal international linkages.

The status of the profession in any province or region will not be improved by the articulation of pious hopes for the future. We simply need to add to the already substantial number of competent and dedicated scholars, researchers, and practitioners in this field who are talking to each other. Thomas (1974) once observed that

> any word you speak this afternoon will radiate . . . around town before tomorrow, out and around the world before Tuesday . . . shaping new and unexpected messages, emerging at the end as an enormously funny Hungarian joke, a fluctuation in the money market, a poem, or simply a long pause in someone's conversation in Brazil. (pp. 131–132)

No less far-reaching effects can be expected when school psychologists speak to each other about matters that bear on the health and welfare of a society's children.

REFERENCES

American Psychological Association Education and Training Board Task Force Task Force on Review of the Scope and Criteria for Accreditation. (January 5, 1987). *Task force report No. 2: Recommendations on accreditation scope* (A limited distribution memorandum). Washington, DC: Author.

Bardon, J. I. (1986). Psychology and schooling: The interrelationships among persons, processes and products. In S. N. Elliott & J. C. Witt (Eds.), *The delivery of psychological services in schools* (pp. 53–79). Hillsdale, NJ: Lawrence Erlbaum Associates.

Dumont, F., & Lecomte, C. (1985). Political and cognitive structures underlying scientific inquiry in the university: The challenge to educational researchers. *The Canadian Journal of Higher Education, 15*(3), 23–38.

Gottsegen, M. G. (1960). Role definition of school psychology. In M. G. Gottsegen & G. G. Gottsegen (Eds.). *Professional school psychology* (pp. 2–17). New York: Grune & Stratton.

Janzen, H. L. (1987, February). American influences on school psychology and a new role for a trainer of school psychology. *The School Psychologist: Division of School Psychology Newsletter*, pp. 4–5.

Mannheim, K. (1936). *Ideology and utopia.* New York: Harvest Books.

Ministère de l'Education du Nouveau-Brunswick. (1982). *Manuel des services de psychologie scolaire* [Handbook of school psychology services]. Fredericton, N. -B.: Author.

Ministère de l'Education du Québec. (1986). *Les services de psychologie à l'école: Guide d' activités* [School psychology services: A guide to activities]. Québec, Qc.: Author.

Monroe, V. (1979). Roles and status of school psychology. In G. D. Phye, & D. J. Reschley (Eds.), *School psychology: Perspectives and issues* (pp. 25–47). New York: Academic Press.

Sarason, S. B. (1977). The unfortunate fate of Alfred Binet and school psychology. In S. Miezitis & M. Orme (Eds.), *Innovation in school psychology* (pp. 19–32). Toronto, Ont.: The Ontario Institute for Studies in Education.

Statistics Canada. (1986, December). *Education in Canada: A statistical review.*

Thomas, L. (1974). *The lives of a cell: Notes of a biology watcher.* New York: Bantam Books.

Weininger, O. (1971). The school psychologist as chameleon. *Canadian Counsellor, 5*, 125–134.

White, M. A., & Harris, M. (1961). *The school psychologist.* New York: Harper.

Ysseldyke, J. E. (1986). Current practice in school psychology. In S. N. Elliott & J.C. Witt (Eds.), *The delivery of psychological services in schools* (pp. 27–51). Hillsdale, NJ: Lawrence Erlbaum Associates.

Chapter Twenty-One
School Psychology in the United States of America in the 1980s

Thomas Oakland
The University of Texas at Austin

BRIEF VIEWS ON SCHOOL PSYCHOLOGY

School Psychology's History

The first psychological clinic, established in 1896 by Lightner Witmer (1897) at the University of Pennsylvania, marks the origin of school psychology in the United States. The following year Witmer began offering courses to teachers and others interested in applying the new methods from clinical psychology. Witmer envisioned the preparation of pedagogical or psychological experts able to work with children who did not profit from ordinary educational methods. He later embodied this vision by serving personally as a school psychologist (Fagan, 1986).

Despite its early beginning, the growth of school psychology as well as other applied areas of psychology was slow during the next 50 years. Psychology departments, dominated by scientists, generally were not interested in applied psychology. Moreover, standards for preparing, credentialing, and licensing school and other applied psychologists did not begin to appear until the 1920s, initially in New York and adjacent states.

By 1950, only 10 universities offered specific programs preparing school psychologists. Although the number increased to 30 by 1964, the period that followed saw a sizeable increase in the number of programs: 79 by 1965, 153 by 1972, and 211 by 1984 (Fagan, 1986). There also was a sevenfold increase in the number of students between 1965 and 1984: from about 1,000 to more than 7,000. Approximately 2,200 school psychology students now graduate yearly (Brown & Lindstrom, 1978).

Who Are School Psychologists?

An estimated 25,000 persons serve as school psychologists. They comprise our nation's most widely dispersed group of professional psychologists and can be found in all 50 states. They are most numerous in states with large populations and in the northeast, upper midwest, and west (e.g., New York, New Jersey, Illinois, Ohio, California). Consistent with historical traditions and with practices in other countries, proportionately more work in urban than in rural areas (Oakland & Mowder, 1981; Ramage, 1984).

About 35% have a doctoral degree and the remaining 65% are prepared at either a specialist or a masters level. Their average age is about 40; most range between 30 and 50. Slightly more than 50% are female. Almost all are White. Many school psychologists seemingly remain in the profession for about 10 years and then go on to other professional positions in education or psychology. The average school psychologist annually earns about $22,000 with a subdoctoral degree and about $26,000 with a doctoral degree. In contrast, the average doctoral clinical psychologist earns about $36,000 yearly (Stapp & Fulcher, 1981), whereas physicians average about $90,000. Most school psychologists work from mid-August through mid-June with a 2-week vacation during the winter and 1 week during spring. They typically work 7 to 8 hours daily, 5 days a week.

School Psychology's Infrastructure Nationally and Within the 50 States

School Psychology's National Infrastructure

A strong infrastructure supporting school psychology exists at the national level. School psychologists have divisional representation (i.e., the Division of School Psychology) in the American Psychological Association (APA) as well as their own professional association: the National Association of School Psychologists (NASP). Other national organizations devoted to the interests of school psychology include the National Association of State Consultants in School Psychology, Trainers of School Psychology, Council of Directors of School Psychology Programs, the Interorganization Committee (between APA and NASP), and APA's Task Force on Psychology in the School.

School psychology also has developed a number of standards that exemplify the profession's values and principles and that serve the needs of service providers, clients, educators, society, and legal bodies (Oakland, 1986). These standards, as prepared by the American Psychological Association, include *Psychology as a Profession* (1968), "Guidelines for Conditions of Employment of Psychologists" (1972), *Ethical Principles in the Conduct of Research with Human Subjects* (1973), *Standards for Educational and Psychological Testing* (1985), *Standards for Providers of Psychological Service* (1977), *Criteria for Accreditation of Doc-*

toral Training Programs and Internships in Professional Psychology (1980), *Ethical Principles of Psychologists* (1981a), and "Specialty Guidelines for the Delivery of Services by School Psychologists" (1981b). The National Association of School Psychologists standards including *Standards for the Provision of School Psychological Services* (1984b), *Standards for Training and Field Placement Programs in School Psychology* (1984c), *Standards for Credentialing in School Psychology* (1978), and *Principles for Professional Ethics* (1984a).

The infrastructure also is strengthened by the four professional journals devoted to advancing the knowledge and practices of school psychology: *Journal of School Psychology, Professional School Psychology, Psychology in the Schools*, and *School Psychology Review*. Sixteen secondary journals and 26 tertiary journals contribute to its literature (Reynolds & Gutkin, 1982, pp. 1169–1172). Scores of textbooks also discuss school psychology (French, 1986; Whelan & Carlson, 1986).

School Psychology's Infrastructure Within States

Infrastructures also exist within the 50 states. School psychologists in almost all states are represented by professional associations that either are within their state psychological association or are separate associations of school psychologists. Also, state education agencies in all states but one certify school psychologists for practice in schools.

Many school psychologists desire to be licensed and thus to retain the option to practice privately in out-of-school settings as a psychologist or school psychologist. Those who hold doctoral degrees in psychology typically are eligible to be licensed by their state as psychologists (note: all states have boards that license psychologists). However, those holding subdoctoral degrees typically are granted permission to practice psychology only under the supervision of licensed (e.g., doctoral) psychologists. This restriction is changing in many states as more nondoctoral-level school psychologists are being granted the right to be licensed and to practice privately as school psychologists.

THE PREPARATION OF SCHOOL PSYCHOLOGISTS

As expected, significant differences exist among the more than 200 programs preparing school psychologists. An understanding of their preparation is enhanced by first describing the three different levels of preparation: masters, specialist, and doctoral levels. No school psychology programs exist at the undergraduate level (i.e., the first 4 years of post-secondary education). Thus, all school psychology programs require students to enter with at least an undergraduate degree. Many students entering these programs have teaching experience, whereas others have not taught but have undergraduate degrees in education or psychology.

However, prior experiences or coursework in education or psychology are not prerequisites for entering most programs.

To enter a program, a student applies to one or more of the school psychology programs in any area of the country. The program faculty selects the most able students as judged by their undergraduate academic records, scores from their Graduate Record Examination (i.e., a measure of cognitive abilities), letters of reference, prior personal and professional experiences, and a statement describing profession goals. Preference often is given to applicants from minority groups (e.g., Black, Mexican American, Asian).

Preparation at the masters level typically requires a 1- to 1½-year program of 10 to 15 courses (each course—or paper as they frequently are called elsewhere—typically meets for 2½ to 3½ hours weekly for about 16 contiguous weeks). Preparation at the specialist level typically requires a 2- to 3-year program of 20 or more courses plus a 1-year supervised internship. Preparation at the doctoral level typically involves a 4- to 5-year program that requires 2 to 3 years of course work (25 to 35 courses), a 1-year supervised internship, and a dissertation. Persons completing doctoral programs obtain the title doctor of philosophy (PhD), doctor of education (Ed.D.), or doctor of psychology (Psy.D.). Approximately 35% of the school psychology programs presently offer doctoral-level preparation, whereas the remaining offer preparation at the masters or specialist levels.

Academic and Professional Coursework

The coursework is intended to enhance a student's understanding of the theory, science, and technology of psychology together with its applications in schools and other applied settings (e.g., juvenile probation, clinics). Students typically take foundation courses in psychology (e.g., learning and cognition, development, personality, social, statistics, psychometrics, and research design) and education (e.g., curriculum and instruction, educational administration, and special education). Longer programs typically require more foundation and applied psychology courses. Between one third and one half of the courses are at the foundations level with the remaining courses directed more specifically to school psychology.

As indicated later in this chapter, many school psychologists devote considerable time to assessment activities. Thus, much of their coursework in school psychology also is devoted to this area and includes introductory courses on tests and measurement and on using intelligence and personality tests; advanced courses also are taken on individual appraisal of learning-disabled and emotionally disturbed children and youth. Students in specialist and doctoral programs also may take courses in behavioral, family, and neuropsychological assessment. Their preparation is not limited to assessment. Students may take one or more courses on consultation; cognitive (e.g., reading, math, intelligence), perceptual, and social–emotional (including counseling and other therapeutic) interventions; evaluation; and organizational development (Copeland & Miller, 1985).

Field-Based Experiences

One's entire academic preparation and the majority of one's professional preparation occur through university-based courses. Some courses have practicum components that require students to work with pupils, their teachers, and parents in field settings (e.g., schools and clinics) under supervision by the course instructor. Internship experiences, on the other hand, typically are supervised directly by professional school psychologists working in the internship location (e.g., schools, mental health clinics) and require the student to work between 20 and 40 hours weekly for 10 to 12 months.

Prevailing Philosophies Guiding Preparation and Practice

A prevailing view, particularly among advocates of doctoral-level school psychology, maintains applications of psychology, including school psychology, should be supportable empirically and theoretically and derived from a body of literature that is held in high esteem. This scientist-practitioner model (Cutts, 1955; Raimy, 1950) emphasizes the importance of reciprocal relationships between the science and practice of psychology; each contributes to the other.

Other views are more pragmatic and stated less formally. They recognize that holding a subdoctoral degree and being restricted to performing appraisal services limit many school psychologists in contributing to the school psychology literature. Although these persons should have a good understanding of psychological literature, practical limitations restrict their ability to make professional or scientific contributions to the profession beyond their immediate work settings.

Viewpoints also are mixed as to whether school psychology belongs in psychology or education. Some persons view school psychology as a specialty within the profession of psychology whose research base is derived largely from the discipline of psychology (Bardon, 1982). Others view school psychology as a profession separate and independent from psychology and more clearly allied with education (Brown, 1982). In fact, most school psychologists maintain some affiliation with both professions. Those who work in schools frequently identify closely with their colleagues in education yet recognize that most of the technology and literature that guide their work comes from psychology.

SOME FEATURES OF THE U.S. SOCIETY

Some knowledge of the U.S. society may help to put information about school psychology in a better perspective. The U.S. population is approximately 240 million with about 20% between ages 6–18. The United States always has been a nation of immigrants. Less than 1% of our population is native American Indian. About 80% of our population traces their ancestors to Europe (i.e., are White), 11% are Black, 5% are Hispanic (i.e., from countries colonized by Spain and Portugal), and 2% Asian. Immigration continues. Immigrants entering the United States constitute two thirds of all immigrants in the world.

The nonWhite (i.e., minority) population tends to be younger and thus constitutes close to 30% of our school-age population. Women's average fertility rates (i.e., the average number of children per lifetime) are 1.7 for Whites, 2.4 for Blacks, and 2.9 for Mexican Americans. The average age of Whites is 31, whereas the average age of Blacks is 25 and of Hispanics is 23. Whites are moving out of their childbearing years as Blacks and Hispanics are moving into them. In some states, the number of minority children exceeds those of Whites. Thus, racial and ethnic diversity is increasing in the United States. By 2,000, one third of our population will be nonWhite.

The United States has a reputation for being a land of plenty, a wealthy nation. The mean level of income is $12,700 per capita (U.S. Bureau of the Census, 1986). However, significant differences can be found among its population. Income levels are higher in urban areas; in the eastern, midwestern, and western states (as opposed to those in the south); for males; among the more highly educated, and among Whites and some minorities (e.g., Jews, Orientals) than among other minorities (e.g., Blacks, Hispanics, and American Indians).

Schooling in the United States

Children typically begin school at age 5 (when they enter kindergarten) and exit at age 18. Approximately 80% of the students enroll in public schools; 20% are in private and parochial schools. School attendance is mandatory in most states until age 16. Upon entering at 5, they remain in elementary school for 6 to 7 years at which point they enter junior high or middle school for a 2- to 3-year program, followed by 4 years of high school. Thus, students typically are in school for 13 years. Following these programs they may elect to continue their tertiary education through business or vocational training programs, community and junior colleges (typically offering 2-year programs), as well as colleges (offering 4-year undergraduate and occasional graduate programs), and universities (offering undergraduate and graduate programs).

An estimated $188 billion is spent yearly on education between Grades K–12. Most costs for public education are paid by state and local governments (i.e., an estimated $163 billion); about 40% of state and local revenues are for education. In contrast, about 5% of the federal government's budget is for education (i.e., $25 billion; U.S. Bureau of the Census, 1986).

Authority for Education in the United States

Unlike many countries in which the federal government plays the dominant role in education, primary authority for education in the United States rests within the 50 states through powers claimed under the Tenth Amendment of the U.S. Constitution. Each state has a board of education (elected by the voters or appointed by the governor), a state education agency, and a commissioner of education. The board of education, together with the state's legislative bodies, establishes policies governing education within the state's public schools; the state education agency, under the direction of the commissioner of education, carries out the policies and monitors practices. The state boards of education also transfer to local school districts many responsibilities for developing policies that govern local practices. Thus, significant differences often exist among the nation's 15,300 school districts with respect to educational goals, the certification and employment of educational personnel (including school psychologists), curricula, school calendars, graduation requirements, and other important features of public education.

However, the impact of the federal government on education is not benign. Each of the three major branches of the federal government influences education in important ways. A few examples are provided.

Congress

Congress passes laws from time to time that establish national standards for education. A clear example is seen in the Education for All Handicap Childrens Act of 1975. The act, also commonly known as P.L. 94–142, offers states assistance for compliance with the extensive goals and procedures set forth in the Act. Congress best expressed its ambitious mission in its statement of purpose as follows:

> It is the purpose of this Act to assure that all handicapped children have available to them . . . a free appropriate public education which emphasizes special education and related services designed to meet their unique needs, to assure that the rights of handicapped children and their parents or guardians are protected, to assist States and localities to provide for the education of all handicapped children, and to assess and assure the effectiveness of efforts to educate handicapped children. (20 U.S.C. 1401(c), 1976)

The act states that procedures must protect the legal rights of the children and their parents. The U.S. Congress has been particularly interested in legislation designed to enhance the care and development of children with physical, mental, or emotional disorders.

Federal Courts

The Supreme Court, together with its lower federal courts, rules on the constitutionality of local, state, and national legislation and of the practices of individuals as well as private and public agencies. During the last 30 years the Supreme Court has diligently attended to allegations of discriminatory school practices.

The 1954 U.S. Supreme Court decision in *Brown v. Board of Education* (347, U.S., 1954) signaled a new era in which the federal court system has been willing to consider the legality of educational policies and practices that affect racial balance, the allocation of resources among and within school districts, and other issues relating to civil and constitutional rights.

Administration

The President of the United States, together with bureaucratic officials working in the Department of Education, is responsible for administering and implementing the policies passed by Congress and judged by the Supreme Court to be constitutional. Many presidents and their staffs have taken an active interest in education and supported particular programs (e.g., teacher aids, foreign language instruction, science and math education, education of gifted and talented pupils, programs for minority pupils).

Administration of School Psychology Services

School psychological services typically are administered by local school districts either through special education or general education. When administered through special education, the services often are restricted largely to assessment and interventions for children and youth referred for special education services. When administered through general education, their responsibilities include both special and general education and often encompass broader areas of service (e.g., assessment, direct interventions, indirect service delivery systems, research and evaluation, administration, and prevention); moreover, they work more closely with counselors, guidance personnel, and others in general education who also have some preparation in psychology.

SCHOOL PSYCHOLOGICAL SERVICES

The title of school psychologist implies that one works in schools. Although a majority do, others work in mental health clinics, hospitals and other medical settings, research centers, private practice, and of course colleges and universities as instructors. Most of the information presented in this paper describes those who work primarily or exclusively in public school settings; few work in private schools.

School psychological services in the United States exhibit considerable differences between states and communities. Their characteristics are influenced by many conditions including federal and state laws, local traditions, policies and practices; financial resources, priorities, and funding patterns; the availability of school psychologists and the nature of their preparation; and national, state, and local professional standards. Furthermore, the quantity and nature of services often differ for preschool, elementary, and secondary pupils. Nationally, school psychologists devote about 5% of their time to preschool (ages 3–5), 60% to elementary (ages 6–12), 20% to junior high (ages 13–15), and 15% to senior high (ages 16–18) pupils (Smith, 1984).

As indicated elsewhere, school psychologists frequently devote considerable attention to the needs of special education, in particular mentally retarded, learning-disabled, and emotionally disabled children. Learning-disabled children comprise the largest number of special education students (about 10% of the school's population), whereas the mentally retarded comprise the smallest number (about 1%). Emotionally disturbed pupils also constitute another important group (about 3%). School psychologists devote about 32% of their time to children with learning disabilities, 22% to those with behavioral and emotional problems, 14% to those with mental retardation, and 16% to the general school population (Smith, 1984). School psychologists also devote smaller amounts of time to the talented and gifted (4%), and to those pupils exhibiting acuity (3%), physical (2%), and speech (2%) disorders.

Six Broad Areas of Service

Although school psychology is a dynamic specialty and one not easily categorized or described, its services tend to fall into six broad areas.

Individual Evaluations

School psychologists frequently conduct psychoeducational evaluations of pupils who may need special attention. The referred pupils typically are identified by teachers as having possible disorders in academic, social, or emotional development. Most referrals occur during the elementary grades and typically are boys, particularly those who are acting out and agressive. School psychologists are likely to conduct evaluations that assess a student's cognitive (i.e., intelligence and achievement), affective, social, emotional, and linguistic characteristics and utilize educational and psychological (including behavioral, psychoneurological, and psychoanalytic) techniques. The evaluations have five goals: to accurately describe a child's development, to develop hypotheses concerning the etiology of the pupil's disorder, to determine if the pupil is eligible to receive special services, to suggest viable interventions, and to establish baseline data that allow for the detection of subsequent changes.

Direct Interventions

School psychologists also participate in planning and evaluating services designed to promote cognitive, social, and emotional development. Their services can include teaching, training, counseling, and providing therapy. Their principal focus frequently is on individual pupils.

Indirect Interventions

School psychologists also offer indirect services to pupils by working individually or with groups of parents, teachers, principals, and other educators. Their indirect services typically involve in-service programs, counseling, consultation, and collaboration. In addition, their organizational development work as members of the education staff often is directed toward making changes in the educational system by working on broad and important issues that impact a home, one or more classrooms, a school building, a school district, a community, or a group of school districts.

Research and Evaluation

School psychologists' knowledge of quantitive methods commonly used in research and evaluation often surpasses that of other educational personnel. Thus, they frequently are responsible for conceptualizing and designing studies, collecting and analyzing data, and interpreting and disseminating the findings.

Supervision and Administration

School psychologists also may supervise pupil personnel and psychological services. In this capacity, they are responsible for conceptualizing and promoting a comprehensive plan for these services, for hiring and supervising personnel, for promoting their development, and for coordinating these services with others in the district and community.

Prevention

Although psychologists are committed to helping those with special needs, they would prefer to establish programs that foster healthy growth and development and that prevent the occurrence of special problems. For example, drug and alchohol abuse, suicide, and pregnancies are occurring at alarming rates among adolescents in some communities. School psychologists are often at the forefront in developing programs designed to prevent these and other problems.

Sixteen Domains of Service

A more detailed view of school psychology practices in the United States is provided by a recent comprehensive review of the school psychology literature (Ysseldyke, Reynolds, & Weinberg, 1984) that identified the following 16 domains as ones in which school psychology has expertise: classroom management, classroom organization and social structure, interpersonal communication and consultation, basic academic skills, basic life skills, affective/social skills, parent involvement, systems development and planning, personnel development, individual differences in development and learning, school-community relations, instruction, legal, ethical, and professional issues, assessment, multicultural concerns, and research and evaluation.

How School Psychologists Do and Prefer to Use Their Time

The six broad areas and the 16 domains are services individual school psychologists provide in varying degrees. Rarely are a school psychologist's responsibilities equally balanced in all six areas and over all 16 domains. When asked how they actually spend their time and how they desired to spend their time, school psychologists indicated they do spend about 54% but would like to spend 40% of their time in assessment activities, they spend 23% but would like to spend 30% of their time in interventions (e.g., counseling, program development); they spend 18% but would like to spend 23% on consultation; and spend 1% but would like to spend 4% on research (Smith, 1984).

SOME SPECIAL PROBLEMS FOR SCHOOL PSYCHOLOGY

Although school psychology is a well-established and large profession, many issues and problems confront the profession and its members (Oakland, 1986).

In Preparation

School psychology needs to strengthen its positions within universities and to improve conditions for faculty and students. More programs are needed at the doctoral level. Also, university instructors tend to be underpaid and overworked, having little time for research and other scholarly activities.

Few scholarships and stipends are available to support students. Thus, many are attracted to other programs that provide better support. Fewer bright female students will be attracted to careers in education and psychology as they increasingly find new and more compelling career opportunities and higher monetary rewards elsewhere. Other students attend school part time, thus delaying the completion of their programs. The significant commitment of money and time needed to obtain a doctoral degree (i.e., 5 or more years of full-time graduate work) compared to the relatively low salaries they receive as school psychologists produces unattractive cost–benefit ratios. The relatively low salaries received by doctoral-level school psychologists may have a deleterious effect by encouraging more students inclined toward advanced professional degrees to consider medicine, law, dentistry, and other more highly paid professions or to encourage students to discontinue their studies after obtaining a subdoctoral degree.

In Practice

Although many potential advantages exist for psychologists working in schools, significant numbers of school psychologists labor under inadequate work conditions (Wise, 1985). They frequently lack adequate supervision, sufficient secretarial support, appropriate assessment techniques, adequate time in which to perform duties, and contact with professional colleagues. Many school psychologists report problems and conflicts associated with (a) diffusing their professional role within an organization (i.e., they are not allowed to regulate their practice of psychology), (b) working in an organization that has a vertical administrative structure instead of the horizontal administrative structure more commonly found among professions, (c) decisions that affect psychological services being made by persons other than psychologists, (d) making compromises between organizational limitations and professional standards, (e) receiving little personal recognition for contributions to the progress of individuals or the organization, (f) too much time and effort being devoted to assessment with little time remaining for providing services in the other five broad areas, and (g) having few colleagues with whom to consult and interact.

Many school psychologists work in settings in which they are the only school psychologist. Feelings of isolation result from this lack of comaraderie with fellow psychologists. Furthermore, many are inclined to identify more with the profession of education than with the profession of psychology.

The demographic characteristics of our profession, like others, do not match the U.S. population. School psychologists are overwhelmingly White and fluent only in English. Current efforts to attract more persons from minority backgrounds and those fluent in other languages have not been sufficiently successful.

The attrition rates for school psychologists seemingly are high. Many leave the field after about 10 years. High attrition rates increase the costs associated with personnel preparation, create the need to continuously attract large numbers of qualified students, encourage lower admission standards, and significantly lower the prestige of the profession.

SOME POSSIBLE FUTURES FOR SCHOOL PSYCHOLOGY

The preparation of school psychologists will be characterized by changes in patterns rather than by continued program expansion (Fagan, 1985). Professional preparation programs, now dominated by persons prepared at the masters level, are moving quickly toward higher levels of training, particularly toward the doctoral level. While many programs in the United States continue to prepare their students as generalists, a number now prepare students for more narrow roles (e.g., to work primarily with issues involving preschoolers, vocational preparation and counseling, rural education, or educational administration).

The United States is a nation in flux. Three important demographic trends are noteworthy that have important implications for the futures of school psychology: Our population is getting older, is becoming more multiethnic, and is increasing in the south and southwest (Oakland, 1984). Older populations tend to be more conservative politically and financially. Moreover, concerns about the elderly are displacing race and gender issues. Also, facing a trillion-dollar federal deficit, the federal government is likely to provide fewer funds for education, thus causing state and local governments to raise taxes. Public schools in many states are likely to receive less financial support, leading to a reduction in the employment of educational personnel, particularly support personnel such as school psychologists.

In the 1980s, eight western states and Florida have shown the largest population growth and the largest increase in minorities. Population shifts bring attendant social and psychological problems to families. The incidence of crime and delinquency, loneliness, drug and alchohol abuse, venereal disease, work and school truancy, and underachievement are often associated with relocation. An estimated 50% of our children will live some time in one-parent famlies. Increased psychological and social problems will require the services of more school psychologists in order to establish direct care and prevention programs in schools and community agencies. Others will enter private practice as child psychologists. With less money to pay for their services, psychologists working in schools may be overburdened with responsibilities and their services may become shallow.

The United States has more than 100 identifiable racial or ethnic groups and ranks fifth among nations in the population of both Blacks and Hispanics. The minority population is younger and growing steadily; this is especially true of Hispanics. In contrast, few school psychologists, probably less than 5%, are from minority groups. Furthermore, few are fluent in a foreign language. Thus, the profession lacks the resources to work effectively with children and their families who evidence sharply different cultural, social, economic, and linguistic characteristics.

As the quality of professional services often is higher in the private sector than in the public sector, our profession must work to ensure the quality of services available from school psychologists working in schools and other public agencies at least matches the quality provided by school psychologists working privately. This constitutes a significant and continuous challenge for the years ahead.

REFERENCES

American Psychological Association. (1968). *Psychology as a profession.* Washington, DC: Author.

American Psychological Association. (1972). Guidelines for conditions of employment of psychologists. *American Psychologist, 27,* 331–334.

American Psychological Association. (1973). *Ethical principles in the conduct of research with human subjects.* Washington, DC: Author.

American Psychological Association. (1977). *Standards for providers of psychological services* (rev. ed.). Washington, DC: Author.

American Psychological Association. (1980). *Criteria for accreditation of doctoral training programs and internships in professional psychology.* Washington, DC: Author.

American Psychological Association. (1981a). *Ethical principles of psychologists* (rev. ed.). Washington, DC: Author.

American Psychological Association. (1981b). Specialty guidelines for the delivery of services by school psychologists. *American Psychologist, 36,* 639, 670-682.

American Psychological Association. (1985). *Standards for educational and psychological testing.* Washington, DC: Author.

Bardon, J. (1982). The psychology of school psychology. In C. R. Reynolds & T. B. Gutkin (Eds.), *The handbook of school psychology* (pp. 1–14). New York: Wiley.

Brown, D. (1982). Issues in the development of professional school psychology. In C. R. Reynolds & T. B. Gutkin (Eds.)., *The handbook of school psychology* (pp. 14–23). New York: Wiley.

Brown, D. T., & Lindstrom, J. P. (1978). The training of school psychologists in the United States: An overview. *Psychology in the Schools, 15,* 37–45.

Brown, v. Board of Education of Topeka. 347 U.S. (1954).

Copeland, E. P., & Miller, L. F. (1985). Training needs of prospective school psychologists: the practitioners' viewpoint. *Journal of School Psychology, 23,* 247–254.

Cutts, N. E. (Ed.). (1955). *School psychology at mid-century.* Washington, DC: American Psychological Association.

Education of All Handicapped Childrens Act. 20.U.S.C, 1401(c), (1976).

Fagan, T. (1985). Quantitative growth of school psychology in the United States. *School Psychology Review, 14,* 121–124.

Fagan, T. K. (1986). The historical origins and growth of programs to prepare school psychologists in the United States. *Journal of School Psychology, 24,* 9–22.

French, J. L. (1986). Books in school psychology: The first forty years. *Professional School Psychology, 1,* 267–277.

National Association of School Psychologists. (1978). *Standards for credentialing in school psychology.* Washington, DC: Author.

National Association of School Psychologists. (1984a). *Principles for professional ethics*. Washington, DC: Author.

National Association of School Psychologists. (1984b). *Standards for the provision of school psychological services*. Washington, DC: Author.

National Association of School Psychologists. (1984c). *Standards for training and field placement programs in school psychology*. Washington, DC: Author.

Oakland, T. (1984). The president's message. *The School Psychologist, 38*, 1–2, 4.

Oakland, T. (1986). Professionalism within school psychology. *Professional School Psychology, 1*, 9–27.

Oakland, T., & Mowder, B. (1981). Selected characteristics of division of school psychology members. *The School Psychologist, 35*, 1–2.

Raimy, V. (Ed.). (1950). *Training in clinical psychology*. Engelwood Cliffs, NJ: Prentice-Hall.

Ramage, J. (1984). Basic characteristics of school psychologists today. *Communique, 12*, 1–2.

Reynolds, C. R., & Gutkin, T. B. (1982). *The handbook of school psychology*. New York: Wiley.

Smith, D. K. (1984). Practicing school psychologists: their characteristics, activities, and populations served. *Professional Psychology: Research & Practice, 15*, 798–810.

Stapp, J., & Fulcher, R. (1981). *Salaries in psychology*. Washington, DC: American Psychological Association.

U. S. Bureau of the Census (1986). *Statistical abstract of the United States: 1986*. Washington, DC.

Whelan, T., & Carlson, C. (1986). Books in school psychology: 1970 to the present. *Professional School Psychology, 1*, 279–289.

Wise, P. S. (1985). School psychologists' rankings of stressful events. *Journal of School Psychology, 23*, 31–41.

Witmer, L. (1897). The organization of practical work in psychology. *Psychological Review, 4*, 116–117.

Ysseldyke, J. E., Reynolds, M. C., & Weinberg, R. A. (1984). *School psychology: A blueprint for training and practice*. Minneapolis: National School Psychology Inservice Training Network.

Chapter Twenty-Two
School Psychology in Mexico

Wayne H. Holtzman, Jr.
University of Texas at Austin

ELEMENTARY AND SECONDARY EDUCATION

A brief description of Mexico's educational system is needed before discussing school psychology in Mexico. Both public and private schools operate at the preschool and kindergarten levels; attendance is optional. Education is mandatory from first through sixth grades, whereas junior high and high school education is optional. The availability of public schools varies throughout Mexico, with urban areas having more resources than rural areas. In some isolated areas of the country, attending school is difficult because of transportation problems, including poor quality of roads and long distances. Much progress has been made during the 1980s, however, to improve the availability of schools. The country's educational resources generally are meager and become more scarce as children advance through higher grades in the public educational system. Because of rampant population growth, children in urban areas typically attend schools in crowded classrooms for 4½ to 5 hours daily either in the mornings or in the afternoons. Evening classes are often reserved for adult education. Although the quality of public education varies between regions, the federal government provides a uniform national curriculum and free textbooks to all pupils.

In contrast to public schools, private schools are located mainly in large urban areas such as Mexico City and state capitals. The tuition in these schools generally is high. Thus, private school pupils largely come from upper middle and upper class families. Because of the economic depression currently affecting Mexico, middle-class families increasingly are finding private education for their children to be too expensive.

The vast majority of public school teachers in the elementary grades are women, with more men working at the junior and senior high school levels. The average income for teachers, principals, and other public school educators is barely at subsistence level because of the country's economic problems. However, the national teacher's union is a powerful force and is the largest union of its kind in Latin America.

Teacher training is conducted through both public and private normal schools. The teacher certification program consists of 4 years of coursework and an additional year to write a thesis, after completing preparatory teacher training in high school. All certification courses are in education and include topics in psychology and educational assessment.

There is a severe lack of special educators and related services in regular education. Special education services generally focus on the more severely handicapped, and are usually provided only in special schools. In 1973, under the presidential administration of Luis Echeverria Alvarez, a consolidation of special education services occurred with the creation of the Department of Special Education as part of the Secretariat of Public Education. In 1976, only 23,500 children were receiving special education services, whereas in 1983, there were 134,431 students participating in specially designed academic programs—an increase of 470% (M. I. Ehrlich, personal communication, January 1987).

Because special education schools exist independently of regular public schools, self-contained classes are the rule and serve the vast majority of children with special educational needs. Since 1976, a separate 6-month program in self-contained classes has been offered to first- and second-grade children who need special instruction in reading and mathematics. The program's objective is to provide for the needs of children who are about to be retained at their grade level. Approximately 70% of first graders enrolled in the program are promoted to second grade, 20% remain in the program for an additional 6 months, 7% drop out of the program, and 3% are placed in a more permanent special educational setting (M. I. Ehrlich, personal communication, January 1987). In addition, free public clinics exist to serve regular education students experiencing learning or behavioral disorders with remedial academic instruction being provided after the regular school day. During 1980 and 1981, approximately 24,000 children utilized the services of the public clinics (Informe Presidencial, 1982).

The Teacher's School of Special Education was founded in 1942 (Diaz-Guerrero, 1984b). Mexico has only a limited number of trained special education teachers. For example, in 1972 the first specialization program in learning disabilities was established through the normal school (Valdes, 1974). From 1972 through 1982, only 42 special education teachers had graduated from the program (M. I. Ehrlich, personal communication, January 1987). Besides courses in pedagogy, those in psychology comprise an important element in the training of these teachers.

UNDERGRADUATE AND GRADUATE TRAINING IN PSYCHOLOGY

The training of psychologists in Mexico was begun formally in 1945 at the National Autonomous University in Mexico City in conjunction with the founding of the Psychology Department within the larger School of Philosophy (Alvarez, 1977). The Department of Psychology became independent in 1973 (Diaz-Loving & Medina Liberty, 1987). As recently as 1964, only 5 universities were involved in the training of psychologists, but 3 years later the number had grown to 10 (Alvarez, 1977).

The largest number of psychology programs currently are found in or near Mexico City. The most well known are the National Autonomous and the Metropolitan Autonomous public universities, and three private universities: The Iberoamerican University, Anahuac University, and University of the Americas. Other federally supported universities that also offer at least a licenciatura degree in psychology are located in the various states.

The philosophic orientations of these schools vary greatly. In 1978, Velasco Hernandez reported that 68% were eclectic, 16% psychodynamic, 12% behavioral, and 4% humanistic. Currently, they appear to be becoming more eclectic.

Many faculty within clinical psychology programs seemingly hold Freudian psychoanalytic viewpoints while others adhere to the theories of Erich Fromm (who lived his final adult years in Cuernavaca, Mexico). Programs in experimental as well as some educational psychology programs more typically employ faculty who are behaviorally oriented. The Universidad Veracruzana in Jalapa, Veracruz, for example, has implemented a popular program dealing with experimental analysis of behavior.

The strongest emphasis and allocation of resources in Mexico are directed toward the undergraduate training of psychologists; few students enter graduate programs in psychology. About 200 students were enrolled in psychology programs at the large National Autonomous University of Mexico in 1956, but that number had skyrocketed to more than 20,000 by 1982. At least 60 institutions of higher education offer undergraduate degrees in psychology while only 6 offer the master's degree and only 2 offer doctoral programs in psychology (National Autonomous University of Mexico and the private Universidad Iberoamericana) (Diaz-Loving & Medina Liberty, 1987).

The undergraduate psychology programs in Mexico award a *licenciatura* degree and are structured differently from undergraduate programs offered in the United States. Rather than providing a broad range of courses in the liberal arts, undergraduate psychology programs in Mexican universities include only psychology courses. During the first 3 years, students take courses on general theoretical, methodological, and applied issues. During the next 1½ years, students choose courses in their major area of interest, including social, clinical, educational, industrial, psychophysiological, and experimental psychology. In addition to completing their academic coursework, all students must devote a certain number of hours during a 6- to 12-month period providing psychological service within the community. The students have considerable freedom in deciding where to provide the services. They typically include research projects and field work in schools, clinics, hospitals, or social agencies. The undergraduate *licenciatura* degree also requires a professional thesis. The qualifications of a graduate holding a *licenciatura* degree in Mexico are similar to those of a master's degree recipient from a U.S. university (Diaz-Guerrero, 1984a).

Students who enroll in a master's program must reside near Monterrey or Mexico City in order to pursue their studies. Many others are educated in the United States due to the close proximity of Mexico to the United States, the willingness of U.S. universities to admit foreign students, and the availability of scholarships and incentives that the Mexican government has made available through the National Council on Science and Technology (CONACYT) to study abroad. This was especially true during the 1970s, when the Mexican economy was stronger and more stable. The number of scholarships granted by CONACYT during the last several years has been severely curtailed to the extent that no psychology scholarships were awarded in 1987. Thus, only students who are able to rely on their personal financial resources are able to pursue graduate study in the United States. On the positive side, however, the generation of Mexicans who were educated in United States and other foreign universities during the 1960s and 1970s are providing important leadership within the academic and professional areas of psychology within both the public and private sectors. These graduates tend to be more productive in research and other scholarship activities than students who obtain doctorates from Mexican universities (Diaz-Guerrero, 1984a).

DEFINITION AND PROPOSED ROLE OF SCHOOL PSYCHOLOGISTS IN MEXICO

The reader may be wondering why much has been written about psychology in general with a total dearth of information regarding school psychology. No independent and well-defined specialization in school psychology exists in Mexico. Furthermore, school psychology has not been distinguished from educational psychology (Alvarez, 1977). It is doubtful that Mexican psychologists could agree on a definition of roles, job description, and responsibilities of school psychologists. Nevertheless, at least some of the school psychology practices that exist in other countries also are carried out in Mexico by either clinical or in some cases by educational psychologists. Most of these psychologists have not had graduate training, although the *licenciatura* degree has been viewed by some to be equivalent to a master's degree from U.S. universities.

Gustavo Fernandez, a Mexican psychologist who received his PhD from the University of Texas at Austin, was the first individual in Mexico to assume the title "school psychologist" (Fernandez, 1974). For Fernandez, school psychologists, like other psychologists, are responsible for providing, changing, or predicting behavior. According to Fernandez, important duties provided by school psychologists include conducting research, individual psychological assessments, implementing behavior modification techniques, and facilitating improved human relations. Traditional roles such as serving as a vocational guidance counselor or occasionally administering a few tests does not qualify one to be a professional school psychologist. More extended and specialized training is necessary. Thus, he encouraged institutions of higher education to change their programs to provide more comprehensive and specialized instruction for individuals being prepared as school psychologists. He recommended courses in statistics and research design, principles of behavior modification, and interviewing. The need for psychological tests developed in Mexico was another consideration. Many translations and test adaptations have been performed during the past few years (Padilla, Roll, & Gomez-Palacio, 1982) although Mexican norms still are needed.

Nieto (1975) also suggested directions school psychology should take in meeting its objective of facilitating the intellectual, social, and emotional development of children. He recommended school psychologists should aid in implementing and evaluating school programs, administering and interpreting standardized tests, serving as consultants to teachers, working as clinicians, preparing paraprofessionals, and helping to develop curriculum materials. Nieto noted that psychologists in Mexico generally work in applied settings and fulfill multiple roles and responsibilities. It is interesting to note that, although the Fernandez and Nieto articles were published about 13 years ago, few changes have occured in the preparation or practices of school psychologists in Mexico.

SCOPE OF SERVICES AND CONTRIBUTIONS

School psychology practices in Mexico most frequently utilize a direct services model that provides individual psychoeducational assessments of children and recommends interventions. Those working in private schools generally devote most of their time to assessment activities. They also may conduct observations of children in classrooms in order to develop behavior management plans.

Although school psychologists are commonly located in private schools, those in public schools are located at centers that serve clusters of schools. Within the public schools, a teacher typically refers a pupil for testing, the psychologist tests the pupil at the center, and then makes recommendations for possible interventions. The WISC–R is by far the most commonly used intelligence test in these assessments.

In contrast to other countries, Mexican school psychologists rarely serve as mental health consultants to teachers or provide inservice programs for them. Research and evaluation activities occur rather infrequently because of the lack of graduate training in these areas. Many research studies focus on behavior modifications of children in classroom settings. Among the 54 universities surveyed, only 14 offered courses in educational evaluation, and few *licenciatura* theses have been done in the area (Reyes Lagunes, 1983). Psychologists working as educational evaluators generally are found only in special centers or governmental agencies located mainly in Mexico City.

Administration

School psychological services either are funded locally through private institutions or nationally through the Mexican government. Most individuals who perform school psychology services work in urban areas, have a *licenciatura* degree, or have completed all coursework for the degree. An estimated 67% or more are women, and the majority are quite young (M. I. Ehrlich, personal communication, July 1987). There are no certification or licensing requirements for psychologists in Mexico. The average salary of school psychologists is estimated to be only between the equivalent of $3,500 and $6,000 per year in U.S. dollars, with salaries at some private schools being slightly higher. Although these figures appear to be extremely low by U.S. standards, most material goods and services in Mexico also are quite reasonable. Thus, the standard of living of school psychologists is higher than might be inferred. Relative to other professionals in Mexico, school psychologists do not fare badly. Salaries are competitive with those of teachers and are usually somewhat higher. Nevertheless, school psychologists must work at several jobs simultaneously in order to avoid severe economic hardships.

Contributions

School psychological practices through applied behavioral analysis is one area in which they made important contributions in Mexico (e.g., Ribes', 1972, book on the use of behavior modification strategies for developmentally retarded children). Other contributions include Reyes-Lagunes' and Lara-Tapia's work in the area of psychometrics, and publications dealing with psychological tests and the collection of data for local populations (Diaz-Guerrero, 1984a).

Several projects have promoted school psychological practices by providing student training and community service. Jimenez and Macotela (1983) described the Center of Human Psychological Studies (*Centro de Estudios de Psicologia Humana*) that began in 1977 to promote student training and to provide special education services within the community. Components of the program included training parents in behavior modification, designing new curriculum materials and methods, and creating behavioral objectives for children. Another project involved training psychology students who work in centers to provide psychological services to indigent families. One center is located in a low-income area and provides services in assessment, training parents to detect learning disabilities, preventing drug abuse and delinquency, fostering creativity in children, and promoting role-playing activities. Although the center serves useful functions, the lack of a permanent staff to provide adequate supervision of students interferes with the quality of services (Gomez del Campo, 1983).

Special Problems and Future Trends

The lack of certification and licensure requirements for psychologists in Mexico has enabled individuals the freedom to call themselves psychologists, regardless of training, and to engage in activities for which they may be unqualified. The quality of psychological services varies greatly; little protection exists for the consumer. Other problems lie in inappropriate use of U.S. developed tests and the lack of restrictions on the sale of psychological tests to the general public. These encourage psychological malpractice, especially in clinics and in private practice settings.

However, consumers are becoming somewhat more sophisticated in evaluating the professional credentials of psychologists. In addition, because of increased competition, it is becoming more difficult for students who have not finished their *licenciatura* theses to locate jobs. Unfortunately, this is generally true for psychologists at all levels of education. The chronic economic situation affecting Mexico forces many psychologists to work at two or three jobs. Thus, there exists a danger in having low-paid university professors devoting less time to research activities and to preparing class lectures, resulting in a lowering of educational standards. This occurs at a time when the severely overcrowded National Autonomous University of Mexico is attempting to implement unpopular reforms aimed to raise admission standards as well as to increase tuition (which has been virtually free for many years). If the country's economic condition worsens, the likelihood of leftist student groups organizing marches, sit-ins, strikes, and other forms of violent civil disturbances is increased.

The need for psychologists to work in public school settings is urgent. Similar to Brazil (Wechsler & Gomes, 1986), a lowering in the standard of living is forcing middle-class parents to transfer their children from private to public schools. These families have relied on school psychological services and may expect them in public schools. Second, the uncontrolled population explosion has made Mexico "a nation of children," in desperate need of school psychological and other support services. As school enrollments grow, the low pay and increased job pressures and stress experienced by principals and teachers result in a need for these professionals to receive psychological and educational support, perhaps through consultation with school psychologists. However, increased school psychological services through the public sector would require a commitment from both the Mexican government and private sources to ensure that psychologists receive adequate training and financial incentives to work in school settings. Because of Mexico's current economic conditions, the Mexican government could make at best only a modest committment to this goal of improving school psychological services. Financial assistance from international organizations also would help.

REFERENCES

Alvarez, B. M. (1977). Educational psychology in Mexico. In C. D. Catterall (Ed.), *Psychology in the schools in international perspective* (Vol. 2, pp. 211–223). Columbus, OH: Calvin D. Catterall.

Diaz-Guerrero, R. (1984a). Contemporary psychology in Mexico. *Annual Review of Psychology, 35*, 83–112.

Diaz-Guerrero, R. (1984b). Transference of psychological knowledge and its impact on Mexico. *International Journal of Psychology, 19*, 123–134.

Diaz-Loving, R., & Medina Liberty, A. (1987). *Foundations of Mexican psychology*. Manuscript submitted for publication.

Fernandez, G. (1974). La funcion del psicologo en las instituciones de ensenanza [The role of the psychologist in teaching institutions]. In L. L. Tapia (Ed.), *Memorias del Primer Congresso Mexicano de Psicologia* (pp. 293–298). Mexico: Imprenta Univ. UNAM.

Gomez del Campo, J. (1983). Centros communitarios de asistencia psicologica: Una alternative a los servicios psicologicos tradicionales [Community centers of psychological assistance: An alternative to traditional psychological services]. *Ensenanza e Investigacion en Psicologia, 9*(1), 27–34.

Informe Presidencial (State of the Union Presidential Address). (1982, September). Mexico, D. F.

Jimenez, M. E., & Macotela, S. (1983). El proyecto del centro de estudios de psicologia humana [The project of the center for studies in human psychology]. In L. L. Tapia (Ed.), *Memorias del Primer Congresso Mexicano de Psicologia* (pp. 363–372). Mexico: Imprenta Univ. UNAM.

Nieto, E. (1975). La universidad de Monterrey y su papel en la formacion de profesionales de alta calidad tecnica en psicologia a nivel de licenciatura [The University of Monterrey and its role in training high caliber professionals in undergraduate psychology]. *Ensenanza e Investigacion en Psicologia, 1*(1), 91–96.

Padilla, E. R., Roll, S., & Gomez-Palacio, M. (1982). The performance of Mexican children and adolescents on the WISC-R. *Interamerican Journal of Psychology, 16*(2), 122–128.

Reyes Lagunes de Carrillo, I. (1983). El papel del psicologo en la evaluacion educativa [The role of the psychologist in educational evaluation]. In F. Garcia Cortes (Ed.), *Una Decada de la Facultad de Psicologia: 1973-1983* (pp. 373–383). Mexico, D. F.: Universidad Nacional Autonoma de Mexico.

Ribes, E. (1972). *Tecnicas de modificacion de conducta: Su aplicacion al retardo en el desarrollo* [Behavior modification techniques: Application for the developmentally retarded]. Mexico: Trillas.

Valdes, S. (1974). Formacion de personal docente especializado en problemas de aprendizaje [Training teachers to be specialists in learning problems]. *Memorias del II Congreso Hispanoamericano de Dificultades en el Aprendizaje de la Lectura y Escritura* (pp. 659–684). Mexico, D. F.: SEP.

Velasco Hernandez, R. (1978). La ensenanza de la psicologia en Mexico [The teaching of psychology in Mexico]. *Ensenanza e Investigacion en Psicologia, 4*(1), 10–24.

Wechsler, S., & Gomes, D. C. (1986). School psychology in Brazil. *Journal of School Psychology, 24*, 221–227.

Chapter Twenty-Three
School Psychology in El Salvador

Marian C. Fish, Regina Varela Vorwald
Queens College
City University of New York

El Salvador is the smallest of the Central American countries. It has a homogeneous, Spanish-speaking population estimated at 5.5 million (Ruiz-Esparza, 1985). The small size of the country coupled with rapid population growth has resulted in high population density. El Salvador has an agriculturally based economy with coffee, cotton, sugarcane, and rice as primary crops (Information Please Almanac, 1986). As with many countries of the region, El Salvador's political history has been turbulent and characterized by coups and civil war; the country has been torn by a civil war since 1979, which has left over 60,000 civilians dead (Human Rights Institute, 1986). Five hundred thousand Salvadoreans have been forcibly relocated, and 1 million have left the country (Lungo, 1985).

The civil war has had different effects on the various socioeconomic groups of Salvadorean society. As is often the case in war-torn countries, the poor have suffered the most from the war (Martin-Baro, 1984). This period of political upheaval has had a significant impact on the government's educational goals, as economic resources have been diverted to the war effort (Ruiz-Esparza, 1985). In addition, during the earthquake of 1986, many schools were destroyed, and there have not been resources to replace them; the remaining schools are overcrowded. Some schools are holding as many as four alternate sessions for students (Varela, personal communication, 1987).

SALVADOREAN EDUCATION

El Salvador's current system of education was established in the First Educational Development Plan (1968–1972), which calls for free basic education for children between the ages of 7 and 15. The formal education system includes preschool, 9 years of mandated basic education in three, 3-year cycles (Grades 1–9), 3 years of secondary education, and post-secondary education varying from

2 to 6 years (Ruiz-Esparza, 1985). Before the earthquake of 1986, for children ages 7 to 15 there were approximately 2,900 schools serving about 1 million students and employing about 19,500 teachers (Ministry of Education, 1986). About 20% of children in this age group receive no schooling. In addition, 6.6% of the 5- to 6-year-old population attend preschools that include day-care and child-care centers in markets, and an estimated 40% of the eligible population attend secondary schools, most of which are located in urban areas (Ministry of Education, 1986). Although public schools outnumber private schools, (88% to 12%) at the basic education level, private schools outnumber public schools (58% to 42%) at the secondary level (Ministry of Education, 1986). Most of the private schools are church affiliated and concentrated in the cities, particularly San Salvador. The literacy rate in the general population is about 72% and is lower in the rural areas (UNESCO, 1985). There is a marked discrepancy between education in urban and rural areas at all levels, with the discrepancy increasing at the secondary level of education. There are no licensing requirements for teachers, and teacher training is not regulated (Ruiz-Esparza, 1985). The majority of teachers at private schools hold bachelor's degrees, whereas those in rural areas and public schools do not. The teacher–student ratio is about 1:45 in the public schools (Ministry of Education, 1985).

Special education services in El Salvador are very limited. The government supports three special schools for youngsters who are deaf, blind, or have cerebral palsy (Rodriguez, personal communication, 1987). At the present time, there are no other special education services available except at the American School. On the other hand, special education services are planned in a few of the private schools (Rodriguez, personal communication, 1987).

All of the Catholic private schools as well as the American School have a psychologist on staff who provides services on a part-time or full-time basis. Very few of the public schools have psychologists, although they may receive the services of a psychology intern for a semester. In fact, there are few support personnel (e.g., nurses, librarians) in any of the schools at this time (Rodriguez, personal communication, 1987).

Finally, the Ministry of Education is responsible for administration, financing, and curriculum development within the elementary and secondary systems of education.

Government expenditures in 1977 on education were 27% of the total budget (Ruiz-Esparza, 1985). This accounted for 90% of the total education expenditures, whereas the remaining 10% came from private sources of support.

THE ROLE OF SCHOOL PSYCHOLOGY

Training in Psychology

To understand the role of school psychology in El Salvador it is necessary to examine the history and scope of the training programs. As recently as 1979 there were only two universities, one public (Universidad Nacional), and one private (Universidad Catolica ''Jose Simeon Canas'' or UCA) in El Salvador. For a period of time following a 1979 coup, the Universidad Nacional was closed leaving the Universidad Catolica and 2-year post-secondary educational institutions to absorb the displaced students. When this happened, professors got together and opened new universities to fill the void. Currently, there are 13 universities with psychology programs (Ministry of Education, 1985). Of these, the Universidad Nacional, UCA, and Francisco Gavida account for over two thirds of the 3,150 psychology graduate students in El Salvador programs (Ministry of Education, 1985). There are approximately twice as many female psychology graduate students as males. Typical admissions procedures for private universities include testing (e.g., achievement tests) and interviews (Cornejo, personal communication, 1987). Of the 13 universities, 8 are situated in San Salvador. The psychology programs offered by the universities reflect a general psychology curriculum and specialization is not offered. The coursework is largely determined by faculty interests at each university, and the emphasis in each may differ. The highest degree offered is the *Licenciatura* (equivalent to the master's), which requires 5 years of coursework and 1 year to prepare a thesis. Training is carried out by psychiatrists as well as psychologists, and often falls into the hands of recent graduates.

Although the psychology programs do not provide specific concentrations, all programs offer components of vocational and school psychology. Extensive coursework is required in areas including general psychology, education, experimental psychology, counseling, clinical, liberal arts, and special education. Field experiences are required at the two main universities, Universidad Nacional and UCA. For example, the UCA curriculum requires interns to provide testing and consultation services in a school setting 1 day a week for a semester. During two other semesters, students spend a day a week in a secondary school where they receive training in psychological and vocational counseling as well as testing. Psychology students are supervised by a professor from the university. In addition, UCA students spend two semesters working at a psychiatric hospital and a semester in an industrial setting. Thus, 3 years of weekly field experiences in varied settings are an integral part of the training.

Given the diversified training, most psychologists simultaneously pursue a variety of tasks. It is not unusual to find psychologists consulting with banks, schools, and/or the military as well as doing private work (Bertin, 1974). Although there are no licensing or certification requirements, there is a Salvadorean Association of Psychology founded in 1964 and this organization established a code of ethics in 1967 (Salvadorean Psychological Association, 1977).

Scope of Services and Contributions

The emphasis of psychologists working in the schools is primarily in the area of assessment. Some of the commonly used instruments include the Bender

Visual–Motor Gestalt Test, WISC–R (Spanish version), Draw-A-Person, Rorschach, and Thematic Apperception Test (Varela, personal communication, 1987). The availability of additional diagnostic instruments is limited. Private school psychologists as well as public school interns spend most of their time testing and consulting with parents. Referrals are generally made by teachers and involve behavioral, emotional, and/or learning problems, but services are generally focused on assessment rather than working with teachers. Because there are no in-school services, students with difficulties are referred out to "clinics"; these are usually psychologists in private practice who do therapy. Few materials are available for remedial work in subject areas. Some vocational counseling is provided by psychologists to 12th graders, and screening programs prior to school admission are in effect in some schools (Cornejo, personal communication, 1987).

In the early 1970s there were only about 30 psychologists working in all of El Salvador (Bertin, 1974), and at the present time there are several hundred (Martin-Baro, 1984). Still, psychological services are spread so thin that there has been little expansion beyond the most basic services.

Given the need for clinical services that psychologists in the schools are facing, it is not surprising that there is little research being carried out. However, a number of graduate students have chosen to standardize test instruments on the Salvadorean school population for their theses that helps address a continuing need in this country.

Special Problems

In a small, populous country such as El Salvador where the demands on the educational system are monumental, there are a number of problems that psychology in general must face as well as some more specific problems that are faced by school psychologists in particular. These can be divided into problems related to professional training, there is currently a lack of regulation of psychology pro- to professional training there is currently a lack of regulation of psychology programs in the universities. This results in inconsistencies in requirements and quality of training. Specifically, there is no body of coursework/experience required for those psychologists who wish to work in schools. The coursework is largely dependent on who is teaching at the time. The problem is exacerbated by a shortage of psychology professionals with expertise in school psychology. Except for the thesis, there is limited research training for students. Testing materials, journals, and textbooks are in short supply. In addition, all courses are taught in Spanish, but the professional materials are frequently in English and must be translated.

The most serious problem in the delivery of school psychological services is the lack of a government mandate for such services. This limits services to private schools almost exclusively. One of the major inequities that results is the marked difference in psychological services between urban and rural areas. Urban areas receive a disproportionate amount of service, whereas the needs of rural areas are not being met. This occurs not only with regard to school psychological services, but also in all areas of educational services (Martin-Baro, 1984).

Another problem to be addressed is the limited role psychologists now have in the schools. There is virtually no preventative or intervention work and apparently very limited consultation. The model followed is one of direct service delivery involving only assessment and parent conferences. There does not appear to be systematic integration of psychological principles within the framework of school settings.

Still another problem has revolved around the use of tests that have not been appropriately validated for El Salvador and for the rural population in particular. Sometimes tests are simply translated and administered; at other times, when standardization is done, it is almost always carried out in urban areas. Disregard for technical considerations of these tests is a continuing concern.

FUTURE NEEDS

The introduction of improved school psychological services is a clear need in El Salvador. However, the broader objectives stated in the First, Second, and Third Educational Development Plans (Ruiz-Esparza, 1985) for improving teacher training, strengthening administration and supervision of education, redressing urban and rural inequities in the schools, as well as providing adult educational opportunities are crucial steps in addressing the needs of the population. Recent literacy campaigns and the expansion of night classes are evidence of some progress in these areas. Although political and economic events have hindered reforms in education and psychology, some attempts have been made to improve services. For example, the two main universities have begun to publish journals of research in psychology, and the Salvadorean Psychological and Psychiatric Associations sponsored a conference for mental health professionals in 1984 and published the proceedings. Some psychologists feel, however, that it is important to consolidate training into one or two central departments rather than to split it across so many universities (Cornejo, personal communication, 1987).

It is apparent that very serious political and economic problems further compounded by a disastrous earthquake in 1986 are affecting the availability of resources necessary to improve psychological services in the schools. Given these difficulties, government recognition and support will be instrumental in improving the scope and quality of psychological services in the schools.

REFERENCES

Bertin, M. A. (1974). *An overview of psychology in Latin America* (Report No. ONR-35). Arlington, VA: Office of Naval Research.

Human Rights Institute. (1986). *En busca de soluciones para los desplazados* [In search of solutions for the refugees]. San Salvador, El Salvador: UCA Editores.

Information Please Almanac. (1986). Boston, MA: Houghton Mifflin.

Lungo, M. (1985). *El Salvador 1981–1984 la dimension politica de la guerra* [The political dimension of the war in El Salvador: 1981–1984]. San Salvador, El Salvador: UCA Editores.

Martin-Baro, I. (1984). Guerra y salud mental [The war and mental health]. In *Primera Jornada de Profesionales de Salud Mental, Junio de 1984* (pp. 27–44). San Salvador, El Salvador: UCA Editores, Publicaciones de la Universidad Centroamericana José Simeón Cáñas.

Ministry of Education (1985). *Estadisticas estudiantiles del ano 1985.* [School statistics of 1985]. San Salvador, El Salvador: Author.

Ministry of Education (1986). *Estadisticas poblacion estudiantil anos 1986.* [Statistics for the 1986 school population]. San Salvador, El Salvador: Author.

Ruiz-Esparza, R. (1985). El Salvador: System of education, In L. C. Deighton (Ed.), *International encyclopedia of education* (Vol. 10, pp. 1647–1651). New York: Pergamon.

Salvadorean Psychological Association (1977, May 17). *Estatutos*, [By-laws]. Publicado en el Diario Oficial No. 91, *255*. San Salvador, El Salvador.

United Nations Educational, Scientific & Cultural Organization (1985). *UNESCO Statistical Yearbook*, Paris: United Nations Educational Organization.

Chapter Twenty-Four
School Psychology in Chile

Nicole Moreau de la Meuse
The University of Texas at Austin

STRUCTURE OF THE CHILEAN EDUCATIONAL SYSTEM

The Chilean educational system consists of the following four stages: preschool, basic (first to eighth grade), middle (first to fourth) and superior education (university,[1] professional institutes, and centers of technical formation). Enrollments in 1985 were 250,000 pupils in preschool, 2,040,557 in basic level, 661,000 in the middle schools, and 196,460 in superior education (*Subsecretaria de Educación*, 1985).

Education in Chile is free from preschool to the end of middle school. Compulsory education extends over 8 years (first to eighth grade). The Ministry of Education provides general guidelines for the school curriculum, including the regulation of subjects taught at each level and the time spent on each subject. However, each school can develop its own curriculum provided that it meets the approval of government officials or can choose to follow the curriculum prepared by the Ministry of Education (*Subsecretaria de Educación*, 1985).

There are 125,548 teachers in preschool, basic, and middle levels of whom 69% are female. The majority (88%) are certified teachers. Compared to other countries in Latin America, Chilean teachers demonstrate higher levels of preparation (*Subsecretaria de Educación*, 1986).

There are 662 private schools (7%), to which 187,894 (6%) of the Chilean students attend and that employ 24,141 (19%) of the Chilean teachers. In contrast, Chile has 9,857 public schools, to which 2,865,554 (94%) of the Chilean

[1]University Education often begins after the middle stage and last between 4 to 7 years depending on the careers.

students attend and that employ 101,407 (81%) of the Chilean teachers. There presently are an estimated 2,000 unemployed teachers, 48% of whom are qualified to teach in the middle level (*Subsecretaria de Educación*, 1985, 1986).

The educational system in Chile has experienced enormous changes during the last 12 years. A brief chronology of recent events is presented here. In 1975, diagnostic centers that are directed toward psychoeducational problems were created. Those centers are intended to prevent, detect, and serve students who have learning problems and difficulties adapting to school. Their services are offered only to public school pupils. In 1980, the administration of most public schools, which had been performed by the Ministry of Education, was transferred to local and regional districts. Before 1981, students who finished their middle education were able to continue their education only at one of eight universities. However, in 1981, a national law created numerous professional institutes and centers of technical formation. Presently, the country offers many alternatives, including 23 universities, 24 professional institutes, and 116 centers of technical formation. In 1982, tests that evaluate the knowledge of students in the fourth and eighth grade were administered to pupils throughout the country. The use of these tests was repeated in 1983 and 1984. In 1986, a program to evaluate the Chilean education system was initiated (*Subsecretaria de Educación*, 1985). All these changes indicate an increasing awareness of the need to improve the quality of the public education and to provide additional opportunities to students to continue their education after they finish middle school.

Special Education in Chile

The special education system in Chile is at an early stage of development. Handicapped children are segregated, and special education programs are offered only in special schools. A few private nursery schools in Santiago have started mainstreaming. However, efforts to integrate special and regular pupils are only beginning.

Separate special education schools exist for students exhibiting problems in each of the following areas: hearing disorders, mental, vision, oral expressions, motor abilities, and for other unspecified disabilities; learning disabilities are not included in these categories. The 278 schools provide services in these areas according to 1985 statistics, of which 206 (74%) are dedicated only to mental deficiency. The special schools are principally located in Santiago (43%). Throughout other areas of the country are some special schools, mainly for pupils who are mentally retarded or have auditory disabilities (*Subsecretaria de Educación*, 1985). Information as to the percentage of special schools that are private or public is unavailable; however, Santiago has a number of private schools dedicated to help mentally retarded children.

The number of students who receive special education services has increased dramatically in the last 15 years. In 1970 only 3,847 students received special services. In 1984, however, 27,384 received services (*Subsecretaria de Edu-*

cación, 1985). Information about the level of training of teachers who work in special schools is unavailable. However, 1% of the teachers in the basic level (first to eighth grade) have a degree in special education.

Because few public schools have the assistance of school psychologists or other similar specialists, children with learning disabilities often go undiagnosed. They generally are considered to be slow learners and frequently drop out of school. Even when a diagnosis is made, the public schools do not provide special services to them.

The conditions in private schools are quite different. Most teachers either refer the children with learning problems to the school psychologist or, if the school does not offer the services, the teachers advise the parents to take the child to a school psychologist in private practice. The majority of the private schools offer some kind of special services to children diagnosed as learning disabled. The types of services vary tremendously between schools. Some children also receive tutorial services provided privately by their parents.

THE DEVELOPMENT OF PSYCHOLOGY IN CHILE

The introduction of psychology in Chile seemingly is associated with Rómulo Peña Maturana. Following the completion of his studies in Germany with Wundt, he returned to Chile and established the first experimental psychology laboratory at the Escuela Normal the Capiapó between 1905 and 1907 (Bravo, 1983).

In 1920, the first "general psychology" course was taught at the Universidad de Concepción and became a requirement for students of the faculty of philosophy and education. In 1927, a course in educational psychology was added (Bravo, 1983). At this university, psychology courses were offered in order to promote the academic and professional development of teacher, not to form a department of psychology.

In 1941, the faculty of philosophy, associated with the Institute of Education at the Universidad de Chile, became the first department to prepare psychologists and to offer a university degree in psychology. Four specialty areas of psychology became available: psychoeducation, clinical, industrial, and criminology. In 1959, a separate department of psychology was created (Bravo, 1983).

The other major university in Chile, Universidad Católica de Chile, created a psychology department in 1955 that was under the faculty of philosophy and education. Its main purpose was to promote teachers' knowledge of psychology. Two years later, the psychology department became independent and offered the professional degree of *psychologist* similar to the one offered by the Universidad de Chile. It is important to recognize that, in both universities, psychology began in schools of education, with its primary purpose to promote teachers' knowledge of psychology. However, both universities quickly created independent psychology departments (Bravo, 1983). When the psychology programs first began, the professors mainly were physicians and educators; very few had a psychology degree. The medical model had a major influence on the professional identity of psychologists, which tended to be confused with the role of the psychiatrist (Morales et al., 1987). The development of psychology in Chile initially was greatly influenced by Europeans and more recently has been greatly influenced by the United States.

Psychologists in Chile have a high level of prestige. In a study done on the prestige associated with careers in Chile, psychology was rated the fourth highest. Only medicine, business, and engineer have higher levels of prestige. Other professions such as law, architecture, dentistry, and journalism had a lower rating (Himmel & Maltes, 1980). This perception of psychology as a prestigious profession has influenced many students in Chile to study psychology. Seven universities currently offer psychology degrees, five in the capital of Chile (Santiago) and two in the south of Child (Concepción and Temuco). In 1981, when the government allowed the creation of private universities, three new universities offered a psychology degree, almost doubling the enrollment in this discipline. In 1986, for example, 183 students were admitted into psychology by the four state universities and 310 by the three private universities (E1 Mercurio, 1987). The criteria for selecting students to study psychology in Chile are quite strict, especially within the state universities. To be accepted, students must obtain very high scores (e.g., $\geq$ 2 standard deviations above the mean) on the *Prueba Aptitude Academica* (a test similar to the U.S. SAT) and high grade-point averages during the last 4 years of high school.

Degrees in psychology take between 5 to 6 years; most universities require 6 years of study. All courses from the freshmen year on are taken in psychology. During their fourth year, students select their area of specialization. These include: clinical, educational (school), and organizational psychology. The number of credit hours required by each specialty are equivalent to between 18 and 21 in U.S. universities. During their fifth year, students complete an unpaid internship in the area of specialization. The minimum requirement is 450 clock hours. Most internships occur in public settings (e.g., schools and hospitals) that provide the students an opportunity to contribute through public services. After completing the required thesis, students receive the title of licensed psychologist. There is no specialization acknowledged in the title nor is there an obligation to work in one's area of specialization.

In Chile no graduate courses are offered in psychology. However, the undergraduate degree previously described is somewhat equivalent to master's degree obtained in U.S. universities—with somewhat less specialization, particularly in school and industrial psychology. According to Morales, Scharager, Díaz, and Sziklai (1985), the universities focus mainly on the specialization of clinical psychology.

Chile has a national association for psychologists, *Colegio de Psicólogos de Chile* (A.G.), to which 72% of the Chilean psychologists belong (Díaz, Sziklai,

Scharager, & Morales, 1985). Also, Chile publishes two professional journals in psychology: *Terapia Psicologica* (Psychological Therapy) and *Revista Chilena de Psicología* (Chilean Journal of Psychology). The former emphasizes clinical psychology and therapeutic interventions and the latter has a broader perspective with articles from different specialities in psychology.

Present Status of School Psychologists

Chile has a population of 11 million people. Approximately 1,350 are psychologists; 31% of these are men (Díaz et al., 1985). Psychologists in general are young professionals, as their average age is approximately 35. According to Díaz et al. (1985), 64% of them have received their degree between 1978 and 1984. Little information exists on the number of psychologists in each specialty because many practice in more than one specialty (Morales et al., 1987). However, there are an estimated 270 school psychologists; this is 20% of the total number of Chilean psychologists. Most psychologists have graduated from one of the two older Chilean Universities (Universidad de Chile and the Universidad Católica) because the others have been offering degrees for only about 5 years. Two percent have been educated at foreign Universities. Although approximately 30% of the Chilean population live in the capital, Santiago, a clear majority of the psychologists practice there (69%). Only 15% practice in other areas of the country and 16% reside in other countries. The ratio of psychologists to the Santiago population is 1:5,067; in contrast, the ratio of psychologists to the Chilean population is 1:9,951. This compares to a physician-population ratio of 1:943 and a lawyer-population ratio of 1:1,129 in Chile (Díaz et al., 1985).

School psychology in Chile has developed mainly in private settings. The majority of school psychologists work in more than one setting: 58% have a private practice, 46% work in private schools, 39% in universities, 14% in juvenile detention centers, 10% in diagnostic centers, and 5% in school districts. Even while more than half of the school psychologists have private practices, the work of psychologists in schools is not exclusively theirs. Twenty-two percent of the clinical and 11% of the industrial psychologist also work in schools. School psychology attracts psychologists from other specialties (Morales et al., 1987).

Most school psychologists (84%) work at least part time within interdisciplinary teams mainly in private schools; many also provide services through private practice (Morales et al., 1987). Although data on the proportion of private schools that employ school psychologists do not exist, an estimated 80% of the private schools in Santiago have a part-time or full-time school psychologist working in their school. The number of private schools has increased dramatically during the last 5 years, especially in Santiago, thus creating many new job opportunities for school psychologists. School psychologists working in private schools devote much attention to the selection of new students. For that purpose, school psychologists administer group and individual tests to applicants for kindergarten. Their opinions count heavily in the selection of new students.

The most common services provided by school psychologist in Chile are to first, diagnose learning disabilities; second, provide intervention plans to teachers in order to modify behavioral problems in the classroom; third, diagnose emotional and behavioral problems in pupils and applying interventions to them and, fourth, select new student applicants, mainly to kindegarten.

Psychological tests most frequently used by Chilean school psychologists include the Wechsler series (e.g., WISC and WAIS), Bender, Raven, Children's Apperception Test, Thematic Apperception Test, Condemarín, sentence completion, and the Draw-A-Person. Except for the Condemarín and some sentence completion tests, the other tests have been developed in the United States. For some (e.g., WISC and WAIS) Chilean norms are available and used.

School psychologists encounter some conflicts with other professionals, mainly psychiatrists, guidance counselors, teachers, and administrators. These conflicts mainly are due to the lack of definitions that differentiate and separate the practices within these professional fields (Morales et al., 1987). This ambiguity in roles weighs strongly in the minds of Chilean psychologists who work cooperatively or coordinately with other professionals. The absence of laws that define the work of psychologists contributes to this confusion (Marassi, 1984). School psychologists also report other work-related difficulties including the lack of economic resources (55%) and the lack of knowledge among the general population as to the nature of the work school psychologists can perform (43%) (Morales et al., 1987).

No Chilean association for school psychologists exists. However, the Association for Children and Adolescents (*Asociación Infanto Juvenil*) has approximately 100 members and is composed of school and clinical child psychologists. This association has shown interest in developing a graduate program for school psychologists (Sepúlveda, personal communication, January 1987). This new possibility will provide opportunities for school psychologists to continue with their professional development. Presently, only 18% of the school psychologists have taken some courses after they have obtained the title of psychologist (Morales et al., 1987).

FUTURE TRENDS AND SUGGESTIONS

Emerging trends in Chile suggest expanded participation of school psychologists at the public level. More school districts have started hiring school psychologists to work in their diagnostic centers, thus creating new job opportunities for school psychologists and enabling them to work with larger portions of the population who have been denied these services.

There is concensus among school psychologists about the need for graduate programs in school psychology. Within 5 years this probability may become a reality. The opportunity to develop greater specialization will enable school psychologists to provide more effective services and to develop a stronger sense of identity among them.

Although psychology in Chile has come a long way since its initiation in the early 1900s, much remains to be accomplished. The following are suggestions for promoting the continuing development of school psychology.

Economic incentives should be offered to school psychologists in order to encourage them to provide services in areas of Chile were they are needed other than the capital. School psychologists should have more active roles in the Ministry of Education in order to plan and to develop the services needed by pupils, their teachers, and other educators. Also, their participation in this most influencial Chilean educational organization might serve to impact other areas of education and may promote the requirement for a school psychologist in each school district. The need for a professional organization exclusively for school psychologists is evident. Such an organization may help to develop a stronger sense of identity, cooperation, and collaboration among its members and to promote the development of a Chilean journal of school psychology. School psychologists need to develop better channels of communication among their colleagues throughout Latin America. Except for Brazil, all Latin Americans speak the same language; therefore, the creation of the Latin American association of school psychologists and a journal of school psychologists for Latin America will provide important channels of communication among Spanish-speaking countries. The promotion of conferences, seminars, and workshops also would enable school psychologists to continue their academic and professional develop and to promote research in school psychology—an area also needing attention.

REFERENCES

Bravo, L. (1983). El origen de la investigación psicologica en Chile [The origin of the psychological research in Chile]. In *Las Ciencias Sociales en Chile 1983*. Corporación de promoción Universitaria, 80–88.

Díaz, R., Sziklai, G., Scharager, J., & Morales, M. (1985). *Aproximaciones al estudio del Campo ocupacional del psicólogo en Chile*. [Approximations to the study of the occupational field of the psychologist in Chile]. Unpublished manuscript, Projecto DIUC 167–84.

El Mercurio. (1987). *Guía postulaciones admision '87* [Guide to '87 postulations and admissions]. Jueves 8 de Enero, 1987.

Himmel, E., & Maltes, S. (1980). El prestigio de las carreras Universitarias en Chile. [The prestige of the University careers in Chile]. *Revista Chilena de Psicología, 3*,(2), 125–132.

Marassi, P. (1984). *Psicología, una profesión en desarrollo* [Psychology, a profession in development]. Cuadernos Consejo de Rectores. Santiago, # 22. Enero–Junio.

Morales, M., Scharager, J., Díaz, R., & Sziklai, G. (1985). *Análisis de las activdades y exigencias profesionales actuales del psicólogo en Chile: un estudio piloto* [Analysis of the activities and professional requirements of the Chilean Psychologists: A pilot study]. Unpublished manuscript, Projecto Diuc 167–89.

Morales, M., Díaz, R., Scharager, J., Sziklai, G., Avendaño, C., & Rosas, R. (1987). *Informe final de investigacion "Campo y rol del psicólogo in Chile"*. [Final report of the research, "Field and role of the psychologist in Chile]. Unpublished manuscript, Projecto DIUC 167-89, Tomo I.

Subsecretaria de Educación. (1985). *La Educación Chilena* [The Chilean Education]. Año 1, número 1.

Subsecretaria de Educación. (1986). *La Educación Chilena* [The Chilean Education]. Año 1, número 2.

Chapter Twenty-Five
School Psychology in Brazil

Solange Wechsler
University of Brasilia

Denise Cristina Gomes
University of Gama Filho

STRUCTURE OF THE BRAZILIAN EDUCATIONAL SYSTEM

The Brazilian educational system has two basic levels, the primary level comprising eight grades and the secondary level comprising three grades. The curriculum is the same for all schools and no differentiation is made between science and liberal arts majors during the secondary level. University education comes after the secondary level and lasts for 4 to 6 years depending on the area of specialization.

The population of Brazil is approximately 121 million. There are approximately 24 million 7-year-old students in the first grade of the primary level (90% in public schools and 10% in private schools). Of these, 3.4 million reach the secondary level (87% attend public and 13% private schools). However, only 1.5 million students enter universities (35% go to public and 65% to private universities). We can conclude that early school withdrawal is a serious problem in our system of education, and that this may be due to a combination of poor teaching techniques and negative economic factors. Consequently, few Brazilian students obtain college degrees, and the majority of those who do belong to middle and upper socioeconomic classes. Despite these figures, the national literacy rate is around 74% among persons who are 15 years of age or older (*Instituto Brasileiro de Geografia e Estatística*, 1982; *Ministério da Educação e Cultura*, 1983).

There are approximately 1.3 million teachers at the primary and secondary levels (*Instituto Brasileiro de Geografia e Estatística*, 1982). In order to teach at the primary level, instructors must graduate from a secondary (normal) school. Secondary school teachers must also have university degrees. Teaching at the university level requires a graduate degree and/or professional experience. The student–teacher ratio is approximately 40:1 in the public schools.

There are approximately 817 public and private universities in Brazil (*Instituto Brasileiro de Geografia e Estatística*, 1982). In order to enter these universities, students must pass an exam based on the subjects that are taught at the secondary level. A typical exam for would-be psychology students covers the areas of physics, chemistry, biology, mathematics, geography, Brazilian history, Portuguese grammar and composition, and a foreign language (English or French).

TRAINING IN PSYCHOLOGY

A professional degree in psychology takes 4 years or more of undergraduate study to complete. After 4 years, graduates can be licensed to teach psychology in the secondary schools. Upon the completion of a 5-year course of study, students obtain a degree in psychology. The curriculum for undergraduate psychology courses is defined by law and by the Federal Council of Education. Federal Law 4119 (1963) defined the curriculum for psychology degrees as consisting of the following subjects: physiology, statistics, experimental psychology, developmental psychology, psychology of the personality, social psychology, psychopathology, psychological assessment, ethics, school psychology, psychotherapeutic techniques, vocational guidance, industrial psychology, psychology of exceptional children, group dynamics, therapeutic pedagogy, and personnel placement. The duration of these courses varies across institutions.

The philosophical orientation underlying the undergraduate or graduate psychology courses comes primarily from the behavioral, functional, and psychoanalytic traditions. Psychology is still a female profession in this country, and approximately 90% of the psychology students are women.

During the fifth undergraduate year, students complete internships in the area of their preference. Supervised internships may last from 1 to 1½ years, and this generally establishes the line that the student will pursue after graduation. However, students are not obliged to work in any specific area, because they receive at graduation only the title *psychologist*. Federal and state legislation does not specify the background or experience for psychologists in each area.

The curricula for master's and doctoral programs are defined by each university. However, each university must have its curriculum approved by the Federal Council of Education. A typical curriculum of a master's program in educational or school psychology covers the areas of research methodology, learning and human development, and exceptional children, as well as an undergraduate teaching practicum. The only subject required by law in all graduate programs is Brazilian socioeconomic problems. Master's programs usually take 3 years or more to complete and require a thesis.

Nine universities offer master's degrees in education/school psychology. There are Pontificia Universidade Católica do Rio de Janeiro, Pontíficia Universidade Católica de São Paulo, Fundação Getúlio Vargas, Universidade de Campinas, Universidade Federal do Rio Grande do Sul, Universidade Gama Filho, Universidade de Brasília, Universidade de São Paulo, and Universidade Federal de Pernambuco. Doctoral degrees in education/school psychology are offered by three universities: Fundação Getúlio Vargas, Pontíficia Universidade Católica do Rio de Janeiro, and Universidade de São Paulo (*Coordenação de Aperfeiçoamento do Pessoal de Nível Superior*, 1982).

Although a considerable number of Brazilians hold graduate degrees in school psychology, it is rare to find professionals with a master's or a doctoral degree in the private or public schools. Graduate-level school psychologists usually teach and conduct research in the universities. By comparison, one can find graduate-level clinical or industrial psychologists not only in the universities but also in private and public clinics and businesses.

Federal Legislation on Psychology

Most professions in Brazil are regulated by federal law. Although school psychology services have operated since the mid-1950s, psychology was legally recognized as a profession by Federal Law 5343/64 only on January 21, 1964 (*Ministério do Trabalho*, 1976).

The functions of a psychologist, according to this law, were defined as the following: use of psychological techniques and methods in order to conduct psychological assessment; vocational guidance and personnel placement; psychoeducational guidance and the treatment of adjustment problems; administration of psychological services in public or private institutions; teaching and supervision of psychology students; and acting as a consultant on psychological issues. Inasmuch as the law does not specify the psychologist's functions in each area of specialization, psychologists interpret the law in different ways.

The Federal Council of Psychology was founded after this law took effect. This entity is subordinated to the Ministry of Labor and was created to oversee the ethics and practice of psychology and to defend the interests of psychologists in all areas of specialization. Regional psychology councils attend to psychologists' concerns from different states and refer them to the Federal Council of Psychology. All psychologists must be registered with their regional psychology councils in order to work as psychologists in public or private institutions or in private practice. In order to obtain this registration, psychologists must present their academic credentials to the council and pay an annual fee. Instructors who want to supervise internships in psychology must also receive credentials as supervisors from their regional psychology council. In addition to an undergraduate degree in psychology, this requires 3 years or more of supervised experience in a specific field of psychology.

School Psychology Services

The Federal Law that regulates the profession of psychology does not require schools, industries, or clinics to have psychologists on their staffs. However, every school is required by law to have an educational supervisor. Therefore, the limited number of psychologists who work in the public schools are frequently subordinated to an educational specialist.

There are more school psychologists working in the south and southeast of Brazil than in other areas, because Brazil's larger cities are located in these regions and because the pay is better there. It is difficult to generalize about what school psychologists are doing throughout the country, there being little publication in this area of specialization. The comments to be presented below pertain to four major Brazilian cities (Rio de Janeiro, São Paulo, João Pessoa, Brasília) where research has been carried out in order to clarify the role of the school psychologist.

Historically, school psychologists in Rio de Janeiro (in the southeast of Brazil) tended to place great emphasis on psychological testing. Novaes (1970), reporting on the organization of a school psychology program that was established in 1959 in the Guatemala School in Rio de Janeiro, indicated that all students were given intelligence and personality tests as soon as they enrolled. This information was used to help teachers in dealing with their students. Children who presented psychological problems during the year were also required to sit for additional psychological tests. All high school seniors received vocational guidance, which was provided on the basis of aptitude, intelligence, interest, and personality test results.

Nowadays, the importance of psychological tests in Rio de Janeiro is diminishing, and the emphasis is shifting toward work with groups of teachers. The topics that are discussed in these groups relate to the psychological aspects of child development and methods of dealing with various problems.

Goldberg (1975), reporting on the school psychologist's work in the private schools in the city of São Paulo (also in the southeast of Brazil), observed that 29% of the school psychologists worked less than 10 hours a week, 23% worked 10–20 hours a week, and only 48% of the school psychologists worked more than 20 hours a week at providing psychological services. Among the 17 school psychologists in her sample, 35% worked as part-time clinical psychologists, 41% as university professors, and 18% as school directors.

The school psychologists in Goldberg's study perceived their roles to be consultants to teachers in the use of behavior modification techniques, advisors to students regarding the need to seek therapy in public or private clinics, and educational researchers. These professionals did not feel that their tasks included vocational guidance or counseling students' families. In general, these psychologists viewed their work as more directed toward helping teachers than to assisting students or school administrators.

Masini (1978) stated that there were 14 school psychologists working in state agencies in São Paulo in 1977. Their work initially involved a heavy emphasis on individual assessment but subsequently involved group work with teachers and parents. Other projects under way at that time in São Paulo were related to compensatory education for disadvantaged children, development of children's perceptual motor skills, preventive group work with mothers, and training school psychology interns.

Macedo, Curchatuz, and Arcos Verdes (1980) described the background and functions of school psychologists in the city of João Pessoa, in the northeast of Brazil. They verified that among 20 school psychologists only 25% completed school psychology internships when they were in college, and that 40% completed their internships in industries and 35% in clinics. After graduation, 20% attended specialized courses in educational psychology, 15% in clinical psychology, and 40% in counseling; and 25%, for lack of funds or interest, did not attend any courses after graduation. On the basis of these results, Macedo et al. (1980) suggested that school psychologists do not feel confident in their roles and that they try to make up for their professional training deficiencies with further training.

School psychologists in João Pessoa (Macedo et al., 1980) felt that their major roles involved vocational counseling and assisting parents in dealing with their children's misconduct. They also reported that their work tended to be more oriented toward helping students than to assisting teachers, and they placed more emphasis on assessment than did school psychologists from other Brazilian cities.

In Brasília, the capital of Brazil, there are approximately 10 school psychologists working in the local public school system who are responsible for the assessment and treatment needs of 398 schools. These figures are especially daunting inasmuch as each school serves 2,000–3,000 students. Consequently, the staff of a public school can seldom ask a psychologist to help with everyday student or teacher problems, and only when students appreciably deviate from the norm are they referred to a school psychologist. The main functions of these psychologists involve providing psychological assessment and counseling for students, vocational guidance for the mentally retarded, and exercises intended to develop perceptual and psychomotor skills. Educational guidance on how to deal with specific learning problems is usually provided by educational supervisors.

The situation in the private schools in Brasília is somewhat better than in the public schools. Albanezi (1979) verified that 9 of the 17 private schools in Brasília had school psychologists on their staffs. Seventy-five percent of these psychologists worked 10–20 hours per week, 8% worked less than 9 hours a week, and only 17% worked on a full-time basis in the schools. Other activities of the part-time school psychologists involved teaching and private practice. The school psychologists in Albanezi's sample view their work as being more oriented to the needs of the individual student than to the needs of teachers. The main work of 75% of these psychologists was individual assessment, direct observations in the classrooms, and parental consultation.

Present Difficulties

The main problem that faces Brazilian school psychologists is that the Federal government does not recognize the importance of the work that they perform. Public schools, throughout the country, can seldom count on the services of a school psychologist. The limited number of psychologists who work for the government generally receive low salaries that are comparable to those of a less-trained school teacher.

Brazilian school psychologists throughout the country are also suffering from an identity crises. Goldberg (1975) indicated that 24% of the school psychologists in São Paulo reported that their main difficulty involved the vague job descriptions that apply to their roles in the schools. Moreover, 20% of these psychologists complained of not being accepted by teachers or schools administrators. Gomes (1984) observed that 27% of the school psychologists in Rio de Janeiro felt that the school staff did not understand their functions, and Macedo et al. (1980) indicated that 33% of the school psychologists in João Pessoa felt that same way. These difficulties may be due to their professional deficiencies, because most of them reported that they were not skilled in advising teachers about educational issues (Goldberg, 1975; Gomes, 1984; Macedo et al., 1980). Indeed, their undergraduate curriculum gives little emphasis to learning problems and is more geared toward training the clinician than to preparing psychologists for work in the schools.

Another commonly experienced difficulty is the lack of technical material. Books written or translated into Portuguese that deal with the practice of school psychology are rare. Moreover, most of the objective tests that are being used were devised in the United States, and these tests have not been properly validated for use in our culture. It is difficult, therefore, to assess children's abilities under these circumstances.

The limited recognition that school psychologists receive as professionals in the public and private schools, and their low salaries, have led psychologists to seek part-time employment in nonschool settings. Consequently, there are not enough school psychologists to screen children with special needs.

A great deficit in Brazilian school psychology is the lack of endemic research and publications. Authors have faced considerable difficulties in gathering information about the status of school psychology in the country. Probably many different research projects are being carried out by individual school psychologists, but with the exception of the activities of a few psychologists whose work is being published, it is almost impossible to report on the progress of these investigations from a national perspective.

FUTURE NEEDS AND TRENDS

The serious economic difficulties that face the country are obliging middle-class parents to transfer their children from private to public schools. This may be beneficial to public education, because middle-class parents may put pressure on government and school administrators to improve the quality of public education. Furthermore, psychologists in schools and in nonschool settings will also have to spend more time with groups than with individuals because increasingly fewer people will be able to afford psychological services on an individual basis. This situation may lead to the development of new group techniques for working in the schools, clinics, or industries.

It is also anticipated that the Federal Council of Psychology will become stronger in order to defend the rights of psychologists in public and private institutions. The Regional Council of Psychology in Rio de Janeiro is already trying to change the official status of psychologists who receive salaries as primary-level teachers. Comparable actions will probably be taken by other regional councils in the future.

Another difficulty that could be addressed by the Federal Council of Psychology is related to the complaints of school psychologists about their curriculum deficiencies. The Federal Council could put pressure on the universities that offer undergraduate and/or graduate degrees in psychology to make them increase the number of courses related to learning problems. These measures would certainly bolster the confidence of students desiring to select a career in school psychology.

Another great challenge in Brazilian education is to find a solution to the problem of elementary grade drop-outs, which is compounded by the fact that most of these children come from impoverished homes and lack academic motivation. In view of this, there is also an urgent need to create remedial educational programs for these students, inasmuch as the misery cycle will be repeated owing to the perpetuation of illiteracy and limited opportunities for employment. International aid would be of considerable use in implementing these programs.

Finally, it is hoped that more international congresses or conferences relating to school psychology will be held in this country—a development that would enable Brazilian school psychologists to exchange ideas with their colleagues and might also generate more cross-cultural research, which in turn could enhance the development of school psychology in Brazil.

ACKNOWLEDGMENT

Reprinted by permission of the *Journal of School Psychology, 24,* 221–227, as published in 1986.

REFERENCES

Albanezi, R. M. B. (1979). *Atuação do psicólogo escolar na cidade de Brasília* [The work of school *psychologists in Brazil]*. Unpublished manuscript, Universidade de Brasília, Departmento de Psicologia, Brasília.

Coordenação de Aperfeiçoamento de Pessoal de Nível Superior. (1982). *Pós-Graduação, catálogo de curso de ciências sociais* [Catalogue of graduate courses in the social sciences]. Report No. 1, 1980, Brasília, DF: CAPES.

Goldberg, M. A. (1975). Concepção do papel do psicólogo escolar [Perception of the school psycholgists' roles]. *Cadernos de Pesquisa, 12*, 29–38.

Gomes, D. C. (1984). Percepção *dos problemas encontrados na atuação do psicólogo escolar em relação ao locus de controle e atribuição de causalidade* [Perception of problems in the school psychologists' work in relation to locus of control and attribution of causality]. Unpublished masters thesis, Universidade Gama Filho, Rio de Janeiro, RJ.

Instituto Brasileiro de Geografia e Estatística, IBGE. (1982). *Anuário estatístico do Brasil* [Brazilian statistical yearbook]. Rio de Janeiro, RJ: IBGE.

Macedo, B. C., Curchatuz, M. S. M., & Arcos Verdes, V. S. (1980). *Formação, função e papéis do psicólogo escolar: un estudo com psicólogos de João Pessoa* [Background, functions and roles of the school psycholgists: A study of psychologists in João, Pessoa]. Unpublished manuscript, Universidade de São Paulo, Departamento de Psicologia, São Paulo.

Masini, E. F. S. (1978). *Ação de psicologia na escola* [Psychology in the schools]. São Paulo, SP: Cortez e Moraes.

Ministério da Educação e Cultura. (1983). *Estatisticas educacionais, síntese* [Synthesis of educational *statistics]. Brasília, DF: INEP.*

Ministério do Trabalho. (1976). *Psicologia-Legislação* [Psychology-Legislation]. Report No. 1 A. Brasília, DF: Conselho Federal de Psicologia.

Novaes, M. H. (1970). *Psicologia escolar* [School psychology]. Rio de Janeiro: Vozes.

Author Index

C

D

E

F

G

M

N

O

Subject Index

E

F

H

I

J

M

N

O

S

T

U

For Product Safety Concerns and Information please contact our EU
representative GPSR@taylorandfrancis.com
Taylor & Francis Verlag GmbH, Kaufingerstraße 24, 80331 München, Germany

www.ingramcontent.com/pod-product-compliance
Ingram Content Group UK Ltd.
Pitfield, Milton Keynes, MK11 3LW, UK
UKHW022116190926
475702UK00013B/1476
9781138973077